Lucy Yeend Culler

Europe, through a Woman's Eye

Lucy Yeend Culler

Europe, through a Woman's Eye

ISBN/EAN: 9783337213046

Printed in Europe, USA, Canada, Australia, Japan

Cover: Foto ©Andreas Hilbeck / pixelio.de

More available books at **www.hansebooks.com**

WITH AN

INTRODUCTION

BY

REV. PROF. W. H. WYNN, PH. D.

PUBLISHED FOR THE AUTHOR.

PHILADELPHIA:
LUTHERAN PUBLICATION SOCIETY,
1883.

INTRODUCTION.

BACON'S Essay on travel, written when the great age of discovery and travel was just opening upon the world, is still the wisest summary of good counsel on the subject that can anywhere be found. The benefit of travel, the objects the traveller should look after and the places he should visit; the aids he should seek and the company he should keep; and, finally, the beneficent uses to which his knowledge and experiences should be applied—all this is condensed in that brief essay not two spans long.

In the closing parapraph ample justification is found for the little book that is herewith sent forth upon the world. "When a traveller returneth home, let him not leave the countries where he hath travelled, altogether behind him, but maintain a correspondence by letters with those of his acquaintance which are of most worth." The same end, however,—that of keeping up the interest of travel among the friends with whom we are anxious to share the marvel of the sights we have seen, and the memory of the thronging experiences through which we have passed, may be attained by writing a book, especially if in that book some definite aim is kept in view. There is no better *souvenir*, and no better way of not "leaving the travelled lands altogether behind."

It is true there are many books of this kind, and it is held that they can have only a transitory interest within a circle of readers that is never at any time large. But there is a peculiar exhilaration attending the reading of a book of this kind, a pleasure somewhat analogous to that which the traveller himself enjoys when in the presence of strange objects and strange people he notes down his experiences and catches and cages the passing joy. And so the popular craving for information and entertainment of this sort seems never to abate, and the "transitory interest," as it is called, has to be repeated every year, in every variety of way. Witness the amount of space given up to the literature of travel in the great magazines of the day, and the enormous expenditure in securing for these articles the best illustrations the pictorial art can supply. Witness, too, the recently revived passion for diaries of times long past, private inventories, so to speak, of incidents and places rendered foreign almost by the long lapse of intervening years. These dusty manuscripts are raked out from the garrets and rubbish corners of old libraries and lumber-rooms, and when published are greedily solicited over seas and all round the world, because of the ceaseless delight we have in anything distant from us either in time or space. We want to traverse these strange spots, hallowed by the stirring events and illustrious deeds of other days, in imagination if not in reality, and momentarily drop out of ourselves into the hearts and homes, the market places, the Senate halls, the busy thoroughfares, the surging tides of human life booming under other skies.

So far books of travel must share their interest with works of history, dramatic compositions, and the engulfing flood of romance, that pours every year upon the world. They keep our "enthusiasm of humanity" aglow when otherwise it might die out. But there is a special sense in which works of this kind may serve a distinctive use of their own. Dr. Johnson was wont to say: "The use of travelling is to regulate the imagination by reality, and instead of thinking how things may be, to see them as they are." That is, it broadens the mind, and enlarges the views, of him whose happiness it is to travel. There is no one who has settled down, as every one ought, into the routine of some way of honorable and beneficent toil, that will not by and by betray the narrowing influence of his surroundings, and even be painfully conscious of the fact. We have no word of encouragement for the spirit of unrest and discontent which is the prevailing malady of the age. One needs only to look in upon the passengers of the next train that halts for a moment at the village depot, to see the unmistakable signs of a restless, fidgety, longing, nervous habit exactly the opposite of the devout sighing of the Psalmist for the wings of a dove—an eager multitude wanting the iron wings of steam to carry them into the uttermost parts of the earth. It is abnormal no doubt. But on the supposition that to the hard-working, painfully-drudging, religiously-faithful man or woman, the time for recreation has fairly come, travel will bring with it not only the recuperating advantages of a change, but the special broadening discipline of which Dr. Johnson speaks. The cosmopolitan spirit he must measurably have. He must know things as they actually are, and not as he might imagine them to be. We are so likely, as Tennyson says, to

>   —" Take the rustic murmur of our bourg
> For the great wave that echoes round the world,"

and so fall short of that broad ample sympathy with the race, which is not only the height of liberal culture, but the sweetest essence of the religion we profess. Travel is an antidote to this.

But what if one is so situated that the hard ligaments of routine will never relax? He cannot go abroad. He must rise and retire, and go through the monotonous round of duties all the working days of the year. Then a vacation by proxy may be furnished to his hand in a book of this kind. He may look upon the strange scenes of other climes through the eyes of some more fortunate one, who has seen not only, but put his choicest impressions into print. What is required to make a book of this kind of substitutional value is, that it be predominantly realistic in its style; that the art of the writer be such, that the reader will follow along easily and buoyantly in the track of the descriptions, and not have his imagination embarrassed by minutiæ of detail nor by a dry, lumbering stiffness of style. Equally fatal is it, if the descriptions of noted places and circumstances are overweighted with comment, or set off with excessive ornamentation from the writer's overflow of rhetorical zeal. Many otherwise valuable works of travel are harmed in this way.

Now of the little, unpretentious book, whose commission to the reading world we are now executing, it may be said by way of cordial unreserved commendation that it may claim exemption from the above-mentioned faults. There is a certain rapidity of narrative, free-flowing, conversational, elegantly easy way of telling what was experienced, resembling very much what might be familiarly communicated by a cultured lady to a circle of parlor friends chatting leisurely the social hour away. Only it is not gossip. You see at once that every point visited, every noted locality upon which this woman's eyes have fallen, has received just that kind of attention that has made conspicuous the objects and aspects of things that, out of the multiplicity of details, are most likely to answer the spontaneous prompting of the reader's mind. Here, for example, is the city of Paris, or the Alps, or Florence, or Rome,—the details of daily observation are infinite, and the woman's art consists in instantaneously catching at the events and sights which out of the great throng of impressions, will best secure for herself, and convey to others a vivid realization of the time and place. It is noticeable how this trait runs throughout the entire narrative, giving it a unique charm of its own. We do certainly go with this delightful companion every step of the way. We see what she sees; we share her pleasures, and even her weariness, when by times that is noted, climbing great flights of steps, or clambering along the mountain side, or battling with the dizziness of the ocean wave. In order to make things real, so that the mind can walk round the object described, or peer into it, or lay hands upon it, or scale its utmost limits, the writer has wisely deemed that the actual dimensions of things so far as such data are accessible to her, are indispensable to the successful limning of her pictures. In general this narrative is to be commended for so attaching us to the society of this cultured woman during all the varied experiences of a European tour, that we regretfully part company when the narrative is at an end.

This, possibly, is the special charm of seeing Europe through a woman's eyes. It is what the penetrating, quick-minded, sympathetic woman sees and enjoys, what the grosser, less nimble vision of man would fail to note, or noting would miss widely from its deeper significance in the sum of things—this that pleases us, this that lures us from page to page to the end. And so we have another proof that the great poet did not fall one whit below that high philosophic standard which everywhere has guided him in his interpretation of human nature, when he makes one of his characters say:

> " From women's eyes this doctrine I derive;
> They sparkle still the right Promethean fire;
> They are the books, the arts, the academies;
> That show, contain, and nourish all the world."

W. H. WYNN.

Iowa State College, Ames, Iowa.

CONTENTS.

	PAGE
Atlantic Ocean	1
Adriatic Sea	103
Antwerp	141
Amsterdam	143
Abbottsford	211
Ayr	218
Brünig Pass	118
Brussels	136
Chamouny	29
Castle of Chillon	33
Cologne	135
Chester	224
Cheltenham	187
Chatsworth Estate	193
Carlisle	218
Danube River	106
Down the Rhine	133
English Channel	8
English Lake Region	223
Edinburgh	199
Florence	95
Frankfort	131
Falls of Schaffhausen	114
Geneva	25
Geneva to Chamouny	27
Genoa	41
Glasgow	217
Heidelberg	128
Haddon Hall	196
Hawthornden	212
Home Again	225
Interlaken	120
Kenilworth Castle	192
Liverpool to London	6
London	148

CONTENTS.

	PAGE
Lake Lucerne	117
Lake Geneva	32
Lake Maggiore	37
Lake Constance	113
Lake Brienz	119
Lake Thun	122
Lucerne	116
Milan	38
Mount Vesuvius	55
Munich	108
Melrose Abbey	209
Naples	47
North Sea	147
Oxford	179
Paris	9
Pisa	44
Pompeii	52
Rome	61
Rosslyn Chapel	213
Strassburg	123
Stratford on Avon	188
Stirling Castle	214
Scottish Lakes	216
Simplon Pass	35
The Hague	146
The Trossachs	215
Versailles	22
Venice	97
Vienna	104
Worms	130
Windsor Castle	177
Warwick	190
York Cathedral	197

EUROPE THROUGH A WOMAN'S EYE.

CHAPTER I.

On the 29th of April, 1882, at three o'clock in the afternoon, the old steamship Egypt, of the National line, that had ploughed the deep for eleven years, steamed out of New York bay, and my husband and I bade good-bye to America, for a few months. For an hour before sailing, the deck was crowded with the friends of those who were about to take the long voyage of three thousand five hundred miles across the Atlantic ocean.

A graceful young lady stepped up to us and introduced herself as a sister of one of my most intimate girl friends (Jessie Beck). She had come as her sister's representative, to bid us "God speed," and at parting presented me a lovely little nosegay, a delicate cream rose encircled with forget-me-nots and geranium leaves. I almost worshiped these few flowers, and kept them fresh for many days; for if there is any place in the world where people *appreciate* flowers it is on the broad, deep ocean, where none of nature's green relieves the eye, but all is water—water everywhere. In two hours the shores of America had entirely vanished from sight. It was with a tinge of sadness that we stood on deck and watched the land until it appeared like a tiny speck on the horizon. We had left America, home and friends behind; but grand old historical Europe, the country we had so long desired to see, was *ahead!*

Everything on the vessel was new and strange, and we flew hither and thither, to learn all we could about what was to be our little world for eleven days. The Egypt is four hundred and fifty feet long and forty-six feet wide. The saloon passengers, ninety-nine in number, occupied one part of the ship, and the steerage passengers the other. The dining saloon is one hundred and fifty feet long, the tables running the entire length, with velvet-cushioned benches for seats, and the floors are carpeted with Brussels. The state-rooms on either side of the dining-saloon are six by eight feet, with quite good accommodations. We had four meals a day; breakfast, at half-past eight; lunch, at half-past twelve; dinner, at five; and tea, at half-past eight in the evening. The meals were simply wonderful. For instance, this is an ordinary bill of fare for dinner:

Mock-turtle and spring soup.
Pigeons on toast, and mushrooms.
Mutton cutlets, curried chicken and rice.
Dresden patties, roast beef and Yorkshire pudding.
Boiled mutton and caper sauce.
Roast lamb and mint sauce.
Roast fillet of veal, corned pork and vegetables.
Corned beef, roast turkey, sausages and cranberry sauce.
Duck and green peas.
Ham and tongue, pickles and asparagus.
Plum and custard pudding, damson tarts, currant pies, Leipzig and plum cakes, Genoese pastry, apple tripple blanc mange, calves-foot jelly, Charlotte russe, macaroni cheese.
Apples, oranges, raisins, and several kinds of nuts.

All of the China dishes bear this stamp, "National Steamship Company," "Pro orbis utilitate" (for the use of the world). The tureens for meats and vegetables are of solid silver, and when the bell taps, the waiters take all the covers off at once, sometimes revealing the most unheard-of mixtures. Mr. Culler took four square meals every day, and did not indulge in sea-sickness. But alas! I was not so fortunate: the first night I fully realized what it was to be "rocked in the cradle of the deep," and the next morning upon raising my head from my pillow, I was initiated into the mysteries of sea-sickness, and it clung to me tenaciously; for seven successive days, I cast up my accounts accurately, several times to the smallest decimal fraction. The feeling is indescribable! If any one had proposed to throw me overboard, I don't know that I should have objected. The kind hands which always minister to my comfort dressed me, and managed to get me on deck in a fainting condition. Wrapped in a heavy sea-blanket and supported on either side, I walked the deck until the color returned to my lips. But when I attempted to recline in a sea-chair the sickness returned, and I was obliged to walk again.—It seemed that I must either walk or die—and thus I spent the entire day. Our second Sabbath out was, however, much more agreeably spent. We had church service in the dining saloon. Pillows piled up on the table and covered with a scarlet cloth served as a pulpit. The Captain read the service of the Church of England, my husband preached the sermon, and the renowned Philip Phillips and his son James sang, accompanied by the piano.

At sea people are more sociable than on land. Nobody thinks of waiting for a formal introduction. All sorts of people are on board, high and low, rich and poor, cultured and ignorant, selfish and generous, joyous and those bearing heavy burdens of sorrow. One lady, whose home was in Texas, started with her consumptive husband for England. He died on the steamer, just as they were entering New York Bay. She buried him in New York, and then embarked in the Egypt. This was a sad, sad trip for her. She returned to her friends in England, whom she left but two years ago to become the happy bride of her lover in Texas. On our homeward voyage, a poor mother among the steerage passengers watched anxiously by the couch of her dying child, and another gave birth to a sweet little baby, who will never be able to say, "This is my own, my native land."

Although life on the ocean wave seems very monotonous to those afflicted with sea-sickness, yet to others it has many attractions. At night the beautiful phosphorescent lights may be seen, looking like sparkling diamonds on the water. Then the pretty rainbows in the spray; and one morning after a shower, the sun shone out brightly and gave us a splendid rainbow, completely spanning old ocean; and one of the grandest sunsets I ever witnessed was on the ocean. The sun gradually slipped out of sight between the sky and the water, leaving its gorgeous robe of gold and purple floating on the ocean blue. We gazed in silent admiration on this grand picture from the brush of the Almighty. It is interesting, too, to watch the monsters of the deep at their uncouth gambols; dozens of whales apparently tried to see which could spout water the highest, and one huge fellow came so near the vessel that we had a good view of his immense back as he came up to blow. And how we would lean over the railing, and never tire of watching the porpoises as they leaped along beside the ship, a whole school of them at a time, chasing each other, darting hither and thither like mad creatures. And the dear, little, harmless, white sea-gulls followed the ship to feed on what was thrown out, occasionally sitting down on the waves to rest.

There are many ways of amusement—reading, writing, chatting, singing, lounging, dreaming. A concert is given each voyage, by the passengers, for the benefit of the Seaman's Orphan Home at Liverpool; and they are quite creditable. One day as we were walking on deck we had the delightful experience of being completely drenched by a playful wave, and we looked as meek as Moses, with our garments dripping with salt water. When one looks out upon the vast ocean, and watches the heaving and swelling of the waves, and thinks of the unfathomable depth of water, he is most solemnly impressed with the greatness and power of God, and the frailty and utter helplessness of man. We had just enough rough weather to get a taste of what a storm at sea would be like. The wind blew furiously; the waves ran high, at times sweeping over the deck in torrents; the rain beat violently; large waves leaped over the tops of the life-boats, high above the deck; the wind was so powerful that the gentlemen could scarcely keep their footing on deck, and the ladies were obliged to content themselves in the cabin. One lady was blown across the deck, and two others who attempted to walk were prostrated. Hats were blown overboard; chairs overturned; dishes broken, etc. As soon as it was safe for the ladies to go on deck, I sat with my husband at the stern of the vessel and watched her breast the waves as they rolled up mountain high. Sometimes the bow of the ship would be submerged in the waves, and it seemed that we must all go under, when up she would come, like a bird on the wing. A storm at sea is a grand sight, *awfully* grand! and the appreciative nature could thoroughly enjoy it, if all fear of the possible results could be dispelled. The sight of a distant sail was always welcomed with delight, and the taking on of a pilot, as we approached land, was another diversion. It is a rule that a vessel must take on the first pilot she meets, to take her into the harbor. The pilot we took, on approaching America, had been sailing about for a month seeking employment. He received $460.00 for his services, so much a foot for the number of feet of water the vessel draws. He came in a pilot boat, and then was brought from that to our steamer in a row boat, as the sailing vessel could not approach very near us. It was a pretty sight to witness the signal of red, white and blue lights by which our vessel reported its arrival off Fastnett rock, on the coast of Ireland. How we strained our eyes to see the first faint outline of land!

We entered the dock at Liverpool at four o'clock a. m. on Wednesday, May 10. There were no sleepy-heads that morning; everybody was up, hurrying and bustling about, seeing to baggage, giving good byes and kind wishes to newly-made friends; confusion reigned supreme. The table stewards, bedroom stewards, the stewardess, the boots, in fact all the servants who had looked at us during the voyage, hovered about expecting a fee, and asked for it if we did not take the hint.

The examination of luggage by the custom-house officials is a very trifling affair to the American tourist, unless he has cigars or fire-arms among his possessions. And during our entire trip, traveling in so many different countries, our baggage being examined twelve times, it was always done courteously, and in a very superficial manner. It is nothing worth getting nervous over.

Oh! how good it seemed, and how safe we felt, when we once more stepped on terra firma. But we soon discovered that we had a very awkward gait, and even that reverend gentleman who walks so excruciatingly straight at home swayed slightly from side to side. For several days I walked as if trying to balance myself, and often thought the floor was moving up and down as on shipboard.

As we had a few hours to spend in Liverpool before taking the train for London, we availed ourselves of the opportunity to visit St. George's Hall. It is a grand building, four hundred and twenty feet long, and ornamented with fifteen magnificent Corinthian columns forty-five feet high; and the massiveness of the structure is greatly enhanced by two colossal stone lions lying at the foot of the steps by which it is approached, and also the equestrian bronze statues of Prince Albert and Queen Victoria. The interior of the hall is very fine, with beautifully gilded ceiling. It is tastefully ornamented with sculpture, and contains a very large pipe organ. It is is used for public gatherings, musical entertainments, etc.

We obtained a lunch at the Northwestern Hotel, and ate with a relish the largest and most delicious mutton chops we had ever tasted.

We left Liverpool at eleven o'clock a. m., in company with Philip Phillips and family, and dear Mrs. Pritchard, whom we learned to know and love on the ocean, on a fast express train over the Northwestern Railway, and reached London about four p. m., a distance of two hundred and ten miles.

The English railway cars are much smaller than our American cars, and are divided into several apartments, each seating eight persons, and occasionally ten. Four ride forward and four backward. The cars are entered from the side, and the windows form the upper half of the doors. The most desirable seats are, of course, near the windows, where one can lower or raise them at pleasure, and obtain a good view of the scenery. There are first, second and third class cars, but they have no fire, water nor conveniences. Baggage is not checked, so that it necessitates a person looking after his luggage very closely, lest it be taken on too far, or not far enough. Valises, satchels, etc., may be taken into the car free, and placed under the seat or in the rack. As our luggage consisted of two valises, it mattered little to us whether they had a check system or not. The guard, or conductor, as we would say, has no means of passing through the train, but is obliged to walk on a narrow platform attached to the outside of the cars, and hold on to an iron railing. He is thus exposed to heat and cold, sun and rain. The engineer and fireman have also no protection in the majority of cases.

The railway stations, however, all over Europe, are much superior to those in America. Some are immense structures, made entirely of glass and iron, with first, second and third class waiting rooms. Others are massive buildings of stone, presenting a fine architectural appearance; and the Swiss depots are perfect marvels of taste, with their display of wood-carving. The first-class waiting rooms are often carpeted with Brussels, and have a cheerful fire in the grate, hearth rugs, easy chairs, etc., which gives the traveler such a home-like feeling, while he is waiting for trains. And I have seen waiting rooms on the Continent decorated with marble statues, and the walls adorned with large oil paintings. I have a distinct recollection of a waiting room in a station at Munich, the walls of which are imitation of different colored marble, and so perfect is the representation, that not until we had tested them in various ways could we believe that they were not marble. The furnishing, too, seemed complete; marble centre table, handsome garnet rep lambrequins, cane-seated chairs, and here and there garnet plush circular sofas.

The ride from Liverpool to London was simply charming! Every foot of ground seemed to be under the most careful cultivation. The lovely green fields dotted with daisies and buttercups, were such a sweet relief to our eyes that had been accustomed to beholding nothing but water for so many days. Not a stick, stone or stump was to be seen. Beautiful green hedges take the place of fences. Even the railways are bordered with them. No pedestrians are allowed on the railway track, and no carriage drives cross the track; but in all cases of intersection, a bridge is built over the track, or the track bridges over the carriage and footway—thus preventing the many accidents common in America.

The buildings in England are all of stone or brick. The scenery during the whole journey seemed like one grand panorama. Bridges over small streams are of white stone, and some of them encircled with English ivy, making such picturesque little views.

When we reached London, we took a hansom, (a small two-wheeled vehicle, with an elevated driver's seat behind; two wooden half-doors in front shut you in, and a dashboard encircling the hind parts of the horse, prevents the mud from flying in one's face), to Mr. Burr's private boarding house, No. 11 Queen Square.

I will not tell you now what we saw and learned in London; but if you will follow us in our trip over the Continent, we will bring you back to London, and tell you what we saw in the two weeks we spent there, and also in other parts of England and Scotland.

At New Haven we took a steamer across the British Channel to Dieppe; were six hours and a half on the water. The shortest route across the Channel, from Dover to Calais, only occupies an hour and a quarter; but we had read and heard so many unpleasant reports about that passage, that we decided to take a route where "wash-bowls" would not be brought into requisition. Old Neptune failed to make any impression on us.

CHAPTER II.

Arriving at Paris, we had a strange experience with the Frenchmen at the depot, but finally succeeded in getting a cab to take us to Mr. J. Eppler's, No. 9, Boulevarde Malesherbes, to whom Rev. Dr. Hamma directed us. These French cab-drivers always expect *pour boire*, that is, a few cents with which to buy drink, in addition to their regular fare; and if you do not give it them they get fearfully angry, and gesture and talk all over.

Mr. Eppler assisted us to find a hotel, centrally located, with comfortable apartments, where English is spoken. The name of the hotel is American Family Home, No. 7, 9, and 11 Rue de la Bienfaisance, near the Boulevarde Malesherbes. It is a very large building, and we lost our way several times, until we became accustomed to its labyrinth of halls. The floors are of dark oiled wood, with the carpets laid on loose. We were struck with the diminutiveness of our wash pitcher, it being only four inches higher than the bowl. Upon inquiry, we found that this was the ordinary size used by the Parisians.

If one had nothing else to judge from, he might suppose them not a very cleanly class of people. But indeed, it is quite the contrary. To my mind, Paris excels all other European cities in cleanliness. The streets are immaculate, its perfect system of sewerage wonderful, and its being built up with lofty structures of white limestone, of the finest architecture, gives it a bright, clean, cheery aspect; such a pleasant change from smoky, foggy London.

Here we entered upon a style of taking our meals essentially different from the habits of our own country. But we afterwards discovered that the same custom prevails all over the Continent, viz., déjeûner (a light breakfast consisting of a French roll and a cup of coffee), which may be had any time after half-past eight in the morning; at twelve comes lunch, the regular déjeûner à la fourchette; and between five and six o'clock comes table d'hôte, a dinner of eleven or twelve courses, finishing up with delicious fruits, especially in Italy. If one eats everything he is offered, he will be sure to have enough.

Wine is as freely used here as water is in America. I once counted the wine bottles on the table and found there were fourteen, besides all the private bottles. We had to call for water, as there was none on the table. The waiters looked at us in astonishment. It takes fully an hour to go through all the ceremonies of this extensive dinner; so one day in Brussels, coming in a little late, we thought it would be a kindness to the waiters, and also to ourselves, not to take all the courses from beginning to end, but select from the bill of fare what we preferred. We did so; and when we came to pay our bill found that they had charged us two francs (forty cents) apiece *more* than if we had allowed the waiters to bring us ten courses, ten clean plates, and ten clean knives and forks! After that experience we permitted waiters to make themselves all the trouble they desired. But I must not omit to tell you what a feast of strawberries we had during our trip. We began to have them about the middle of May in Paris, and continued to have them in different countries until the last of August, when we bid them good-bye in Scotland.

Paris! The very name has a charm, but one cannot imagine its beauties and attractions. They must be seen to be realized. The boulevards, of which we have heard so much, are streets ninety-nine feet wide, with an addition of thirty-five feet of pavement on either side. They are macadamized, and are flanked with beautiful shade trees. These great thoroughfares, some sixty in number, are universally admitted to excel all other cities in the grandeur of their architecture, the attractiveness of their shops, and the briskness of their traffic. The vehicles which traverse these boulevards daily, from the superb private equipage to the ponderous wagon, are more than twenty-five thousand. The population of Paris is two millions. Late in the afternoon on the day of our arrival we took a walk to the Place de la Concorde, situated between the Garden of the Tuileries and the Champs Elysées, where stands the wonderful obelisk of Luxor, with a picturesque fountain on either side. This obelisk is a single block of reddish granite, covered with hieroglyphics, from the quarries of Syene, in Upper Egypt. It is seventy-six feet in height, and weighs two hundred and forty tons. The pedestal of Breton granite is thirteen feet high, and is also a single block. The steps raise it three and one-half feet above the ground. It was presented to Louis Philippe by the Pasha of Egypt, and it cost four hundred thousand dollars to move and erect it. It formerly stood in front of the Temple of Thebes, fifteen hundred years before Christ. This delightful Place de la Concorde, to which crowds of visitors are attracted by the obelisk and the sparkling fountains, could tell of many a dark historic deed if it could speak. It was here, during the French Revolution in 1793, that the guillotine, a horrid machine used for beheading people, was set up to execute Louis XVI.; and soon after his wife, Marie Antoinette, was subjected to the same cruel fate.

The French people kept this infamous instrument warm with the blood of human beings until its victims numbered more than two thousand eight hundred persons. Here it was, during the celebration of the marriage of Louis XVI. and Marie Antionette, that the accidental discharge of some rockets caused a panic, and twelve hundred people were trampled to death. And in 1871, during the Franco-Prussian war, this square was literally soaked with the blood of the slain. As we turned our steps toward our hotel, we could not but think, what a happy transformation! These beautiful fountains shooting up their crystal streams seem to be trying to wash away all traces of the bloody scenes enacted here.

The dress of the French ladies we met on the street appeared to be faultless, from the nicely-fitting glove to the dainty boot, although I cannot indorse the French heel. As a natural consequence, the ladies of this city, in which all our fashions originate, have exquisite taste. If *they* put a spray of blossoms or an ostrich tip on a bonnet, tie a bow, or drape an overskirt, it at once possesses the charm of gracefulness. A French milliner has probably more grace in the tips of her fingers, than in her heart.

When we saw Paris by gas-light, we fully realized that we were in the "gay capital." Yes, evening is the time to see the gayety of Paris. The innumerable gas jets and electric lights make the city almost as light as day; the fashionable people in luxuriant attire are promenading; the vast number of cafés are brilliant and attractive; and outside, on the pavement, seated at small tables, are crowds of ladies and gentlemen sipping their favorite beverage from their dainty wine-glasses; and the display in the shop windows exceeds anything I ever saw elsewhere. The artistic taste in the arrangement of articles is wonderful! The jeweler's French plate glass windows, with rows of gas jets on the *outside* as well as inside, flashing and sparkling with diamonds, gold, silver and precious stones, attract you like a magnet—men just as well as women. Open-air concerts, entertainments of all sorts, to suit the different classes of people, operas, balls and games, serve to while away the time; and this gayety is kept up half the night, as they do their sleeping in the morning.

One day, passing through the magnificent arcades in the Rue de Rivoli, its shop windows rich with splendor, we at length reached the Louvre, that world-renowned museum, a perfect gem of architecture, and covering a space of forty acres. It is a vast palace in the form of a square, with an open court in the centre, thus giving a good light to all parts of the building. As the admission is free, these halls are thronged with visitors daily; and you can form some idea of the number, when I tell you that more than twenty thousand dollars per annum is received for depositing canes and umbrellas at the door, for which you pay a penny or two. People are not allowed to take canes, umbrellas, etc., into any picture gallery in Europe, as some would be thoughtless enough to use them for pointers.

This museum is a perfect wilderness of pictures, statuary, curiosities, relics from all parts of Europe and Egypt and Assyria. The Gallery de Apollon is the most beautiful hall in the Louvre, and is considered one of the finest in the world. It is two hundred and ten feet long. The ceiling paintings are very fine, and around the edge of the ceiling is the most beautiful statuary standing out in high relief. There are handsome inlaid tables and other furniture, dating from the time of Louis XIV. Glass cases in the centre contain objects of art, rare gems, etc. The collection of enamels is the most extensive and valuable in the world. One room of French porcelain consists chiefly of dishes adorned with snakes, frogs, fish, lizards, plants and flowers moulded from nature, and the coloring perfect, standing out life-like. Just fancy at one of your family gatherings, having a roast turkey on a platter of this description, and as the turkey diminished you would discover a huge snake coiled up in the bottom, with his head raised and tongue extended. The Egyptian sphynxes, sarcophagi, and the immense Assyrian winged bulls, four in number, are ponderous. It seems almost impossible that they were brought all the way from Africa and Asia; yet when we think of it, many seeming impossibilities are overcome by mechanical skill.

We walked through room after room of statuary, and finally found the one piece of sculpture of all others that we had been looking for—the celebrated Venus of Milo. The face is very handsome, delicately carved and full of expression ; but both arms are broken off, and it is otherwise mutilated. In passing through the almost endless number of picture galleries, said to contain seven miles of pictures, we found so many to admire that we will not attempt to mention those which pleased us most : suffice it to say, that we saw many, many masterly productions by Rubens, Raphael, Titian, Vandyke, Rembrandt, Paul Veronese, Albert Dürer, Claude Lorraine, Murillo, Holbein, Leonardo de Vinci, Quentin Massys, and many others.

The marine and ethnographical departments are very extensive, instructive and interesting.

Although we spent three days in this museum, continually feasting our eyes on things ancient, new, curious, beautiful and interesting, yet we felt that it would take as many months to become familiar with it all.

The Garden of the Tuileries being in close proximity to the Louvre, we upon one occasion took it in on our way home. It is seven hundred and eighty yards in length, and three hundred and forty-seven yards in breadth. On the west it is bounded by a shady grove of lofty trees. There are beautiful spacious walks running in all directions, lovely flower-beds, fountains, statuary, inviting green grass plats, with rustic seats here and there, and two long rows of orange trees in tubs, some of them four hundred years old. This happened to be a holiday, and so the garden was crowded with pleasure-seekers, playing all sorts of games, making a gay, festive scene.

On Sabbath we attended services in the morning at the Madeleine. The music was very fine, but the Catholic performances seemed like mockery to us. This is considered one of the grandest of the modern churches in Paris. It is built in imitation of a Greek temple. It is three hundred and fifty-four feet long and one hundred and forty-one feet wide, and is surrounded by fifty-two magnificent Corinthian columns, each seventeen feet in circumference. The tympanum of the façade contains a high relief in marble, representing Christ as the Judge of the world. The figures are all colossal. On the right of the Saviour are the elect and the Angel of Salvation, and on his left the Angel of Justice and the damned, with Mary Magdalene interceding for them.

This church is built exclusively of stone, and is entirely destitute of windows, the light being introduced through three dome-shaped sections in the ceiling. It is approached by a flight of twenty-eight marble steps, extending across the whole front of the structure. The interior is one large hall, with three chapels on either side, each containing a marble statue of its patron saint. It is gorgeous with frescoes, gildings, carvings, and statues. The floor and walls are of solid, polished marble, and the high altar consists of an elegant group of statuary, representing Mary Magdalene being borne into Paradise by two angels.

In the evening Mr. Culler went to the Wesleyan chapel. After the services, he with several others was invited to drink a cup of tea with the minister. The few Protestant clergymen in this city have up-hill work. The Sabbath is not regarded except by religious people. We saw men doing all sorts of work— masons and carpenters as busy as on other days; circuses, theatres, and many places of business open; heavily-loaded carts continuously passing in the streets; many enjoying it as a gala day; military companies drilling and parading; women selling flowers on the street corners; others sewing, patching and darning, as though the Lord had not called upon them to rest on this His holy day. By invitation we spent part of a day with Mr. Eppler's family. Their residence is just outside the city walls, on a part of what used to be Louis Philippe's park, now divided up into many grand residences. This we found to be a lovely home, elegantly furnished and adorned with pictures and ornaments, but only one rocking-chair! and that a very peculiar one. European people know nothing of the comforts of a rocking-chair. I saw but two during our entire trip. They have handsome, upholstered easy-chairs in almost every shape and style, but no rockers. The yard was most delightful!—filled with flower-beds and rare trees, the loveliest roses of all tints, pansies of immense size, daisies, forget-me-nots, syringas in rich profusion. The training of the fruit-bearing trees was both novel and interesting to us; apple trees with but two branches running in opposite directions, were tied to a wire about a foot from the ground; they were trimmed when very young, and bent into the desired shape. Cherry, peach and pear trees were trained up against stone walls like grape vines. They say the fruit grows much larger and more abundant in this manner. I counted the pears on a small bush of this kind, about five feet long and three feet high, and found sixty-five little, green, healthy pears. Several ladies called while we were there, and

Mr. Eppler saluted them with a kiss on either cheek, which seems to be the French style.

We went to see the Notre Dame cathedral. This magnificent Gothic structure was founded in 1163; but has been much altered. The external architecture is exceedingly beautiful. It has two great square towers in front, over two hundred feet high, with a superb stained-glass rose-window, thirty-six feet in diameter, between them; and the three portals, richly ornamented with sculpture, are fine specimens of early Gothic workmanship. The interior consists of a nave and double aisles, crossed by a transept. The vaulted arches more than a hundred feet high, supported by seventy-five pillars, give one a good idea of the style of all Gothic cathedrals. A fine organ with five thousand two hundred and forty-six pipes, and eighty-six stops, is over the entrance door. The choir and sanctuary are separated from the nave by ornamental railings. On the right side of the nave are small chapels with confessional boxes in them, where the people, on bended knees, confess their sins to the priest. We saw them so frequently afterwards, that we became quite familiar with the "*modus operandi.*" The priest shuts himself in the confessional box, sits down, rests his head on his hand, with his ear close to a little side window. The sinner kneels without, on a step, and through the window confesses his sin in the ear of the priest. Poor deluded mortals! Why do they not go to "the *great high priest*, that is passed into the heavens, Jesus the Son of God," who will freely and fully forgive all their sins if they but ask him.

One chapel was tastefully decorated with blooming plants and cut flowers, preparatory to some special service which was to take place. This church is four hundred and seventeen feet long, and one hundred and fifty-six feet wide. Pere Hyacinthe used to pour forth his eloquence in this sanctuary.

At the rear of this edifice is a small building called the Morgue, where people who have been drowned in the river Seine, or have been found dead anywhere in the city, are left for recognition; and if not claimed in three days, the city provides a burial. Here we saw a woman with flowing raven locks, which had evidently been drenched in the river, with a face expressive of vice and degradation; and a man in his working dress, blue blouse and cap, with soiled hands, looking as though he had suddenly stopped work. Many of the lower classes were passing in and out.

We next visited the Pantheon, a church of imposing dimensions; its form that of a Greek cross. The interior is very beautiful, decorated with paintings and other works of art of a national and historic character. It is three hundred and sixty-nine feet long, and two hundred and seventy-six feet wide; surmounted by a dome two hundred and seventy-two feet high. We ascended to the top of the lantern, above the dome, where we had a fine view of the city. We also descended to the vaults or crypts beneath the building, which are very extensive, and so dark that it is necessary for the guide to light the way with a lantern. Here we saw two sarcophagi, erected as monuments to Voltaire and Rousseau; but the remains of both of these philosophers have been removed from these coffins. Several eminent men are buried here. In one part of these vaults a remarkably loud echo can be heard. We with several other persons stood in a row against the wall; the guide struck the wall with his tobacco box, and it sounded like the discharge of a cannon. When hands were clapped, it sounded like peals of thunder; and it was very funny when he talked, to hear the echo follow him up so distinctly and quickly.

From here we went to the "Jardin des Plantes" (garden of plants), covering an area of seventy-five acres. The grounds are handsomely laid out, including a very fine Botanical garden, to which professors and medical students resort; a Zoological garden, containing boa-constrictors, crocodiles, alligators, bears, lions, tigers, monkeys, birds innumerable, and in fact I suppose nearly all the animals in existence are represented; also galleries of botany, mineralogy and zoology, and laboratories for lectures. Winding walks bordered with shrubs and flowers led us to new attractions whichever way we turned; and finally, foot-sore and weary, we went down to the river Seine, which flows near by, and took a short ride of three miles, in a swift little steamboat. There are swimming-schools, bath-houses, and long houses where the poorer classes go to earn their daily bread by washing, built out in the river.

The Champs Elysées is the most fashionable promenade in Paris. One end of this magnificent avenue widens out into a park, seven hundred and fifty yards long and four hundred yards wide, joining the Place de la Concorde. This park is a favorite resort for Parisians in the evening, when it is brilliantly illuminated. And certainly it is a gay spectacle! There are elegant cafés, with crowds of richly-dressed people sitting in front, watching the splendid turnouts, liveried coachmen and prancing horses, as they pass hither and thither along the broad avenue; bands of music filling the air with sweetest strains; Chinese lanterns suspended from the trees; platforms filled with dancers; Punch and Judy shows; revolving swings with wooden horses for children to ride, and games of chance and amusement, while the air is laden with perfume from the many bright flower-beds. One sunny, glorious morning, we took a walk the entire length of the Champs Elysées, from the Place de la Concorde down the broad avenue flanked with handsome buildings, a distance of nearly a mile and a half. We passed the Palais de l'Industrie, erected in 1855, for the first great Exhibition of Paris. This grand avenue terminates at the Place de l'Etoile, on the slight eminence of which rises the Arc de Triomphe, the largest triumphal arch in the world; begun by Napoleon I. in 1806, but not completed until thirty years afterwards.

This superb monument, built to commemorate the victories of the French, is in the form of a rectangle, and rises to the lofty height of one hundred and sixty feet, and is one hundred and forty-six feet wide and seventy-two feet thick. The great central arch is sixty-seven feet high and forty-six feet wide, and is intersected by a transverse arch which forms an entrance through this splendid structure, which cost more than two million dollars. The exterior is adorned with richly-carved groups, representing battle scenes, and on the walls of the interior are the names of French generals and victories won, cut in the solid masonry. We were not satisfied until we had climbed to the top by a spiral staircase of two hundred and sixty-one steps. This was rather fatiguing; but what a rare treat when we gained the summit! There were those twelve grand, broad avenues radiating from that centre like the spokes of a wheel, stretching out into the distance, presenting a view which cannot be obtained from any other point of observation. While standing there, we thought of the armies and processions that had passed under this arch from time to time. The German army passed *triumphantly* through it in 1871.

In the afternoon, strange as it may seem, we took a trip through the sewers. Paris is said to have better drainage than any other city in the world. There were about two hundred ladies and gentlemen in the party. Of course we dressed very warmly, to protect ourselves against the cold and dampness. With our permit from the Préfet de la Seine in hand, we repaired to an iron trap-door in the pavement, near the Madeleine. Prepared to put our handkerchiefs to our noses at the first offensive odor, we descended a long flight of stone steps, which terminated in a massive stone tunnel, with great iron pipes overhead by which the city is supplied with pure water; also telegraph wires, enclosed in lead pipes. These channels are of ample dimensions, the smallest being four by seven feet, and the largest sixteen by eighteen feet, all constructed of solid masonry, and lighted with lamps. They communicate with the streets of the city above by means of iron ladders; and the names of the streets are posted along the walls, so one knows just what part or the city he is beneath. We could discover no unpleasant odor; and, upon inquiry, found that these channels are frequently dragged with a vertical iron gate or sort of comb, and the sediment conveyed away in barges, to be used for fertilizing the soil. Visitors are only allowed to enter immediately after this cleansing process. The total length of the principal sewers of Paris is six hundred and ten miles, and they are kept so sweet and clean that a lady may wear a silk or satin dress to explore them without fear of pollution. And what an admirable means of conducting troops from one part of the city to another in case of war!

Well, we rode in these sewers for about an hour, part of the time in a boat drawn through the water by six men, who walked on narrow stone sidewalks, three on either side; and part of the time in a car, under the management of five men, two to pull, two to push, and the other on the car to use the brake. There was quite a long line of cars, but disconnected. Away we went, our men-horses running at full speed, creating quite a breeze, and giving zest and excitement to the excursion. It was a novel and wonderful experience.

When we ascended to the upper regions and again beheld the light of day, it was almost unbearable at first. We looked about us, and found we were a long, long way from home; so we procured seats on top of an omnibus—and by the way, this is the most successful way to see Paris; for many of the private residences are so shut in by high stone walls, that unless one takes an elevated position he is wholly ignorant of the charm of wealth and grandeur within. The very fragrance of the flowers with which the lawns are ornamented cannot escape. But perched upon an omnibus one may take in everything, from the rich heavy crimson curtains, half-opened, revealing creamy waves of lace, to the bare sombre basements where a tin reflector steals from the street a few rays of sunshine, and pale little faces peer out, which put one in mind of the growth of geranium leaves that have been excluded from the sun, with their long, slender, sickly stalks.

The church of St. Augustine is built in a modernized Romanesque style, and is very large and handsome. The Palais Royal occupies a whole square, and is just opposite to the Louvre. It is very showy and attractive, as the ground floor is mostly taken up with jewelry shops. These shops are of two kinds, those which contain the real, pure gold and precious stones, and those containing the imitation. Of course the latter looks equally as good, to the unpracticed eye, as the former, and many an inexperienced person might be "taken in" were it not a law that a sign, announcing the fact that they are imitation, shall always be displayed. Here may be seen imitation Roman and Florentine mosaics made out of wax, imitation diamonds made of polished rock-crystal, mock coral, painted jewelry which looks like inlaid stones of different colors, etc. Wouldn't this be a feast for many of our American girls, who delight in wearing shoddy jewelry?

Our next sight was the Palace of Luxembourg. This is a grand edifice externally, and a part of the interior is devoted to the Musée de Luxembourg, which contains a choice collection of paintings, drawings and sculptures by modern artists. I was particularly struck with Rosa Bonheur's "Oxen Ploughing," and an oil painting by Leyendecker, of three birds hung up by a string, as natural as could be. It scarcely seemed possible that it could be a picture. The statue of Psyche interested me because I have a picture of her in my parlor at home; and my sympathies were immediately aroused for the "Wounded Dog" in bronze, so true was it to nature. The gardens surrounding the palace are beautified with flowers, fountains and statuary.

From this place we took a cab to the Hotel des Invalides. This is an institution for disabled soldiers, and is an immense building with a chapel for the soldiers to worship in; and strangely appropriate seems the decoration of this chapel with all of the flags captured by the French in their many battles. There are a number of rooms in this institution filled with warriors made of wood, and some of wax, dressed in full uniform, from every country in the world. Our North American Indian had a bracelet made of human double-teeth strung on a string. The west wing of the building contains an interesting collection of four thousand specimens of weapons of war, suits of armor of the sixteenth and seventeenth centuries, etc. We also peeped into the culinary department. The tomb of Napoleon is a recent addition to the building. Its dome, which is lofty and gilded, is conspicuous from all parts of the city. The vault or crypt is directly under the dome, and the same shape; it is thirty-six feet in diameter. You look down over a white marble railing, into the crypt, in which is the reddish-brown marble sarcophagus of Napoleon the first. His remains were brought here by Prince Joinville from St. Helena in 1840. On the floor of the crypt, encircling the sarcophagus, is a beautiful mosaic wreath of laurels, wrought of green marble, or serpentine, as it is called. Around the walls of the crypt stand twelve colossal statues of pure white marble, facing the tomb, representing victories. They look as though they might be guardian angels. The light falling through the handsome stained-glass windows into the crypt, produces a delicate violet tint, giving it a strange and softened beauty. The high altar, back of the crypt, is a gilded canopy supported by four columns of mottled marble, twisted in the most graceful manner. Beneath the canopy is a golden cross on which is the crucified Redeemer. Over the entrance to the crypt is the following extract from the Emperor's will: "I desire that my ashes may repose on the banks of the Seine, in the midst of the French people, whom I have ever loved."

We could not think of leaving Paris without visiting Versailles, the most beautiful and interesting of all its environs. So, in company with Mr. and Mrs. Gibb, of Southport, England, most companionable people, we made this little excursion of about twelve miles by rail. We approached the palace, which is the centre of attraction in this place, through the park, which is simply charming! Lovely shaded avenues run in all directions, the tall graceful trees meeting overhead. Upon a nearer approach, there are pretty green terraces (stone walls completely covered with vines, or trees trimmed so as to look like vines), in the shape of a half circle. On the upper terrace is a row of evergreen trees trimmed in the shape of cones, reminding every scholar of the figures in his geometry. Then a grand flight of stone steps leads to the large gravel space in front of the palace. Immediately below the terraces are two large, exquisitely beautiful fountains, and tastefully-arranged flower-beds, with their rich scarlet, pink and white blossoms, setting off to good advantage the closely-shaven lawn. I often think of these beautiful pleasure grounds, and am unable to decide in my own mind which is the most charming spot, *this*, or the Chatsworth estate in England.

There seems to be no end to the fountains, artificial lakes, statuary, pebbly walks, and other attractions. But the fitting up of these grounds cost the treasury of Louis XIV. the enormous sum of two million dollars, and the poor people of France were heavily taxed that this sovereign might have every foolish whim and fancy gratified. The palace is a majestic pile of immense proportions. The façade towards the park is a quarter of a mile in length. In one part of the palace is the royal chapel, which is a perfect gem of beauty, with its handsome mosaic pavement, elegant Corinthian columns, elaborate paintings illustrating Bible scenes, statuary, bas-reliefs, and magnificent high altar, rich with different-colored marbles. And this chapel is no small affair; it is one hundred and fourteen feet long and sixty feet wide. Louis XVI. and Marie Antoinette were married here in 1770. There is also a theatre of great splendor in this palace, brilliant with mirrors, chandeliers, scarlet, purple and gold, richly ornamented boxes, etc., and a large ball-room, two hundred and forty feet long, with seventeen massive arched windows, commanding an extended view of the lovely park already described. The opposite wall is a mass of elegant mirrors, the ceiling one grand battle scene, painted in glowing colors, and the floor dark, oiled wood, so shiny and sleek that none but an agile Frenchman dare tread it with anything like composure. We passed through gallery after gallery filled with rich paintings by distinguished artists, most of them portraying the victories of the French, until the eye became wearied, and the brilliant tints, form and expression ceased to attract, and we were glad of the change when the guide took us through the private apartments of Louis XIII., Louis XIV., Louis XV., Louis XVI., and those of the wife of the latter, Marie Antoinette. There are several of these gorgeous rooms belonging to each. Some have furniture upholstered in pale blue satin, others light green, orange, and a variety of deep as well as delicate shades. The window curtains are of satin and silk. The rooms fitted up for Queen Victoria when she visited Paris are truly royal. The walls and ceiling of the bedroom are in gilt; gold bedstead with a canopy over it, silk bed-spread, rose-color and gilt upholstered furniture, and everything else to correspond. In nearly all these apartments were handsome clocks made by Louis XIV. One looks like a bouquet of gilt flowers. This sovereign seemed to have a mania for clocks.

CHAPTER III.

AFTER a most delightful stay of ten days we left Paris for Geneva, accompanied by Miss Hortense Camp, a niece of Philip Phillips. Eight of us rode all night in one of the car apartments, with about twenty-five valises all told, little and big, and were so crowded that we could scarcely move our feet. We passed through Dijon and Macon, and arrived at Geneva, Switzerland, about ten o'clock the next morning. After the first peep of day the scenery was delightful. Fleecy clouds floated about half-way up the sides of the Jura mountains, and at the foot the Rhone river wound in and out, following the mountain chain. Charming bits of landscape here and there effectually opened our drooping eyelids and freshened us up for the day.

Geneva, with its population of about 50,000, is the largest and wealthiest town in Switzerland. It is prettily situated at the south end of Lake Geneva, and is built in quite a modern style. It has some broad streets flanked with handsome buildings, and also some narrow crooked ones. This was the birth-place of Rousseau; and Calvin, second to none but Luther in the great work of the Reformation, resided here twenty-eight years, and his humble cottage is still pointed out to tourists. We walked down to the jetée or pier, which is adorned with shade-trees and rustic seats, and there had our first view of the Alps. With the aid of an opera-glass we could clearly distinguish Mont Blanc, with its snowy peaks, glistening in the sunlight, looking like white thunder-clouds in the distance.

The monument of Duke Charles II. of Brunswick, who willed four million dollars to this city, is lavishly adorned. It is wrought of different-colored marbles, in the form of a six-sided pyramid. On the top is an equestrian statue of the duke in bronze, and in the interior is also a reclining figure of the duke.

The reliefs, pillars, and the entire ornamentation, are exquisite in design.

As Geneva is world-renowned for its manufacture of jewelry and watches, of course we made it a point to explore some of these establishments, and in none of the shops did we find plated jewelry. Everything is 18 carats fine. Five thousand people are daily employed in this business. In the Jardin du Lac (garden of the lake), we listened to a very fine orchestral concert, given by thirty performers. There were five bass viols, violins, flutes, brass horns, hautboys, and kettle-drums. The compositions were by Strauss, Faust, and other masters. The gardens were crowded with music-loving people, yet perfect order prevailed everywhere. There were two large music-boxes at our hotel, which sharpened our desire to see more of these sweetest of all musical instruments. So we went to the manufactory, where we saw musical vases, fruit dishes, cake baskets, Swiss cottages, clocks, ink-stands, bears—in fact, everything in the shop was converted into a music-box. I became wearied with standing so long, and dropped into a chair, when lo! it broke forth in such sweet musical strains that I immediately rose to my feet, when it suddenly ceased its mirthful tune, and could not be induced to proceed until I was re-seated. The proprietor wound up what appeared to be a secretary or book-case, and it at once began to play in exact imitation of a pipe organ accompanied by a full orchestra. It would play twenty pieces of classical music. Why does not every rich man who has any music in his soul, but none in his voice, and no one in his home to make any, purchase an instrument of this kind, that will produce the most difficult and soul-enchanting strains by simply winding it up? I could not refrain from buying a beautiful fruit-dish with a Swiss scene in the interior exquisitely painted in oil, with money presented to me by the ladies of our congregation in Newton, Iowa. When I pass fruit to my friends it plays lively little waltzes, but modestly stops when placed upon the table.

One of the sights of Geneva is the junction of the Rhone and

Arve rivers. The Rhone is a clear, swift-flowing river, emerging from the lake, and the Arve is a sluggish, dirty stream coming from the glaciers at Chamouny. We did not experiment, but were told that where they flow together, a person can put one hand in the tepid water of the Rhone, and the other in the icy-cold Arve, and that they flow in the same channel for some distance before they mingle. We attended services in the Episcopal church, which is small but neat, and was well filled with devout worshipers.

Bright and early Monday morning, we started on a fifty-four mile drive to Chamouny, in a diligence (a vehicle having two stories, the top one covered with canvas; a peculiar looking thing drawn by four horses). We paid extra and obtained a seat in the upper story, thus having a charming view of the grand mountain scenery as we passed along. We were quite a lively company, twenty persons in all, and were soon chatting as gayly to each other as though we were friends of long standing. They changed horses frequently, so as to drive on a keen trot all the way, requiring twenty-four horses to take us through. All teams on the street, everybody and everything, are required by law to make clear the way for the diligence all the distance from Geneva to Chamouny. It was too funny to see them scamper to get out of our way. One man, driving a team, did not give us the middle of the road, but crowded us almost to the edge, and but for careful managing we might have been overturned. As soon as we had safely passed, our big French two-hundred-pound conductor jumped off, ran after the team, and hit the man a furious blow on the head. The other retaliated by trying to strike back with his whip. After some expressive language on both sides, our man ended the fracas by throwing a stone at the other, and then drove rapidly on. A coarse-looking peasant woman leading a calf, grasped it by the horns, and with her strong arms held it, in spite of its struggles, until we had passed. Every mile of the fifty-four presented most picturesque and varied scenery; ancient ruined castles on rocky heights, charming cascades, magnificent views of Mont Blanc, with its dazzling snowy peaks, towering majestically in the distance. We passed through long avenues of trees, through tunnels, over bridges, following the Arve, winding around the lofty mountains. A rocky projection of the mountains is called the profile of Louis Philippe, the green grass at the top forming the hair. Crosses of all descriptions are set up by the roadside, bearing the word Mission, and the date. One was a bronze cross on a stone pedestal, with the figure of the crucified Saviour, where Catholics come to pray. This seemed very strange to us, but we afterwards saw an innumerable number of them scattered through Italy.

Driving through the country and towns in this manner, enabled us to form a good idea of French and Swiss peasant life. For instance, it was wash-day, and everybody washed in the streams; some on flat stones, and others on slabs of wood; some scrubbed the clothes with brushes, others beat them with sticks; and such-looking clothes! An American woman would be ashamed to have them hang in her yard. One female was washing greens for dinner by stamping on them with her bare feet in a brook. Women were laboring in the fields, doing all sorts of farm work. We also saw them knitting under various circumstances; one away up on the mountain side, seated on a stump, *knitting* and watching two cows pasture; others standing in the streets *knitting*, riding in carts *knitting*, carrying baskets filled with lunch and bottles of wine on their heads, *knitting*. I began to think that the Swiss people must be "very hard on their stockings." A family moving, was another diversion; the man driving a pig, the woman leading a goat, and another following in the rear with the baby—the three essentials to Swiss housekeeping. A huge boulder which had rolled down the mountain, was utilized as one of the side-walls of a rude dwelling.

As we passed through the town of Cluses, we discovered it was market day; and a novel affair it was! The streets were strewn with merchandise of all kinds. Pieces of canvas were spread down in the dusty streets, and on them were piles of bright-colored ribbons, embroidery, dry goods and notions;

also a department for cattle, goats and pigs. We met several men coming home from market, each with a span of small pigs, with harness and lines made of rope; women in broad-brimmed, high-crowned hats of straw, with a band of ribbon and faded artificials. A pretty sight it was, to see flocks of goats feeding on the dizzy heights; and little stone cottages here and there, far up on the mountain side, where people live in the summer season, and make cheese from goats' milk. Many times during the trip, our passengers threw pennies to poor, blind, deformed, lame and idiotic beggars, who sat in shady nooks by the wayside, holding out their hands for charity. Dirty, ragged children would run along by the diligence and want to sell us crystals, pretty stones, and tiny bouquets, which they had gathered on the mountains.

We reached Chamouny about half past six o'clock in the evening, and went to the Hotel des Alpes. The village of Chamouny is nestled between lofty mountains; the grand old Mont Blanc chain bounding it on the south-west. It consists principally of hotels and guides; and is a fashionable summer resort.

The next morning we ate an early breakfast, and started out on mule-back to ascend Montanvert. Our party was made up of Mr. George Lavino, consul for the Netherlands, a gentleman *without* a title, Miss Camp, my husband and myself. We each had a guide and an Alpine stock (a long stick with an iron spike in the end.) As I was the most timid, they gave me my choice, and I selected the meekest-looking mule, having a side-saddle with an iron hoop around it, to prevent one from falling off backwards. My guide immediately informed me that I had chosen the oldest and most reasonable of them all, it having passed its fifteenth birthday. Before mounting, however, I gained from him the promise that he would lead the mule every step of the way. We were quite a merry party winding up the mountain, one after the other, the mules keeping the narrow path and never slipping once. We reached the top, an ascent of six thousand three hundred and three feet, in two and one-half hours. We rested for a short time at a hotel, perched away up here, and examined the choice crystals and precious stones found on the mountain. Then we walked a short distance until we came to the Mer de Glace, a glacier or huge stream of ice twelve miles long, and from one to three miles wide. This glacier resembles a sea suddenly frozen, with the great waves somewhat blunted. These waves are intersected by crevices, the interior of which appears as blue as indigo. This vast sea of ice fills the highest gorges of the chain of Mont Blanc. "It has been calculated that two hundred years would elapse before a mass of rock, lying on the surface of this glacier at its upper end, would reach the valley of Chamouny."

We crossed this glacier on foot. I took my guide's arm, and used my Alpine stock in the other hand. Great rocks and boulders lay in our path before reaching the mountain on the other side, which took us an hour and a half. In the most dangerous places steps were cut in the ice, and we often had to cross over great yawning chasms, hundreds of feet deep, where a misstep would have soon ushered us into eternity. We descended the mountain on the other side, by a narrow path, to the celebrated Mauvais Pas (the bad path) a steep rocky mountain side, where the path is hewn in steps and flanked with an iron railing anchored to the solid rock. I clung nervously to the railing with one hand, while the other was placed in that of the guide. I did not dare to look down into the awful abyss below. We were glad when this was over, and we reached the little hut where we procured dinner for ourselves and our guides. These little summer houses are found at certain distances, all along up the sides of the mountains, where we stopped and refreshed ourselves with nice, cold, rich goats' milk.

Soon after dinner, the boys, who had taken our mules by a different route, while we crossed the glacier, met us, and we again mounted; but I did not ride very far, for the descent was so steep and the path so narrow that I was terrifically frightened. The turns were so abrupt that when my mule, in the attempt to make them, dexterously collapsed, by putting several of his feet in the same place, I felt that he was going to "step down and out." I suppose he wanted to show me how smart and surefooted he was, and how near he could go to the edge of the precipice without slipping off; for he would insist on walking just on the "ragged edge" all the time. Miss Camp, accustomed to riding, was brave through it all, and often halted a moment and allowed her guide to assist me in turning the corners.

At last my head began to swim, as I looked down thousands of feet below, and I called to my French guide to take me down. But he only replied, "Courage, Madam!" and not until the tears came with fright, and I slipped my foot from the stirrup, did he comprehend my meaning. Then he lifted me down carefully, and I clung to some roots above, while the whole party passed, and then skipped along on foot until the descent was more gradual. And be it known, to the shame of the gentlemen, that not one of them attempted to ride down this steep declivity; for, after dismounting, I looked back, and saw them meekly *following* their mules.

Our next jaunt was to ascend Mount Flégère, five thousand nine hundred and twenty-five feet high, where we had still another view of the highest point of Mont Blanc, the monarch of European mountains, fifteen thousand seven hundred and thirty-one feet high. I had no desire to ascend that. A party of eleven persons perished in a snow-storm, in 1870, while trying to make the ascent. It seems to me I never saw such an exquisitely grand picture in nature as while descending the Flégère. There was the valley of Chamouny below, dotted with pretty villages, the Arve river winding like a silver thread through the beautiful green meadows, with a background of lofty mountains, covered with evergreen trees of many shades and varieties; and back of and towering above all, the majestic snowy peaks of old Mont Blanc. I was lost in admiration, and for the time forgot that I was on a mule's back. The mountain air sharpened our appetites, and we did justice to the inviting evening meal.

The next morning I awakened to the fact that I was stiff and sore in every joint and limb; but nevertheless, as the others were in tolerably good trim, we left Chamouny at seven o'clock in the diligence, and reached Geneva at three p. m. We went to the same hotel, de Geneve, and stayed all night.

Next day, in a pretty, commodious steamboat, we rode nearly the whole length of Lake Geneva, the largest of the Swiss lakes, being fifty miles long and a mile and a quarter wide, in the shape of a half moon. The day was perfect! The kindly sun tempered his rays to just the right degree of comfort and pleasantness. The lake was as smooth as glass; not a ripple disturbed its peaceful bosom of azure blue; and the soft sweet notes of the brass band lent additional enchantment to the surroundings. The lake is bounded on the north by gently-sloping hills, clothed with the cedar of Lebanon, chestnut, walnut and magnolia trees, and luxuriant vineyards, with smiling villages peeping out here and there. On the opposite shore a grand panorama of mountains stretches as far as the eye can see. An ancient castle, with five towers, presents a pretty picture. It being the first of June, or opening of the season, many of the little villages where the boat halted were celebrating the day.

The landing at Lausanne, was beautifully trimmed with flowers. Arriving at Chillon, we immediately secured the services of a man to take us over to the Castle, a distance of half a mile, in a dainty little row-boat with canopy, brussels carpet and cushioned seats; and as we approached the castle, which is built on an isolated rock sixty-six feet from the shore, with which it is connected by a drawbridge, and were told that the water beneath us was seven hundred feet deep, I must confess I trembled at the frailty of our bark.

But soon we were under the very shadow of this ancient castle, the foundation of which was laid in 830, with its massive walls, narrow loop-holes, six towers and battlements, made immortal by Byron. When once within its gloomy walls, we proceeded immediately to the dungeons beneath, as this was the part we came to see. These dungeons consist of several cells dug out of the solid rock upon which the castle stands, so that it must have seemed like a living grave to the many prisoners who have been confined there, beneath the surface of the lake. We held our breath when we entered the cell which is the scene of Byron's poem, entitled "The Prisoner of Chillon," it seemed so real; for there stood the seven huge stone pillars with heavy iron rings, to which the chains were attached. There are the narrow loop-holes through which a few golden rays of sunlight might creep, to remind the prisoner how the world without is lighted with his full-orbed splendor. See how the stone pavement around the pillars is worn in hollows by the weary pacing of the captives! We could almost fancy we saw their forms in the dim light, and heard the clanking of their chains. I cannot refrain from quoting a few lines from Byron:

> " There are seven pillars of Gothic mould
> In Chillon's dungeons deep and old,
> There are seven columns, massy and gray,
> Dim with a dull imprisoned ray,—
> A sunbeam which hath lost its way,
> And through the crevice and the cleft
> Of the thick wall is fallen and left,
> Creeping o'er the floor so damp,
> Like a marsh's meteor lamp,—
> And in each pillar there is a ring,
> And in each ring there is a chain;
> * * * * * * * *
> They chained us each to a column stone,
> And we were three, yet each alone;
> We could not move a single pace,
> We could not see each other's face,
> But with that pale and livid light
> That made us strangers in our sight;
> And thus together, yet apart,
> Fettered in hand, but pined in heart;
> 'Twas still some solace, in the dearth
> Of the pure elements of earth
> To hearken to each other's speech,
> And each turn comforter to each
> With some new hope, or legend old,
> Or song heroically bold;
> But even these at length grew cold.

> Our voices took a dreary tone,
> An echo of the dungeon-stone,
> A grating sound,—not full and free
> As they of yore were wont to be;
> It might be fancy,—but to me
> They never sounded like our own."

Among the hundreds of names cut in these pillars by visitors, are those of Byron, Victor Hugo and George Sand. Bonivard was chained to one of these pillars for six weary years, and lived thirty-five years after his release. One would suppose that being deprived of God's pure air and sunshine, and the inactivity of his physical and intellectual powers for so long, would have brought him to a premature grave; but not so—he lived to the good old age of threescore and fifteen years.

On our way to the station we saw a handsome Swiss cottage, that was actually taken to the Exposition at Paris. Our route presented most picturesque scenery of mountains, rivers, tunnels, cascades, waterfalls, several ruined castles, the bleak, yellowish slopes of a vast semi-circular crater and the Gorge du Trient.

We arrived at Brieg in the evening, tired and hungry. Went to the hotel d'Angleterre, an old-fashioned house, with no plastering over the bare stone walls within; stone floors and staircases with no carpets; huge doors like those of a prison, with heavy iron locks and bolts; but good, wholesome, well-prepared food, and withal, the most popular hotel in the little village. At half-past four o'clock the next morning, we started by diligence, to go over the wonderful Simplon Pass of the Alps into Italy. We traveled the road constructed by Napoleon Bonaparte, in 1800, or rather begun then; it took six years to build it and cost $3,600,000. It is a grand memento of his perseverance and skillful engineering, winding back and forth up the mountain; in some places built up of solid masonry, in others rocks blasted off to form the track; running through galleries, hewn out of the solid rock, one ninety-nine feet long; having snow-sheds built of stone over the track in the most dangerous places, as a protection from the avalanches, which slide down the side of the mountains at times.

Soon after leaving Brieg we saw a small pilgrimage church away up on the side of the mountain, to which a winding path leads by a number of stations. We had a fine view of the Kaltwasser Glacier, the Rant Glacier, the Rossboden Glacier, and many others. The finely shaped Mount Fletschhorn, 12,853 feet high, seemed so near to us and yet how far distant! It took four hours to ascend to the summit of the pass, but when there, we had a charming retrospective view of the village of Brieg, resting in the valley, thousands of feet below us, and the surrounding scenery was indescribably beautiful!—snow-capped mountains, others dressed in living green, wonderful, awe-inspiring glaciers, and lovely cascades. It was a new experience to us to be riding over the snow, the beautiful snow, the second day of June, warmly wrapped in blankets and robes, yet cheered by the friendly sun. Up and down this mountain pass there are nine places of refuge for travelers. The culminating point of the Simplon Pass is 6,595 feet high. Here is the Hospice of St. Bernard, consisting of two large buildings. One contains the church, the dwellings of the brethren, and numerous apartments for the reception of travelers, and the other is a refuge in case of fire, and contains the storehouse and lodging for poor wayfarers. They were built in the sixteenth century. The brotherhood consists of fifteen monks and seven attendants, who entertain strangers, free of charge, and assist travelers who are exposed to the dangers of heavy snow-storms. Their snowy season lasts nine months. The famous breed of dogs, employed at the hospice, is known the world over. Their acute sense of smell enables them to trace and find people who are perishing, although they may be completely covered from sight by the snow; and many lives have been saved by these noble animals.

A short distance from the hospice is the morgue, a receptacle for dead bodies found in the snow; and I have seen it stated that the features of the deceased are sometimes recognizable years after death, as the coldness and dryness of the air retard decomposition.

In descending the mountain pass we rode nearly all the way

through the Ravine of Gondo, one of the wildest and grandest gorges in the Alps. It is *terrific* grandeur, *awful* sublimity. At some places the rocks on both sides stretch up to the dizzy height of two thousand feet. In other places its precipitous walls of mica-slate overhang the road. Huge boulders fill up the bottom of this ravine, and over and under and around them dashes the river in mad fury, "helter-skelter, hurry-skurry." We approached a huge black rock or cliff that appeared to completely block the way, but when we came to it we found that it is pierced with a tunnel seven hundred and thirty-five feet long, called the Gallery of Gondo. Upon emerging from this tunnel a lovely cascade is precipitated over the rocks at the left, coming from the heights above, a mass of feathery foam, leaping and dashing in frolicsome glee; and its beauty is all the more appreciated on account of its position—at the mouth of a tunnel. It seems to be playing bo-peep with travelers, springing upon them in this most unexpected place. Its very name is fanciful, Fressinone Waterfall. Through this gorge our horses went on the keen trot, and from our hearts we thanked God and Napoleon that there was a solid stone wall four or five feet high on the side of the road next to the gorge, for our driver had taken too much wine. A column of granite marks the boundary between Switzerland and Italy. When we reached the town of Domo d'Ossola, we went to a restaurant and had some good beefsteak, potatoes and coffee; then again took seats in the diligence and rode to Arona.

CHAPTER IV.

For two hours, at twilight, we rode along the right bank of the celebrated picturesque Lake Maggiore. Oh! that my pen could portray its loveliness! A painter's brush could tell but half its charms! We saw it in its prettiest dress and happiest mood, and evening light brings out its shadows to perfection. This beautiful expanse of water, stretching out thirty-seven miles in length, a clear, placid, deep, blue sheet, striped with all the tints of the rainbow; its clearly-defined shadows, its noble background of irregular mountain peaks in their emerald robes; and behind them, peeping over their heads, the older hills in their snowy caps, was soul-stirring! We looked up there, and saw *stern* grandeur, old winter's frosty breath. We turned to our right and saw the luxuriance of a southern clime, vines, laurels, mulberry, fig, olive, oleander, magnolia, lemon and orange trees. It seems that every art that man can devise has been added to increase the beauty of this unparalleled natural scenery. The road winding along the bank of the lake is hard and smooth and white, and is flanked on the right with numerous habitations, costly mansions of superior architecture, picturesque fairy-like Swiss cottages, every dwelling that might otherwise seem unsightly, artistically covered with creeping vines and ivies; the lawns exquisitely shaven, and vying with each other in flowers and adornments. Hanging over the low stone wall which separates the lawns from the street, were huge rose bushes in close proximity, literally covered with dark, velvety, red and cream-colored roses, the shades alternating. One of these elegant residences, a handsome brick, called Villa Clara, is the one which Queen Victoria honored with her presence in the spring of 1879. Perhaps the prettiest spot on the lake is that in which the lovely group of Borromean islands appear, clothed with their rich verdure, and ornamented with costly edifices. Those who have seen both, say that just here Lake Maggiore rivals Lake Como in grandeur and softness of character. The dainty row-boats dreamily floating on its surface, with their gayly-attired occupants, and the birds on the wing, put the finishing touches to this glorious landscape. No wonder that people of wealth and leisure and artistic taste come here to spend a few months, and drink in the pleasures which surround them.

In this vicinity is a fine granite quarry, and when we saw how extensive it was, we began to mistrust that this must be the place where all the tall granite telegraph posts came from that we had been passing for many miles back. I must say, we could not help contrasting them with the slender, wooden, tottering telegraph poles in our own beloved America.

We reached Arona at nine o'clock p. m., a distance of seventy-eight miles by diligence from Brieg. We immediately boarded a train and reached Milan at midnight. That same night Garibaldi, the true, noble-hearted, patriotic friend of the Italian people, died. Our sole object in going to Milan was to see its wonderful cathedral; so, immediately after breakfast next morning, we hastened thither, determined on giving up the day to this world-renowned object. In passing through the streets we discovered that the ladies of Milan have a pretty fashion of wearing elegant, rich lace shawls on their heads, draped in the most fantastic manner, without hat or bonnet. The cathedral loomed up before us, a majestic pile of white marble, the exterior of which is lavishly adorned with more than two thousand statues, and the roof with its ninety-eight Gothic turrets, and tower three hundred and sixty feet high, pointing heavenward.

We walked around this magnificent structure at a sufficient distance to take it in as a whole, and we could at once comprehend how people always go into ecstasies over the "Gothic Cathedral of Milan." It was built in the fifteenth century, and next to St. Peter's at Rome is the largest church in Europe. The interior is four hundred and seventy-seven feet long, and one hundred and eighty-three feet wide, supported by fifty-two pillars which are twelve feet in diameter, and instead of having capitals, they are ornamented at the top with eight or more beautifully-carved canopied niches containing statues; and against a great many of these pillars are hung fine oil paintings. The mosaic pavement is of many different colored marbles. The vaulted roof is so skillfully painted that a person looking up at it would not doubt for a moment but that it was delicately perforated stone work. Three hundred and fifty Bible scenes are portrayed on the three large stained-glass choir windows. The structure and decoration of the choir itself is very superior. The Cathedral has double aisles, and there are also aisles in each transept. All along the side aisles are chapels, with rich marble altars and tombs. One of them contains an old wooden crucifix, which in 1576 S. Carlo Borromeo carried barefooted, on his mission of mercy during the plague. Directly under the dome is the crypt containing the tomb of this saint. We reached it by descending a short flight of steps, passing through a passage with beautifully-polished marble walls, and a door with rich columns bearing gilded capitals. This crypt or sepulcher is octagonal in shape, and its walls are covered with eight silver bass-reliefs, historical representations of events in the saint's life; and eight silver statues stand in the angles. For five more francs (one dollar) the attendant would have opened the sarcophagus and shown us the saint, covered with diamonds and precious stones; but we shook our heads.

The most remarkable piece of sculpture which adorns the church, is the marble statue of St. Bartholomew, by Marcus Agrate. The saint is represented flayed, with his skin thrown carelessly over his shoulder. The head, face, hands and feet of the skin are exactly the same shape and size as those of the statue, which stands up, looking like the pictures in our Physiology with the muscles, tendons and arteries chiseled out, astonishingly true to nature. One can not help but stand and gaze at this wonderful work of art, and pity the poor fellow who was so ruthlessly robbed of his last garment—his skin. Here we also saw a valuable bronze candelabrum (candlestick), in the form of a tree, elaborately ornamented with precious stones, which is about six hundred years old. Nearly all these cathedrals have what is called a treasury, a room in which are kept gold and silver vessels, precious stones, crosses, valuable relics, and treasures of untold wealth. Here we saw life-size statues of St. Ambrogio, and St. Carlo Borromeo in solid silver; the ring and staff of the latter; lamps, censers, candelabra, goblets, etc., rich in splendor, oddly shaped and covered with rare and beautiful designs. I could not help but wonder what the Lord thought of all these treasures, "laid up in a napkin," while his poor crouch at the very door of the sanctuary, with outstretched hands for charity. This cathedral is so large that the hammer of the stone masons in a distant part of the church sounded but as the ticking of a clock. We saw the priests burn incense, and heard the grand peals of the organ. As the roof of this cathedral is perhaps equal to the interior in grandeur, we ascended a flight of one hundred and ninety-four broad white stone steps and reached the roof, where we suddenly found ourselves in a perfect labyrinth of statues, pinnacles, exquisite carvings and tracery, flying buttresses, arches and pillars. One can form but little idea of the immensity of this roof unless he attempts to walk over it. We ascended three hundred more steps and reached the highest gallery of the tower, where we sat and rested and looked down over the forest of white marble turrets beneath us, and out over the city of Milan, which is seven miles in circumference, and contains two hundred thousand inhabitants.

The next day being the Sabbath, we turned our steps once more to the Cathedral. As we approached, the broad front steps were crowded with people clothed in rags, selling oranges, lemons, cherries, lemonade, photographs, and all sorts of fancy cakes. Just imagine having a lot of Italians run up to you and offer things for sale on Sabbath morning as you are entering church! Most of that audience stood on the cold stone floor during the whole service. The chairs were not sufficient to supply one quarter of the people, and those who did occupy them had to pay a penny apiece before they were allowed to sit down. The Italian tongue of the priest, together with the cold, formal ceremonies, made us long for our own little church at home.

On Monday we went by train to Genoa. This city is most picturesquely situated on the Gulf of Genoa. It is built in terraces from the water's edge up the mountain side. It is strongly fortified, having ten forts situated on the heights above the town. And back of all, reaching to the mountain-top, is a luxuriant growth of orange, lemon, fig, olive, and other tropical trees. It is the chief commercial town in Italy, having a good harbor, which was filled with a perfect forest of masts. Its population is one hundred and thirty thousand. It has many handsome buildings, among which are the palaces of the Genoese nobility. Some of the streets are wide, but most of them are narrow and crooked. One street up which we walked was about eight feet wide; but they have a fashion there of extending the second story a foot or two farther into the street than the first, the third story that much further than the second, and so on, till actually the roofs of two houses, on opposite sides of the street, did meet six stories above our heads. Of course this darkens the streets, and when filled with vile odors, as they sometimes are, they do not make very delightful promenades.

Genoa is noted for its manufacture of silver filigree work. We went into one shop that had nothing in it but this silver-gilt filigree work, wrought of very fine wires into exquisite patterns, roses, pansies, butterflies, etc., for the pins and earrings, and all sorts of fantastic designs for bracelets, rings and chains. It is so fine and delicately made that it looks like lace-work. Although it tarnishes after a few months' wearing, yet it looks like solid Etruscan gold, and makes a showy, novel appearance in the shop-windows, and Americans always go in to see what it is.

The finest church in Genoa is that of St. Annunziata. Its principal beauty consists in the vaulting being supported by twelve fluted white marble columns, ornamented with gold. In the church of St. Lorenzo is a large handsome painting of the Crucifixion. It is kept covered with a heavy curtain of green rep, so that the light will not fade the colors. It was taken to Paris when Napoleon I. captured Genoa, but they afterwards regained possession of it. The side aisles have several handsome chapels. In one of them they claim to have the relics of John the Baptist, preserved in a richly-carved marble tomb, which stands on four pillars of porphyry brought from Egypt. Mr. Culler went in to see *it*, and the chain with which John was bound while in prison; but Miss Camp and I were not allowed to go in, because it was through a woman that John the Baptist lost his head.

We went to see one of the grand palaces, called Palazzo del Municipio. In the vestibule is a fine statue of Mazzini. In the Council Chamber were the portraits of Christopher Columbus and Marco Polo, beautifully wrought in mosaic. The former was born in Cogoleto, about sixteen miles from Genoa. In an adjoining room is the picture of the Madonna between two saints; a large bronze tablet of A. D. 117, recording the judgment of Roman arbiters in a dispute between Genoa and a neighboring castle; letters of Columbus' writing; and a cabinet in the wall, lined with pink satin, contains the violin of Paganini under a glass case.

The greatest sight in Genoa, however, is the Campo Santo (burial place). It is situated on the slope of the valley, a mile or two from the city, and is built in the form of a square, with an open court in the centre. This court is filled with unpretending tombstones, some of them simple slabs, and others in the form of a cross; but from nearly all of them is suspended an artificial wreath of flowers in black and white, presenting a very sombre appearance.

But it seeems to be a custom among the Catholics everywhere, thus to decorate their tombstones. The handsome stone building which incloses this court is the burial place of the wealthy. And truly it is sumptuous! There are sepulchers, niches made in the solid stone walls, in which the coffins are placed, and then sealed shut with a marble slab, upon which is engraved the epitaph. Two sides of this square are extremely beautiful and impressive. The space is divided into family burial places, with the statue of each person who has died beautifully carved in white marble. The features of these statues are exactly like those of the departed, also manner of wearing the hair, style of dress, etc. It is perfectly wonderful! Lace and embroidery, ribbons, ties, fringe, all of white marble, yet of such superior workmanship that one almost fancies these statues are real people, whose garments are covered with snow. One statue of a dear old grandma, in her ruffled cap, with wrinkled but sunny face, and the veins standing out on her thin hands, brought to mind the passage of scripture: "These are they which came out of great tribulation, and have washed their robes and made them white in the blood of the Lamb."

This sight is very impressive to a stranger. At a glance one can see just whom the Messenger of Death has snatched from each family circle. Here is the sweet little baby in its long robes, there sunny youth, there the fond sister, there the young husband in the full strength of manhood, there frosted orange blossoms, there decrepit old age. On the hill-side shaded by cypress trees is the vault of Mazzini, who died in 1872. Looking in through the bronze doors, we saw the sarcophagus of this most remarkable man of modern Italy. His wife's tomb is just outside.

The chapel in connection with the cemetery is very handsome. The dome is supported by sixteen columns of black marble; each column having cost three thousand two hundred dollars, and are each nine feet in circumference.

Not far from the depot is the statue of Columbus. It stands on a pedestal ornamented with prows of ships. A figure representing America kneels at his feet. The monument is surrounded by allegorical figures representing geography, wisdom, strength and religion.

The scenery between Genoa and Pisa is very striking. For miles we ran along the shore of the Mediterranean Sea. This broad expanse of water, so smooth and peaceful, dotted with white sails, is the very identical body of water I had so often pointed out on the map when a school-girl! But it was difficult to reconcile that little black spot in the geography with this glorious sight. The Apennine mountains, with old ruined castles here and there perched on their summits, extend down to the sea-shore in many places, and the railroad is carried through numerous promontories by means of cuttings and eighty tunnels, which are short, causing a continual change from sunshine to shadow. We whirled past many orange and lemon groves, olive and fig orchards, palm and oleander trees, and immense cactuses in wild luxuriance from six to eight feet high, with their broad, tough, thorny leaves.

We arrived at Pisa too late in the day for sight-seeing, but were up betimes in the morning to explore the wonders of the Piazza del Duomo, in which is situated an unparalleled group of buildings, viz., the Cathedral, the Leaning Tower, the Baptistry, and the Campo Santo. We first entered the Cathedral. This beautiful edifice is built of white marble in the form of a Latin cross. The nave, flanked with double aisles, is three hundred and twelve feet long, and has a flat, richly-gilded ceiling. In this part of the Cathedral the swaying of a bronze lamp, which is suspended from the roof by a cable about eighty feet long, suggested to Galileo the idea of the pendulum. In the interior of this church are sixty-eight ancient Greek and Roman columns, which the people of Pisa captured in war, and many grand paintings add to the richness of its beauty. The elliptical dome is decorated with pictures, wrought in mosaic. In the right transept the basin for holy water, adorned with the Madonna and Child was designed by Michael Angelo.

The Baptistry is a handsome circular structure, considered the most elegant one in Italy, built also of white marble. It is one hundred and ninety feet high, and one hundred feet in diameter inside the walls, which are nine feet thick, and is so delicately and elaborately carved that it looks as if veiled in white lace. A child would probably think it looked like a huge pyramid cake frosted in beautiful patterns. I felt that I was in a great, white marble bell; and certainly the fine echo produced here is sweeter than the tones of any bell. The guide sang a few notes, and the echo came back like the full rich tones of a pipe organ. In the centre is a marble octagonal font fourteen feet in diameter, lavishly ornamented with reliefs and mosaics. The children of the church are brought here to be baptized. Here, also, is the celebrated hexagonal pulpit, supported by seven columns, the masterpiece of Nicola Pisano. Each side is covered with bass-reliefs of surpassing beauty—1. Annunciation and Nativity; 2. Adoration of the Magi; 3. Presentation in the Temple; 4. Crucifixion; 5. Last Judgment; 6. Allegorical figures. We afterwards saw many plaster casts of this wonderful pulpit in different museums throughout Europe; so we were particularly glad that we had seen the original.

We next visited the Campo Santo. A shade of disappointment stole over our faces when we remembered the fresh beauty of the Campo Santo at Genoa. Of course this is nearly six hundred years older than that; this having been built in the thirteenth century, and that in the present. However, this old, faded, historic beauty is the most interesting after all. They are similar in shape, a vast corridor or arched cloisters extending around the four sides of an open court, which is called the Garden of the Dead. Fifty-three ship-loads of earth was deposited here, brought from Mount Calvary in Jerusalem, in order that (according to a superstitious notion) the dead might be buried in holy ground. This structure is four hundred and fourteen feet long, one hundred and seventy-one feet wide, and forty-eight feet high. The walls are covered with frescoes by painters of the fourteenth and fifteenth centuries; some of them are almost effaced by time. Perhaps the Triumph of Death is the most celebrated and striking, in which horrible devils are snatching away the wicked and carrying them off to perdition, some of them by the hair of the head, others are being hurled into the flames head first; the devil and angels are contending over others, the former dragging them down, and the latter lifting them up. Three kings mounted on their gallant steeds are approaching three open coffins; the horses, by their outstretched necks, distended nostrils and frightened attitude, seem to realize that death is near at hand. At the right of the picture are some of the blest sitting under palm trees, and others ascending to heaven. Another picture called "The Last Judgment," portrays the Judge in the centre, with the saved on the right and the damned on the left. A third picture represents "Hell,"— a horrible spectacle, in which the damned are writhing with agony in the fiery furnace, entwined with serpents; and misery of all sorts is graphically depicted. On another side of this building the book of Genesis is portrayed—the Creation of the World, the Creation of Eve, the Fall, Expulsion from Paradise, Cain killing Abel, Lot's wife turned into a pillar of salt, etc. The pavement on which we walked was formed of tombstones, some of them so old that we could not begin to read the inscriptions. Along the sides of the walls are Roman, Etruscan and mediæval sculptures, many of which are crumbling to pieces and black with age.

We next turned our steps to the Campanile, or as it is more commonly called, the Leaning Tower, as it leans thirteen feet out of the perpendicular. It is built of white marble, and was begun in 1174, but was not completed until one hundred and seventy-six years afterwards. It is a perfect cylinder fifty-three feet in diameter and one hundred and seventy-nine feet high. It consists of eight stories, eight tiers of columns supporting arches, thus forming open galleries around the tower. Inside is a winding staircase of broad, easy steps, two hundred and ninety-four in number. In making the ascent, when on the side which leaned we ran, but climbed on the other side. We could go out and walk around on any of these galleries, which project seven feet. At last we reached the belfry, in which is a chime of seven bells, the largest weighing six tons. But ambition spurred us on to climb to the very tip-top, and going to the edge and holding on to the iron railing on the leaning side, we looked down. I was afraid we might tip it over, but we made no more impression upon its solid masonry than if a canary bird had for a moment rested there. The view from the top is very pretty. The eye takes in the city, the distant hills and mountains, and the grand old Mediterranean Sea with all the details that go to make up a charming landscape. Everybody asks, Was it built that way on purpose, or by accident? History tells us that the most probable solution is that "the foundation settled during its erection, and in order to remedy the defect, an attempt was made to give a vertical position to the upper part."

We had so much veneration for these four buildings that, although the beggars were bold and numerous, the weather warm and depressing, yet we left Pisa with pleasant thoughts; taking train for Naples, riding all night long, changed cars at ten o'clock at Rome, and reached Naples at half-past six o'clock next morning. For twenty miles we could see the smoke rolling up from the chimney of old Mount Vesuvius. Somewhat fatigued by our night's journey, we immediately sought out the handsomely-furnished, comfortable hotel Geneve. After indulging in a warm bath and a delicious breakfast, we felt somewhat refreshed, and went out, not to "See Naples and die," but to live, and tell others of its strange conglomeration of happy, joyous, indolent, slovenly, squalid, hungry, naked, dirty human beings; of its beautiful situation and its ancient curiosities. Naples has a population of four hundred and fifty thousand eight hundred, and has one of the most lovely situations in the world, being built in the form of a crescent on the beautiful Bay of Naples. The lavish gifts of nature bestowed upon this spot of God's footstool seem to atone somewhat for the want of energy, pride and enterprise of its inhabitants. Although some of the streets are spacious and airy, and paved with square blocks of lava, yet the most of them are narrow and dingy, flanked with high, narrow, flat-roofed houses. The noise of the wheels, and drivers, and whips, and donkeys, and children, is enough to set a nervous person wild. The streets of Naples are full of sights! We saw lazy, ragged, dirty women seated on the curbstones (perfectly indifferent to the passers-by) giving their children various acts of attention, such as searching for and ruthlessly slaying the tenants of the upper story, etc. Filthy hard-looking men were stretched out asleep on the pavements, and dozens of them asleep on stone walls, lying face down like a lot of lizards basking in the sun. Entirely nude children three or four years old were running about the streets promiscuously. People in the fourth or fifth stories were bargaining for cherries, etc., in the street below; letting down their money in a basket, and drawing it up full of fruit. Merchandise of all sorts was laid right down in the dusty streets. Three or four people were ravenously eating macaroni from one big, yellow bowl.

Men, women and children pestered us at every step to buy matches and all sorts of notions. Horrible beggars with all sorts of deformities followed us for squares with outstretched hands, repeating a lingo in a monotonous style. At every turn a cabman would drive up to us and ask for employment. Porters fairly take your baggage out of your hands. Beggars run to open a door for you, and then expect five or ten centimes in return. We saw several ungainly-looking teams—a cow and donkey, an ox and a horse harnessed together; and frequently we saw a little homely donkey drawing an enormous load, built up so high and out so wide that you could not mistrust how it was put in motion, unless you were fortunate enough to get a front view.

Our attention was attracted to a rope hanging down outside a shop, the end of which was smoking a little; we could not imagine what heathenish custom that was, until we had seen an unlimited number of them, and observed that men lit their cigars with them; whereupon the following question arose: Are these Italians too lazy or too poor to strike a match? A dirty indolent boy was engaged in unrolling stubs of cigars to have made up again. The fellow who smokes a cigar made out of that will have one that has been in a variety of mouths. Great wagon loads of bread pass through the streets, and filthy women carry baskets of bread on their heads, and yards of bread under their arms.

Oranges and lemons are very cheap here—a penny a piece.

The coral shops make an elegant and showy display. We visited the Aquarium, which occupies the ground floor of a building situated in the Villa Nazionale, a beautiful pleasure ground embellished with palm-trees, flowers, sculpture and shady walks, affording the fashionable promenade of Naples. The Aquarium consists of large tanks extending around the building, reaching from the floor to the ceiling, inclosed in glass cases, containing an extensive stock of curious marine animals of all descriptions, and is considered one of the most interesting establishments of the kind in the world. Most of the animals are from the Mediterranean, which is the richest in animal life of all European seas. It is certainly a most enchanting sight to watch these millions of sea-animals with their different shapes, sizes, colors, and habits. Beautiful fish of delicate shades of pink, lavender, green, in fact all sorts of tints, striped and spotted, dart hither and thither, glittering in the sunshine. And oh, the beautiful specimens of *living* coral! We had often seen pretty white and red branches adorning a mantel-piece or incased in a museum in our own country; but here we actually saw it in living form, and found by study and observation that these beautiful branches and twigs are stony substances produced by the coral polypes which have secreted it as the common support and skeleton of their soft vital parts. The living branch of coral is covered with a softer rind, just as the trunk of a real tree is covered with bark, and the little coral insects may be seen, like delicate white flower-cups with eight feathery leaves, unfolding themselves at innumerable points on the surface of the branch. The pretty Medusæ, another specimen of marine life, with their graceful motions and splendid colors, look like anything rather than animals, as you can discover no arms, legs or head. They are merely a sort of shallow cup resembling a mushroom or umbrella, and move by the contractions of their bodies. On the edge of the cup are the organs of sight and hearing, and from the centre of the hollow of the cup hangs a long, gelatinous, transparent stem, which is provided with a mouth orifice. The tank containing the Annelids looked more like a garden planted with miniature palm-trees of various rich colors, than a collection of worms. There, shoot forth bright red tassels from a white calcareous tube; there, wave feathery spiral crowns on slender stems; there, a confused mass of tubes seem set with hundreds of dainty colored brushes; and yet all these creations are real worms. They are so sensitive that a passing cloud or a slight disturbance of the water will cause these tiny crowns to be drawn into the tube, to wait until the supposed danger is over, then cautiously something resembling a camel's-hair brush, will begin to peep out of the mouth of the tube, and finally unfold its gorgeous beauty. One could watch them for hours! The electric ray is a peculiar and interesting fish, having a flat, round, naked, slimy body, with a large bean shaped electric organ on each side. The nervous electricity is collected in this apparatus, and discharged when pressed with the thumb and finger. The back is positive and the belly negative.

The keeper of the Aquarium caught one of them, and Mr. Culler received quite a shock by pressing it in this manner. Of course (being a woman) I was too cowardly to touch it. Some of the animals have a very disgusting appearance, as the Octopus Vulgaris, with a body like a bag which we could distinctly see breathing. The small head at the top contains two big eyes, and eight long, slimy arms branch out from the head, with which it creeps, climbs, and seizes and holds its prey. We watched the keeper feed it with great interest. It is continually contracting and expanding its long arms, wriggling and twisting about, and appears to be trying to turn itself wrong side out. They are very strong, and drag quite good-sized stones into a heap and then hide behind them. They grow to a considerable size in the ocean. The arms of some of them which have been caught, measured twenty-five feet in length. These in the Aquarium are young, with arms only three or four feet long. If ever I am so unfortunate as to be drowned in the sea, I hope one of these creatures will not take after me. The star-fish, sea urchins, young sharks, the murex, from which was obtained the purple fluid with which the ancients dyed their royal robes, and in fact everything we saw there, was intensely interesting and enjoyable.

We began to change our minds about Naples and think it was rather a nice place after all. The museum at Naples, containing excavated treasures from Pompeii, Herculaneum and other valuables, forms one of the finest collections in the world. Seven rooms and a corridor are filled with ancient frescoes from the above-mentioned cities. Among the finest are Medea brooding over the murder of her children, the Dancing Girls, the Three Graces, various representations of Cupid, and some very fine mosaic pictures, the most remarkable of which is the Battle of Alexander. These works are almost the only specimens of ancient painting which have been handed down to our generation, and are therefore of priceless value. They give us an idea of the style, shading and coloring of the ancients, and many of them are beautifully designed and richly executed, including animal life, landscapes, fruit pieces, designs for architecture, historical and mythological subjects. They were painted between A. D. 63, and A. D. 79. The sculpture and bronze are exceedingly fine. We studied carefully the celebrated colossal marble group of the Farnese Bull. Two strong young men are engaged in tying a helpless woman to the horns of a furious bull, which is plunging violently, and in the background stands a female figure. The story which it represents is as follows: "The two sons of Antiope, Amphion and Zethus, avenge the wrongs of their mother by binding Dirce, who had treated her with the greatest cruelty for many years, to the horns of a wild bull. Antiope in the background entreats them to forgiveness." Near this group stands the so-called Farnese Hercules. They both belonged formerly to the Farnese family. There are three rooms filled with books and papers, scrolls rolled up that were burned black at Pompeii and Herculaneum, and are now being carefully unrolled by a chemical process, and the writing on them read and transcribed into a book. They are then hung around the walls of the room for exhibition. We saw a bracelet, pair of ear-rings and chain, found on a female skeleton at

Pompeii. In this museum are hundreds of bottles from drug-shops, fruits, raisins, prunes, walnuts, honey, bread, meat, sugar, eggs, fish, wheat, coffee, all found at Pompeii. Think of them being so securely locked up for seventeen centuries. In addition to these ancient relics the museum is rich in books and manuscripts, modern paintings, an extensive and valuable collection of handsome vases of immense proportions, exquisitely painted, mosaics, gold and silver ornaments, and gems; altogether too much for one pair of eyes to take in.

About eight o'clock one morning we took train for Pompeii, a distance of fifteen miles. We became almost feverish with excitement, and the train did not run half fast enough to suit us, for we were on our way to see that wonderful city that had been buried for seventeen centuries. And when we were actually within its walls, we felt like holding our breath and treading softly. The earliest record that we can gather from history of Pompeii is B. C. 310. It was once a prosperous city of thirty thousand inhabitants. On the twenty-fourth of August, in the year A. D. 79, by the eruption of Mount Vesuvius, Pompeii was covered with a shower of ashes three feet deep. The ashes were followed by a shower of red-hot pumice stones of all sizes; then ashes again, and so on until the mass was about twenty feet thick. Excavations have been made from time to time, but during the middle ages Pompeii was entirely unknown. In the years intervening between 1861 and 1872 there were found eighty-seven human skeletons, and those of three dogs and seven horses. The whole number of those who perished is estimated at two thousand. An average number of eighty men are constantly employed in excavating. They watch visitors with a jealous eye, for fear they may discover and pick up anything valuable. We saw a bed-room that had only been excavated four days, and a skeleton that was found only six months before. It is estimated that if the work progresses at the present rate, the complete excavation will take seventy years longer. Only about one-third of the town is unearthed at present; but it is probably the most important part, as it includes the principal public buildings.

We took a guide to show us through the ruins, and there we walked all the forenoon, looking at these old, old things of the past. The movable objects found, as well as the most important frescoes, have been removed to the museum at Naples, as they would soon be ruined by exposure to the sun and rain. However, quite a number of the frescoed walls remain, so one can get an idea of what it once was; also some beautiful fountains in mosaic work, marble statuary, etc. One of the old wells has been cleaned out, and the water found to be sweet and pure; so we had our guide draw up a pail full, and after he had tested it, we took a good draught from this crystal fountain. Think of drinking from a well seventeen hundred years old! The streets are straight and narrow, about twenty-four feet wide, and some only fourteen feet; but they are well paved with blocks of lava, and have a very narrow pavement for foot-passengers, about twelve inches higher than the carriage road. At street corners are public fountains ornamented with the head of a god, lion, flowers, etc.

The houses are built of brick with corner-blocks of stone, and by the staircases it is plain to be seen that they were generally two or three stories high, although they are roofless. They are built with an open court in the centre, and the side facing the street was usually occupied by merchants and shopkeepers. All their best rooms were on the ground floor, and the servants or slaves occupied the upper floor. Many of the business places are recognizable by the signs painted on the front of the building. Thus two men carrying a large jug indicated a wine shop, a goat signified that milk could be bought within, a man whipping a boy, indicated a schoolroom, and houses of ill-fame are even marked with an indelicate figure over the door. Vice is as old as the world!

We went into the Basilica, the Temple of Venus, the Forum, Temple of Mercury, Temple of Jupiter. We ascended to the top of the latter by a flight of steps, where we had a fine panorama of Pompeii, with its ruined walls, broken columns, and grand old Mount Vesuvius, her destroyer, over yonder, quietly puffing out its smoke, looking down upon her in the most complacent manner. On we went to the Pantheon, the Triumphal Arch, the bathing-houses—these are in quite good preservation, with some of the ceilings complete; the Temple of Isis, the Great Theatre, the Forum Triangulare. In a chamber in this theatre, used as a prison, were found three skeletons with iron stocks for the feet. Sixty-three persons in all were destroyed in this building. The Amphitheatre was begun seventy years before Christ, and would seat twenty thousand spectators. We also peeped into the houses of Homer, the tragic poet, Sallust and Cicero. Whether these old fellows of Latin lore ever lived here, I don't know; but that is what the guides say. Perhaps the house of Diomedes is as interesting as any building we explored. Allow me to quote its description by another: "A flight of steps with two columns leads at once to the peristyle of fourteen Doric columns, whence the bath is entered to the left. Opposite are terraces, which rise above the second and lower portion of the house. The garden, one hundred and seven feet square, with a basin for a fountain in the centre, is surrounded by a colonnade. From the terrace a staircase descends to the left (another, from the entrance from the street, to the right). Below this colonnade, on three sides, lies a vaulted cellar, lighted by small apertures above, and approached by staircases descending at each end. Seventeen bodies of women and children, who had provided themselves with food and sought protection in this vault against the eruption, were found here. But impalpable ashes penetrated through the openings into the interior, and too late the ill-fated party attempted to escape. They were found with their heads wrapped up, half-buried in the ashes. The probable proprietor of the house was found near the garden door, with the key in his hand, and beside him a slave with money and valuables."

We explored soap factories, dyers' establishments, taverns, mills, bakeries, butcher-shops, stores, surgeons' offices, drug stores, and many private residences with handsome mosaic floors. We walked through the Street of the Tombs, as it was their custom to bury the dead in vaults by the side of the highway. A small museum has been erected here, where are in glass cases the bodies of eight persons found in the ruins. Although the flesh had decayed, the forms remained imprinted on the ashes, which afterwards hardened. The bones were carefully removed and the cavities filled with plaster by an artist, and with the aid of the impression on the ashes, he has succeeded in preserving the figures and attitudes of the deceased. Here is a young girl with a ring on her finger, a man lying on his face, another on his side, two women, one much larger than the other, locked in each other's arms, probably mother and daughter, sharing their dreadful fate together. Here are also skeletons of cats, dogs, chickens and horses, loaves of bread found in brick ovens, etc. A cold shudder crept over me as I thought of the past, and pictured in my mind the horrible catastrophe which wiped out this city in a day. Will the last Great Day be anything like that?

At Pompeii we engaged three horses, a guide who could speak a few words of English, two Italian boys to lead our horses, and proceeded to ascend Mount Vesuvius. As usual, they allowed me to take my pick, and I chose a little gray pony, which proved to be a plucky little fellow, though not at all vicious. Miss Camp selected a brown horse of more style, which soon gave us an exhibition of his expertness in kicking. Mr. Culler's horse was quite frisky, and was anxious to make the journey as soon as possible. After about half an hour's ride we came to a small village, which had evidently suffered from an eruption, filled with dilapidated houses, and dirty, lazy people. Our guide took our horses by the bits and stopped them in front of a little public house. The proprietor immediately came out with wines, and expected us to buy. We shook our heads. They insisted; the guide telling us that we could not make the ascent without a stimulant. We positively declined. Then the guide wished us to treat him. "No," said my husband, "I don't drink myself, and I won't give any man money to buy liquor with."

After some parley we again proceeded, and I thought, "Well, this is the last spot on earth I should select for a dwelling place—at the foot of this burning mountain." But the human race, with their different habits and dispositions, will live anywhere and call it home. Some live in houses of ice and snow, in Lapland's dreary clime; the Chinese have their little floating houses on the water; some live in "dug-outs" in Kansas; some live on snow-capped mountains; others in coal mines; and some dare to live on the side of old Vesuvius, in the very shadow of its smoke, within sound of its mutterings!

For some time we rode through luxurious vineyards; then came ashes. Our Italian boys, seeing we could manage our horses tolerably well, let go the bridle and walked by the side. Mr. Culler's horse dashed off on a keen trot. Miss Camp, being a good horsewoman, sat erect in her saddle, and followed hard behind, pausing occasionally for her horse to give a few vigorous kicks, of which I had the full benefit, being in the rear. My little gray pony could not bear to be left behind, and suddenly put down his head and galloped off in pursuit. Regardless of my reins, I nervously clung to the horns of my saddle with both hands, bore down in my stirrup, and managed to keep my seat when not in the air—at least I did not fall to the ground. Our garments floated in the strong breeze. Our Italian boys, fearing they could not keep up, caught the ponies by the tails, and by dint of close application succeeded at least in heightening the novelty and picturesqueness of the scene. The ridiculousness of the whole affair so took possession of me, that I became perfectly reckless of all danger, and laughed until the tears rolled down my cheeks. Picture it, think of it, reader, and if you know me you will laugh too.

This chase was kept up for some time, until the mountain became steep and rough with the lava of 1848 and 1868. Then, slowly picking our way along a winding path, sinking into the ashes at every step, we at last reached the point where the horses could go no farther, and we dismounted at the foot of the cone. There were three strong, wiry men, who seemed to be waiting for us, and at once offered their services to pull us up the precipitous cone, consisting of slag and loose ashes, and rising at an angle of 35°. Mr. Culler, thinking himself equal to the task, refused assistance, but secured the services of two men for us ladies. I held on to a stick with both hands, to which a rope was attached. The guide put the rope over his shoulder and pulled me up, up, for one long hour. Sometimes we sank nearly to our knees in loose ashes. The third man, who was unemployed, followed us and tried in every possible way to force his services upon us. He would say to my husband in his few words of English, "Too much fatigue." Then he would take hold of him and try to assist him. Mr. Culler would shake him off, scowl, and tell him he did not want help. Then he would say, "Too much fatigue, lady," and point to me, immediately stepping up behind me and pushing at my back. I pushed him away. Then he beset Miss Camp. Meeting with no approval from her, he began over again, and kept up a constant annoyance. And to add to our discomfort it set in to rain violently. The ashes became wet and soggy, and our shoes were soon penetrated with the dampness. Our flannel dresses and heavy shawls were weighed down with moisture. Breathless with fatigue we toiled on. I was ahead. Mr. Culler in the rear called out to halt! Overwhelmed with the thought of our cruel exposure to wind and rain, together with the extreme exertion necessary, he feared we ladies might die in the attempt to ascend, and for our sakes would willingly sacrifice the pleasure of gaining the summit, and thought we would better retrace our steps immediately. Then said Miss Camp: "Oh yes, Mrs. Culler, let's go back. It's wicked for us to attempt to go further." For a moment there was a great struggle within me between duty and ambition. I replied: "No I can't go back. I came all the way from America to see Mount Vesuvius, and I *must* go to the top. See, it's not much farther! We shall *not* take cold. This is our last chance. We shall never be here again. We *must* go up!"

We trudged on, steeper and steeper at every step, wearily lifting our feet, pausing at intervals for breath and courage. I trembled with fear lest something might happen to one of us, and then I should be to blame. Almost desperate, I turned around; Miss Camp was resting for a minute, with face and lips as pale as death, with her big blue eyes cast upward in an imploring attitude, and I almost thought she would faint. My husband was also pale with fatigue, having received no assistance, and being constantly bored with that extra guide. I told Miss Camp to pull hard on her rope, and let the guide do the climbing. Then, fearing it might take some of Mr. Culler's strength to answer the frequent questions of this unfortunate guide, I beckoned him to me, and, laying my hand on his shoulder, almost too breathless to speak myself, I said, "Don't you dare to speak another word to my husband till we reach the top." He understood me. We stuck to it, and were soon walking over the ropy-looking lava which had cooled and hardened.

"Hurrah! we are at the top of the cone."

"And not likely to take cold either, for it's too hot."

Our damp soles soon dried, and would actually have burned if we had not kept moving about. Here we walked over a furrowed, fissured mass of crisp, crackling lava. There were great crevices through which we could look down into the boiling, seething mass below, and cracks from which issued flames of fire. Our guide put in one end of his long staff, and it immediately caught fire. Sulphur fumes came up through these openings, which bleached the color out of my blue flannel dress in streaks, and nearly suffocated us. Then suddenly the smoke from the crater would envelop us; and, afraid of being strangled to death, we ladies clung to our guides, so blinded by the smoke that we could not see where we were going.

The crater changes its form after every great eruption. At present the cone in the crater is higher than the rim, and lateral openings have been made, out of which the lava escapes. From one of these openings the red-hot lava poured in a wide stream, like thick oil, or like we see red-hot iron in a foundry. We looked into it (but only for a moment, as it was so scorching hot), and saw the seething mass and fiery flames. Our guide fished out some of the red-hot lava for us, pressed some pennies in it, and when it cooled it became as black as iron.

There we were, four thousand feet above the city of Naples, and the bay with its beautiful islands, Capri and Ischia. But it is not the most comfortable point of observation in the world, and we were soon ready to start down the mountain. Our curiosity and ambition having been satisfied, the rain having abated, and the tug of war over, the descent was quite different from the ascent. We all took hold of hands, and went pitching through the ashes, knee deep, with remarkably long and rapid strides. Our steps or jumps must have been at least three yards long.

Reaching the point where our horses were to meet us, we saw them a long way in the distance. While waiting for them, the guides invited us into a little place enclosed with a stone wall, and there tried to extort more money from us, our guide whom we took from Pompeii also siding with them. We gave the extra guide two francs (forty cents) for dipping out the lava for us, and then stoutly refused to give any more than previously agreed upon.

> "Fie on thee, wretches! 'tis pity that thou livest
> To walk where any honest men resort."

Then they insisted on our going to another town, instead of going back to Pompeii, to take the train for Naples. We had return tickets, and insisted on going back to Pompeii; but we did not know the road, and were at their mercy; and in spite of all we could do and say, they took us to the proposed station. I was uneasy every minute, for I had heard and read so much of the murders and robberies committed by Italian guides in making this excursion, that I was afraid to have Mr. Culler ride in the rear, as they probably knew that he carried the gold. However, we arrived in safety at the station. Miss Camp and I remained seated on our ponies while Mr. Culler and the guide went in to see if our tickets were good from there. We did not propose to give up our horses until we knew that everything was straight. All the little ragged beggars in this miserable town gathered about us like a swarm of bees, stretching out their hands for money. When we refused they made all sorts of horrible faces at us, yelled and screamed, and whipped Mr. Culler's horse so that it jerked away from the boy who was holding it, and went scampering about the town. Our horses were restless, and we were glad when Mr. Culler came and said all was right.

While waiting in the station for the train, we had an opportunity to examine our shoes. The black was entirely scraped off, having a yellowish-red appearance, and they were burnt and torn shamefully. It took us just five hours to make the ascent and descent. It was hard work, but it paid! However, I don't think I could be tempted to repeat it.

"At the time of the eruption in 1872, a torrent of lava descended in a stream three thousand feet wide and twenty feet deep. At the same time, amidst terrific thundering, the crater poured forth huge volumes of smoke, mingled with red-hot stones and lava, to a height of four thousand feet; whilst clouds of ashes, rising to double that height, were carried by the wind a distance of one hundred and forty miles. It is a fact that all the principal volcanoes are situated near the sea or ocean; and it is believed that the enormous clouds of steam generated during eruptions, are due to some temporary communication of the water with the burning liquids of the interior of the earth; and that the premonitory earthquakes are occasioned by the vapors and gases as they expand and endeavor to find an outlet."

On the train to Naples, an Italian gentleman, who could speak English with some difficulty, informed us that the way to get rid of beggars and guides, is to throw back the head, elevate the nose, and say *no!* We afterwards found it worked like a charm. We bade good-bye to Naples, and reached Rome in about seven hours by train.

CHAPTER IV.

"ROME, that sat on her seven hills, and from her throne of beauty ruled the world." We entered the Eternal City at half past ten o'clock at night, and took up our abode at the hotel Minerva for a stay of eleven days. This large establishment is situated just back of the old Pantheon, and from our room we could look out upon this venerable pile. Statues of the goddess Minerva adorn the roomy, handsome dining hall, and every piece of china was stamped with her graceful figure. The meals were excellent and bountiful, with always a good supply of luscious Italian fruit; and the gentlemanly clerk, who could speak the English fluently, was no small addition to our comfort and enjoyment.

Rome was founded about B. C. 750. It is built on both banks of the yellow, muddy Tiber, and is surrounded by a brick wall, fourteen miles in circumference, and fifty-five feet high. It is entered by twelve gates, the most important of which is the Porta del Popolo. The far-famed "Seven Hills," upon which stand the ruins of ancient Rome are the Capitoline, Quirinal, Viminal, Esquiline, Palatine, Aventine, and Caelius, ranging from one hundred and fifty-one feet to two hundred and forty-six feet in height. Modern Rome is principally confined to the plain. The modern city is divided by the Corso or principal street. The part bordering on the Tiber consists of narrow, dirty streets. The population is two hundred and eighty-five thousand; and more than one-third cannot read or write. Among the first sights which we saw in Rome was the funeral procession in honor of the renowned Italian statesman Garibaldi, which passed through the Corso. For an hour before anything was to be seen, the street was lined with hundreds of people, scarcely leaving sufficient space for a team to pass. There we were surrounded by people of all classes chattering in Italian, and anxiously looking for the procession. Suddenly there was a dreadful panic among the crowd, the cause of which we could not find out. But the people screamed and ran over each other; strong men were knocked down flat on their backs; women and children were trampled upon. Mr. Culler managed to keep on his feet and keep my head from the ground, while my body was carried with the crowd. Twenty-eight persons were badly injured, some having limbs and arms broken, and others were jammed against the solid stone buildings. We were all terribly frightened. The pale faces, crying of children, and the expectation of being trampled to death, are indelibly impressed upon my mind.

Finally, after two or three excitements, the people, seeing there was no danger, became calm, and the grand and imposing procession came in sight. I managed to get in a place where I could run at the least alarm. There was a fine display of different orders in rich costumes, soldiers in gay uniforms, splendid banners, etc., seemingly endless in number. At last came a magnificent funeral car, beautifully and tastefully trimmed with floral offerings, and on the top was a pure white marble statue of Garibaldi, and a gracefully-carved female figure beside him, placing a wreath of laurels on his brow. I have seen several other funeral cars, but none to compare with this.

As the Pantheon was so near our hotel, we visited it at our earliest opportunity. It is the most perfect of the ancient buildings of Rome, and has stood here, braving wind and storm, ever since twenty-seven years before the birth of Christ. This huge circular structure is one hundred and forty feet high, and one hundred and forty feet in diameter. The massive brick walls are twenty feet thick, and were originally covered on the exterior with marble and stucco; but, having been stripped of this costly covering, and also of reliefs and statues, it presents a shabby appearance on the outside. The portico is supported by sixteen granite Corinthian columns, each thirteen feet in circumference. This church has no windows, being lighted by a round opening twenty-eight feet in diameter in the centre of the dome, through which peeps the blue sky of sunny Italy. When it rains, of course, it comes down, but there are several holes made in the floor, through which it escapes. The interior of the dome was formerly decorated with gold leaf, but it was stripped of this hundreds of years ago. This edifice was built for a heathen temple, and there are seven empty niches in which used to stand the statues of the gods. It was consecrated as a Christian church in A. D. 609. King Victor Emmanuel, who died January 9, 1878, is buried here, near the high altar; and also Raphael, who died in 1520. Over Raphael's tomb is hung his first painting, a little thing about six by eight inches. It represents three people in bed, and one saying his prayers before the Virgin Mary.

We went outside and walked entirely around the building, looking at its old, old walls, blackened with the breath of ages, and yet it stands firm as a rock. Byron beautifully describes it in the following lines.

> "Simple, erect, severe, austere, sublime—
> Shrine of all saints and temple of all gods,
> From Jove to Jesus—spared and blest by time;
> Looking tranquility, while falls or nods
> Arch, empire, each thing round thee, and man plods
> His way through thorns to ashes—glorious dome!
> Shalt thou not last? Time's scythe and tyrants' rods
> Shiver upon thee—sanctuary and home
> Of art and piety—Pantheon!—pride of Rome."

We walked over to the church of S. Maria Sopra Minerva, which stands at the right of our hotel. It is the only Gothic church in Rome, and is only about six hundred years old. In the interior is a piece of statuary by Michael Angelo, viz., "Christ with the Cross." The right foot is protected by a bronze shoe from the lips of worshipers. In one of the side chapels are life-size wax figures, representing Mary and Joseph watching over Jesus, who is represented by a wax baby in a cradle between them. Mary is dressed in a blue delaine suit, with jewelry, etc. We saw several poor deluded people kneel down and pray to these images.

Cab fare is very cheap in Rome, and it is well for tourists that it is; for we found it too warm and fatiguing to do much walking, and besides the streets in some parts are so exceedingly narrow and crooked, and running at all angles, that a stranger would soon lose his reckonings. I came to the conclusion that they must have put up the buildings first, and then made the streets to run between them. Little, cavern-like holes of shops occupy the ground floor of the houses. Some of them which I peeped into I am sure could not have been more than six by ten feet in size. They looked something like bears' dens, filled with fruits and vegetables; and the slovenly women, with uncombed hair, who kept them, did not add to their attractiveness.

We engaged a cabman to take us to St. Peter's. We crossed the Tiber over a handsome bridge, borne by five arches, and adorned with ten colossal marble statues eleven feet high. Directly in front of us rises the castle of St. Angelo or tomb of Hadrian. It is a massive stone monument, in the form of a cylinder, and is nine hundred and eighty-seven feet in circumference. On the summit is a bronze figure of the arch-angel Michael, with his flaming sword. Beneath is a large clock. This structure is more than sixteen hundred years old. From the time of Hadrian to Septimus Severus, all the emperors and their familes were interred here. Since 537 it has been used as a fortress. The celebrated Beatrice Cenci, whose beautiful face we have so often seen portrayed, is said to have been imprisoned in one of its dungeons.

There was a grand display of fireworks from the summit of this castle one evening, a general public jubilee, something like our "Fourth of July;" but it was on Sabbath night, so we did not go to witness it. We were soon in sight of St. Peter's, and recognized it immediately from the many pictures we had seen of it. In front is a grand piazza or elliptical space enclosed by the extended arms of the church, or colonnades branching out from each side of the façade, sort of sickle-shaped. These colonnades are one thousand one hundred and ten feet long, and each contains four series of Doric columns, in all numbering two hundred and eighty-four; forming three covered passages; the middle one being wide enough for two carriages abreast; and on the roofs are one hundred and sixty-two statues of saints. In the centre of this open space stands the great red obelisk, which weighs five hundred tons: brought from Heliopolis, and is the only monument of the kind at Rome which has never been thrown down. On each side of the obelisk is a lovely fountain, which throws up its sparkling water in graceful curves to be caught in a marble basin. The effect of the whole seems very appropriate for the entrance to the largest and most imposing church in the world. St. Peter's stands on the site of the circus of Nero, where many Christians were martyred, and where St. Peter is said to have been buried after his crucifixion. The present edifice was begun in 1506 and finished in 1626. Its area is twenty-six thousand one hundred and sixty-three square yards. The façade is surmounted with statues of the Saviour and apostles, nineteen feet in height. The portico, two hundred and thirty-four feet long, is sumptuously decorated, and has equestrian statues at the ends. The church is built in the form of a cross, with nave, aisles and transepts. The length of the interior, including the portico, is six hundred and ninety-six feet. The height of the nave is one hundred and fifty feet; and the dome (constructed by Michael Angelo) from the pavement to the top of the cross is four hundred and thirty-five feet high. Emerson says:

> "The hand that rounded Peter's dome
> And groined the aisles of Christian Rome
> Wrought in a sad sincerity—
> Himself from God he could not free—
> He builded better than he knew—
> The conscious stone to beauty grew."

Beneath the dome rises the grand bronze canopy borne by four spiral columns, magnificently gilded. Under the canopy is the high altar, where the pope reads mass on high festivals, and stands directly over the tomb of St. Peter. The church contains thirty altars and one hundred and forty-eight columns. The confessio is surrounded by eighty-nine lamps, which are kept burning constantly. The descent to it is by a double flight of marble stairs, and between the two flights is the statue of Pius VI., kneeling. The church has chapels on each side of the nave, the whole length, containing beautiful statuary. In one is an admirable group of Michael Angelo's, carved by him when he was twenty-four years old. It represents the Virgin with the dead body of the Saviour on her knees. Under the stupendous arches are many monuments to the different popes of Rome—of the same general character, elegant in design and workmanship. One is a monument to Gregory XIII., the rectifier of the calendar. In the nave, seated on a white marble throne, is a bronze life-size figure of St. Peter, holding the inevitable key in one hand, and the other is raised in the attitude of bestowing a blessing. The right foot is considerably worn away by being so frequently kissed by devotees. This bronze figure was made in the fifth century. I saw a man approach it, and was curious enough to watch the performance. After kissing the toe three times, he crossed his forehead and passed on.

Many fine paintings adorn the walls, among which are "Christ and Peter on the Water," "Peter Raising Tabitha from the Dead," "Healing of the Lame Man by Peter and John," "The Crucifixion of Peter with His Head Downwards," and also several good pictures in mosaic, perhaps the finest of which is a copy of Raphael's "Transfiguration," which is four times the size of the original. Over a small door of egress is "Time," a golden skeleton with his head partly hidden by a flowing robe made of brown marble, so beautifully executed that the folds are easy and graceful. The bony legs extend into the doorway. It is wonderful.

There are confessionals for eleven different languages, where the sinners confess, and the priest claims to pardon their sins. At the different altars were priests busily engaged in their religious rites and ceremonies, which were meaningless to us. A little page lifted up the long white robe of a priest, and rang a bell under it. Was it to drive away Satan? We were charmed with the pope's choir, a male quartette, accompanied with the full, rich tones of the pipe organ. The musical strains sweeping through the lofty arches of this grand cathedral reached the remotest recesses as a sweet refrain, or a gentle echo.

There are no seats of any kind in this superb edifice, and there is no way of heating it, and its floor is of marble wrought in mosaic work. I imagine that on a cold, chilly day I should prefer a snug little church, carpeted and heated, to all this wealth of papal splendor. One cannot realize the immensity of anything in this church unless he knows the exact measurement of objects. Its proportions are in such perfect harmony that one is easily deceived. For instance, as we stood beneath the dome, gorgeously decorated with mosaic pictures, gazing up at its beauty, the inscription running around it appears to be composed of ordinary-sized letters, but those letters are actually six feet high. The infant cherubs that support the basin of holy water, wrought in the shape of a pretty shell (which is near the entrance), are really giants in size. And thus it is with everything.

We pushed aside the heavy leathern curtain (which hangs before the open doors of the cathedrals of Europe) and passed out into the sunlight once more, overawed with the solemn grandeur, and marveling at the enormous sum of money that this structure cost, viz.: fifty million dollars; and its running expenses are about thirty-seven thousand five hundred dollars per annum. But when we think that in 1517, Pope Leo X., needing large sums of money to complete St. Peter's, authorized the sale of indulgences for the commission and pardon of sins, and a notorious Dominican monk, John Tetzel, went through parts of Germany carrying on this nefarious traffic from town to town, it takes away half its glory.

Having obtained a permit to visit the Vatican, the largest palace in the world, containing eleven thousand rooms, the greater number of which are occupied as a museum, and the remainder by the papal court, we entered at the end of the right colonnade of the piazza of St. Peter's; passed the Swiss guard, whose pretty gay uniforms called forth our admiration, and ascended the Scala Regia, a grand flight of stairs, each step being about two feet wide, and the risers not more than four inches, making the ascent very easy. Would that all the staircases in Europe were like this! At a door on the right we entered the world-renowned Sistine Chapel. The upper parts of the walls of this chapel are decorated with frescoes by Florentine masters of the fifteenth century. The ceiling is painted by Michael Angelo. It is divided into sections. *First*, God Almighty is represented in the form of a man, who with the motion of his arms separates light from darkness. *Second*, He creates the sun and moon. *Third*, He commands the waters to bring forth fish, etc. *Fourth*, The creation of man. *Fifth*, God takes Eve from Adam's side. *Sixth*, Satan tempts Eve. *Seventh*, The sacrifice of Cain and Abel. *Eighth*, The flood. *Ninth*, The drunkenness of Noah. These pictures are simply marvelous! and the more you study them the more fascinating they become, as you think the thoughts of the artist after him. Nearly thirty years after completing the ceiling, Michael Angelo painted on the altar wall the Last Judgment, reaching from the floor to the ceiling, and sixty-four feet in width. The light is very unfavorable for this picture, and it has become faded and dim with age. In the upper part are groups of angels, with the cross on which Christ suffered, and the column at which he was scourged. In the centre are Christ and Mary surrounded by the blessed. Beneath are the rising dead, breaking from their graves at the sound of the trumpet. On the right, the saints are supported by angels, and those on the left strive in vain to rise. At the bottom is hell, where people are writhing in a lake of fire. A boat is full of miserable wretches, and the boatman, Charon, is driving them overboard with his paddle, where an expectant group of demons encircles them "with many a scaly fold."

We ascended another flight of stairs, and passed through the several rooms in the department called Raphael's Stanze. Of the beautiful frescoes here displayed, it is stated in history that "They are unquestionably the foremost among the creations of the master, and are unrivalled by any modern works of art in existence, except the ceiling paintings in the Sistine Chapel. Among all this wealth of pictures representing allegorical and mythological subjects and Bible history, the one which most completely captivated me was the "Liberation of Peter;" representing his deliverance from prison, in three sections. The centre scene is Peter in the dungeon, sleeping between the soldiers, his wrists chained fast to both of them, and awakened by the angel. The armor of the soldiers glistens in the bright, shining, heavenly light which encircles the angel. On the other side of the dungeon, through a grated window, flashes the red torch-light of the guard without, and the pale beams of the moon add their feeble light, enhancing the artistic effect. On the right he is conducted away; and on the left the watchmen awake. It is indescribably beautiful, and so natural that I caught myself holding my breath lest the soldiers might awake before Peter made his escape.

Raphael's Loggie is a long hall, with scarcely anything left on the walls, but the ceiling is elegantly frescoed. Each of the thirteen sections of the vaulting contains four square pictures, which taken as a whole are called Raphael's Bible. It contains forty-eight scenes from the Old Testament, and four from the New. A Bible student can readily read the "Stories of Old" by looking up at these wonderfully graphic and handsome paintings. The four from the New Testament are the Adoration of the Shepherds, the Wise men from the East, Baptism of Christ, and the Last Supper.

Climbing another flight of stairs, we reached what is called the Picture Gallery of the Vatican. This, excepting the Borghese Gallery, is the most important collection of pictures in Rome, occupying four rooms only, but the works are very choice and select. I will mention those which I gazed upon the longest, ever finding some new beauty to admire: The Dead Christ, with Mary Magdalene annointing his wounds, by Giov. Bellini; Communion of St. Jerome, one of the best works of Domenichino; the last great work of Raphael, The Transfiguration, which is certainly wonderful. The expression of the faces, attitude, form, coloring; all are perfect. Beneath this picture the artist's body lay in state before his funeral. This Bible story is here minutely and thrillingly told on canvas, "Jesus taketh Peter, James, and John, his brother, and bringeth them up into a high mountain apart, and was transfigured before them; and his face did shine as the sun, and his raiment was white as the light. And behold there appeared unto them Moses and Elias talking with him. A bright cloud overshadowed them; and behold a voice out of the cloud, which said, This is my beloved son, in whom I am well pleased; hear ye him. And when the disciples heard it they fell on their face, and were sore afraid." At the foot of the mount are a multitude of people, and prominent among them is the father presenting his lunatic child to the disciples to be healed of them. The demented expression of the boy's face, and the anxious entreaty of the father's countenance, speak a volume of sorrow.

Twenty centuries after this scene was enacted on Mount Tabor occurred the "Battle of Mount Tabor," so valiantly won by Napoleon Bonaparte.

Headley poetically says: "Can there be a stranger contrast than the battle and the transfiguration of Mount Tabor? One shudders to think of Bonaparte and the Son of God on the same mountain; one with his wasting cannon by his side, and the other with Moses and Elias just from heaven. But no after desecration can destroy the first consecration of Mount Tabor; for baptized with the glory of heaven, and honored with the wondrous scene of the transfiguration, it stands a sacred mountain on the earth."

A fourth enchanting picture is the Madonna of Foligno, with the town of Foligno in the background, by Raphael; also the Coronation of the Virgin, by the same master; The Entombment, one of the ablest works of the naturalistic school, by

Caravaggio; the Doge of Venice, by Titian, and the Crucifixion of St. Peter, by Guido Reni.

In order to reach the Museum of Statues, we were required to descend to the piazza and go around St. Peter's to another entrance of the Vatican, which proved to be such a long, warm walk that we were wiser the next day, and hired a cab at the door of St. Peter's.

Just think of a church covering so much space that one must hire a carriage to go around it.

In one of the Pope's apartments of the Vatican, on the ground floor, we saw three golden chariots belonging to the Pope; and saddles and harness rich with splendor.

The Vatican collection of antiquities, the finest in the world, consists of the Museo Pio Clementino, Museo Gregoriano, Museo Chiaramonti, Braccio Nuovo, Egyptian Museum, and Raphael's Tapestry. There are more than one thousand pieces of sculpture in these museums; but we shall confine ourselves to the mention of a very few.

We had proceeded but a short distance, when our attention was drawn to a lovely basket of flowers wrought in mosaic work on the floor. The arrangement of buds, blossoms, and leaves displays rare taste and artistic skill. And in another room an admirable circular piece of mosaic nearly covers the floor. We were captivated with a two-horse chariot, or Biga, it is called, drawn by spirited horses, exquisitely chiseled out of snowy marble. The body of the chariot, which was used for centuries as an Episcopal throne in St. Mark's Church in Rome, is richly adorned with leaves and scroll work. Lions' heads form the hubs of the wheels, and the pole has a ram's head at the end. The horses are standing on their hind legs, as if restless to be off. The colossal group representing the river Nile, consists of a man of giant proportions, half reclining, with one arm resting upon a sphynx. Sixteen cute, chubby little babies are clambering over him; one is cunningly perched on his shoulder, pulling his ear; another poised on his thigh; others clinging to his arms and legs, and one dear little dot, with folded arms, is plunged to his waist in a cornucopia of grapes. The sixteen children are emblematic of the sixteen yards which the river Nile rises. Hercules looms up before us, a statue twelve feet high in gilded bronze, found in 1864 near the theatre at Pompeii. He is leaning upon his club, with a lion's skin thrown over his arm. But the one group of statuary we desired to see most of all in this collection was the Laocoön, the great wonderful original! It was found in the ruins of the Palace of Titus in 1506, and, according to Pliny, was executed by the three Rhodians, Agesander, Polydorus and Athenodorus. This famous group represents Laocoön, with his two sons, strangled by serpents. The intense agony depicted upon the countenances, the strain of the muscles, the contortion of the bodies, seem so true to nature that no wonder Michael Angelo termed it "a marvel of art." According to classic legend, "Laocoön was a priest of Apollo, who in vain warned his countrymen of the deceit practiced by the Greeks in their pretended offering of the wooden horse to Minerva, and was destroyed, along with his two sons, by two enormous serpents, which came from the sea. They first fastened on his children, and when he attempted to rescue them, involved himself in their coils."

In the midst of this vast wilderness of statuary, possessing beauties beyond description, one scarcely knows which to study most. Here is a beautifully-draped statue; a bearded Bacchus, and an effeminate Bacchus; Ephesian Diana, from the villa of Hadrian; a female runner from the same place, with banged hair (aped by the girls of the present generation); bust of Zeus, the finest in existence; Posid; the goddess Minerva, crowned with the familiar helmet; Posidippus and Menander, comic dramatists seated in easy chairs; Saturn; head of Menelaus; torso of Hercules, dating back to the first century B. C., and found in the sixteenth century near the theatre at Pompeii; torso of an archaic Penelope, in a sitting posture of fine workmanship; a head of Neptune; Venus; a drowsy spinster; bow-bending Cupid; Tiberius, a colossal sitting figure; daughter of Niobe; Augustus; Mercury; Apoxyomenos, an athlete cleaning his right arm with a scraping-iron. Here, also, we saw two large sarcophagi in porphyry, of the daughter and mother of Constantine the Great; a colossal camel's head, formerly used as the aperture of a fountain; a magnificent basin of porphyry, twenty feet across and four feet deep, brought from the baths of Diocletian; the Barberini Candelabra, found in Hadrian's villa; a wind indicator, found in 1779, near the Colosseum; a fine, large basin of delicately-tinted marble, and one of alabaster; sarcophagus of L. Cornelius Scipio Barbatus, great grandfather of the illustrious Africanus, and consul B. C. 298. The Etruscan Department contains twelve rooms of antiquities excavated about fifty years ago in the Etruscan cities of Vulci, Toscanella and Chiusi. Four of these rooms are filled with vases, ornamented with different figures, such as Achilles and Ajax playing with dice, in a variety of colors. One room consists of early paintings, with stiff angular-looking horses and men; another of bronzes, old, rusty, mouldy things; a bronze chariot, fairly green with age and verdigris; an immense bronze arm; bronze kitchen utensils, etc., etc. Although repulsive to look upon, they form an interesting link in the history of Italian art, and afford information concerning the habits of the almost prehistoric Etruscans. Here are also ancient weapons, ornaments and jewelry. A large glass case contains golden Etruscan jewelry of all descriptions, wrought in the most delicate and elegant designs, something like filigree work; and no wonder that it is sadly in need of a thorough cleaning, for it is three thousand years old. A table about three feet in diameter, made of small pieces of stained glass, artistically arranged, from church windows found in ancient Rome, is an object of great beauty.

Passing into the Egyptian Museum, the mummies, hieroglyphics, model of a pyramid, birds, cats, dogs, beetles, idols, and other objects in bronze and stone, made the Roman and Etruscan relics seem quite modern. The mummies, as usual, were tightly bound with heavy linen bandages, with just the face and toes visible; the skin black and dried, but the teeth well preserved: others of greater age, with the skin entirely gone.

The Egyptian art of thus embalming the dead is at least as old as two thousand years B. C. One of the earliest recorded embalmments is that of the patriarch Jacob, and the body of Joseph was preserved as a mummy. One of the most expensive processes of embalming the dead was as follows: A deep incision was made on the left side beneath the ribs, and the entrails and lungs were removed; the brain was extracted through the nose by means of a crooked instrument; the cavity of the body was filled with resins, cassia, and other substances, and the incision stitched up; peculiar drugs were passed through the nostrils into the skull. The mummy was then steeped in a native carbonate of soda for seventy days, then tightly wrapped up in linen bandages, cemented by gums, and set upright in a wooden or stone coffin, the cost of which was more than three thousand dollars. I should think it would be a miracle if they did not keep, after such a pickling. "The Egyptians thought that the preservation of the body was necessary for the return of the soul to the human form after it had completed its cycle of existence, of three or ten thousand years." How strong the faith of this heathen nation, even in its darkness, in the immortality of the soul, and how earnest the efforts to save it!

We did not inspect the library of the Vatican, as there is too much to be seen in this wonderful palace without poring over musty books and manuscripts, even though one had the opportunity.

In order to satisfy the curiosity of my readers, I will here state that we did *not* see the Pope. We had but one opportunity of being admitted into his presence, with a large party, and missed that. It was no great disappointment, however. I suppose he is made of flesh and blood, like other people, walks, eats and sleeps; and, no doubt, closely resembles the other inhabitants of the earth in many points, if not all.

We were delighted with Raphael's tapestry, executed from cartoons drawn by Raphael in 1515 and 1516. Each piece of this tapestry, wrought at Brussels, with marked skill, in wool, silk and gold, cost about three thousand five hundred dollars.

They are the most wonderful things I ever beheld in the form of tapestry. The whole looks like a beautiful oil painting, so perfect are the tints, forms and shading. Even the veins, muscles, wrinkles, clouds, mountains, foliage, expression—*all* are faultless! These pictures are perhaps twenty by eighteen feet in size. The principal scenes represent the Conversion of St. Paul; The people of Lystra about to offer sacrifice to Paul and Barnabas; St. Paul healing the lame man in the temple; Paul preaching at Athens; Miraculous draught of fishes; St. Peter receiving the keys; Slaughter of the Innocents, in three large pictures; Death of Ananias; Christ appearing to Mary Magdalene; The supper at Emmaus; Presentation of Christ in the temple; Adoration of the Magi; Resurrection; Adoration of the Shepherds; Ascension; Stoning of Stephen; Religion between Justice and Mercy; Descent of the Holy Ghost, and Paul in Prison at Philippi.

Having seen the principal sights of the Vatican, knowing how utterly foolish it was to try to take in everything, we turned our attention in another direction.

We were in Rome two Sabbaths and attended services in St. Paul's American Episcopal Church, there being no church of our own denomination in the place.

One bright beautiful morning seated in an open barouche we were whirled off in the direction of the Colosseum. Passing the ruins of the Roman Forum and the Palace of the Cæsars, at last the great, circular structure, so poetically described by historians, loomed up before us, with its giant proportions, the largest theatre and one of the most imposing structures in the world. It was eight years in building, and was finished by Titus A. D. 80. Only about one third of the original edifice now remains. It is circular in form on the outside, and the arena is elliptical. It is built of huge blocks of stone, some of them five feet high and eight or ten feet long, originally held together by strong iron clamps. It is one third of a mile in circumference and one hundred and fifty-six feet high. The arena is two hundred and seventy-nine feet by one hundred and seventy-four feet, and above this open space rise tiers of seats intersected by steps and passages, most of which are in a ruined condition. One side, however, is preserved sufficiently, to give a good idea of what it once was. At one side of the arena are two pillars upon which was a platform where the Emperor, senators and vestal virgins used to sit. The first tier above them was occupied by the knights; the next tier by the plebeians; the next by the ladies, and the upper tier by the slaves. These raised seats would accommodate eighty-seven thousand people. At one of the most perfect parts of the outside wall we could see four rows of columns, one above another; the first Doric, the second Ionic, and the third and fourth Corinthian. In the arena, the bull fights took place, gladiator combats, games, and so on; and Christian martyrs were forced into the arena and torn to pieces by ravenous wild beasts. Adjacent to the foundation of the inner wall were chambers and dens for wild beasts; also prisons where martyrs were confined a few days before they were sacrificed. The wild beasts were brought to the Colosseum by an underground passage for some little distance, from a sort of rocky den, which we peeped into. We picked up some pieces of the crumbled walls and a small brick from the floor, as souvenirs. Our guide who thought he could speak English thoroughly made the following remark as we were searching for some relics. "I find a piece of marble once on the top, and wen I finds it I gives you to it." Allow me to give what Dickens says about the Colosseum. "To see it crumbling there, an inch a year; its walls and arches overgrown with green, its corridors open to the day; the long grass growing in its porches; young trees of yesterday springing up on its ragged parapets, and bearing fruit—chance produce of the seeds dropped there by the birds that build their nests within its chinks and crannies; to climb into its upper halls, and look down on ruin, ruin, ruin, all about it; the triumphal arches of Constantine, Septimius Severus, and Titus, the Roman Forum, the Palace of the Cæsars, the temples of the old religion fallen down and gone; is to see the ghost of old Rome, wicked, wonderful old city, haunting the very ground on which its people trod. It is the most impressive, the most stately, the most solemn, grand, majestic, mournful sight conceivable." We clambered around wherever it was safe to go, and looking away down into the arena, we imagined as being enacted, some of the bloody scenes of which we had read; and which occured here with such frequency in bygone days. Our guide whom we had hired for the day pointed out to us from our elevated position the ruins which lay scattered about us on every side. Close at hand are the remains of a fountain where the gladiators used to wash after the fights; the Triumphal Arch of Constantine is also near, and is the best preserved structure of the kind, built in 311, when Constantine boldly declared his belief in Christianity. Slowly and carefully we descended the stone steps and still lingered for a time within its old, old walls, which are silently crumbling with age.

> "While stands the Colosseum, Rome shall stand,
> When falls the Colosseum, Rome shall fall,
> And when Rome falls, with it shall fall the world."

A short walk from the Colosseum is the Church of S. Pietro in Vincoli (St. Peter in chains) which we entered expressly to see the celebrated statue of Moses by Michael Angelo; one of his most famous works. It is a colossal sitting figure, with strong muscular arms and limbs. He is represented as having horns, and his long flowing beard falls to his lap in graceful waves; and his eyes (unlike anything I ever saw before in statuary) are full of expression; they fairly speak to you. It is a grand ideal of the man of God, appointed to lead the chosen people out of bondage, through the Red Sea, and the long weary journeys of the wilderness, even to the borders of the Promised Land

> "Statue! whose giant limbs
> Old Buonarotti planned,
> And Genius carved with meditative hand,—
> Thy dazzling radiance dims
> The best and brightest boasts of Sculpture's favorite land."

"What dignity adorns
 That beard's prodigious sweep!
 That forehead, awful with mysterious horns
 And cogitation deep,
 Of some uncommon mind the rapt beholder warns.

"In that proud semblance, well
 My soul can recognize
 The prophet fresh from converse with the skies;
 Nor is it hard to tell
 The liberator's name—the guide of Israel."

"Well might the deep respond
 Obedient to that voice,
 When on the Red Sea shore he waved his wand,
 And bade the tribes rejoice,
 Saved from the yawning gulf and the Egyptian's bond."

"Fools! in the wilderness
 Ye raised a calf of gold!
 Had ye then worshiped what I now behold,
 Your crime had been far less—
 For ye had bent the knee to one of godlike mould!"

We next went to take a closer inspection of the ruins of the Roman Forum, which in times past echoed to the sound of Cicero's orations, alas! now nothing but a heap of fragments, with here and there a broken column, a shattered arch, and the site of temples marked only by a group of lonely pillars. There stands the arch of Septimius Severus, erected A. D. 205, and although badly mutilated, yet the reliefs of battles, sieges, marches, etc., with which it is covered, are interesting to the lover of history. Eight handsome granite columns are proudly standing to mark the site of the temple of Saturn, built forty-four years before Christ; the column of Phocas gracefully rises to the height of fifty-four feet, and those three beautiful Parian marble columns with their Corinthian capitals and ornamental entablature, mark the spot where the Temple of Castor and Pollux stood. Three great arches belonging to one of the aisles of the Basilica of Constance, and the ruin of the Three Columns, or Temple of Venus and Roma, are silent witnesses of the past, of the splendor of ancient Rome.

We passed behind the Arch of Septimius Severus and came to a small church at the foot of the Capitoline Hill, beneath which is the Mamertine Prison, one of the oldest relics of Rome, having been restored 22 B. C. It was originally built over a well, and was afterwards used as a prison. St. Peter and St. Paul are said to have been confined here for nine months. It consists of two stone apartments, one above the other. A monk who has charge of the little church, provided us with candles and led the way down a flight of stone steps into the dark dungeon, where not a ray of light enters. The lower dungeon is reached by a little circular staircase now, and is nineteen feet long, ten feet wide, and six and one-half feet high; the roof is formed by the gradual projection of the side walls until they meet, and in the centre of the ceiling is a round hole where the prisoners were thrust down. It seemed horrible to be away down there in that dark dungeon groping our way about with our little candles and thinking how Jugurtha starved to death here in this cheerless, comfortless hole, after being deprived of food for six days, and how many days and nights of solitary gloom had been passed here by many others. Following our guide we held our candles close to the wall and there saw the busts of Peter and Paul; and in one corner is a well with nothing to protect one from inadvertently stepping into it. The guide drew up some water and we tasted it after him. Near the spring on the wall is a bronze relief illustrating the legend that the disciples miraculously caused the water to flow in order to baptize the jailor. Whether it be a fact or only a legend that the apostles were imprisoned here, it was thrilling to think that I was walking over the very floor which, perhaps, Peter's feet had pressed—he who had so often walked with Jesus.

From here we went to the Capitol, approached by a grand staircase, at the foot of which are two lions of Egyptian porphyry, and at its head the ancient colossal statues of Castor and Pollux. At the left of the steps are a pair of caged wolves, kept in reminiscence of the story that Romulus and Remus, the founders of Rome, were suckled by a wolf. In the centre of the open space or square between the buildings is the renowned statue of Marcus Aurelius, "the only perfect, ancient, equestrian statue in existence." On the right is the Palace of the Conservatori, on the left the Museum of the Capitol, and on the third side of the square is the palace of the Senators. The bell in the tower of the latter is only rung at the opening of the Carnival, or when a pope dies. We first entered the museum, filled with very fine statuary. Here we found the celebrated Dying Gladiator, to which Byron so touchingly refers in his Childe Harold. One room is filled with statues of philosophers, another with busts of emperors, Victor Immanuel, Dante, Columbus and Galileo are also here. The room of the Doves is so called from the mosaic picture on the wall, of some doves sitting on the edge of a vase, drinking and pluming themselves. It is mentioned by Pliny, and is certainly very pretty. You may see scores of copies of it on mosaic breastpins in the jewelers windows in Rome. The Capitoline Venus is an admirable piece of statuary.

We crossed the square to the Palace of the Conservatori, where we walked through two rooms with modern lists of Roman magistrates, then through a long corridor containing a collection of busts of celebrated Italians—scholars, painters, architects, sculptors, and poets. One room was filled with all kinds of bronze utensils; another with terra cottas (pitchers, jars, lamps, etc.) Among the bronzes is the Capitoline Wolf, with Romulus and Remus, supposed to have been in existence as early as 296 B. C.; and the Thorn Extractor, a boy removing a thorn from his foot, which brought to mind the scenes of country-school scholars extracting thistles.

The Picture Gallery, though not extensive, has some very good pictures, one of the most striking of which is St. Petronella raised from her tomb and shown to her bridegroom.

The Tarpeian Rock, from which the ancient Romans used to hurl the condemned, is on this hill, and proved quite a disappointment, as it is nothing more than a high stone wall with a dirty street at the bottom. I had my mind made up for a formidable, projecting rock, yawning precipice, etc.

On our way home we stopped to look at the outside of the Theatre of Marcellus, which dates back to 13 B. C. It is something after the style of the Colosseum, and accommodated twenty thousand spectators. Twelve arches of the outer wall are now occupied by blacksmith and other shops. As you look in and see the flaming forge under one of the arches of this massive stone building, it looks like a little fire-place with an enormous mantel-piece. But an Italian just wants room enough to turn around in, in a shop. It's astonishing what small quarters a cobbler can be happy in. I have seen them under a little shanty with the roof scarcely high enough to accommodate them when sitting, something like a dog-kennel.

Our next drive was to Piazza di S. Giovanni, in Laterano. On the east side of this public square is a small building containing the Scala Santa, or Holy Stairs. At the foot of this staircase, which is very wide, is a piece of statuary representing Christ before Pilate, on one side; and on the other, Judas betraying Christ with a kiss, holding his bag of money behind him. These stairs consist of twenty-eight marble steps, now covered with wood to protect them, and can only be ascended by penitents on their knees. Here and there are round holes in the wood, exposing a portion of the marble. We watched two elderly women ascend these stairs on their knees, and kiss these spots of marble as they came to them; and when they painfully reached the top they kissed the floor where is a figure of Christ with the wounds in his side, hands, and feet. On the wall, at the top of the stairs is a picture of Christ on the cross. These marble steps were brought from Jerusalem to Rome in the year 326, and are said to have belonged to Pilate's house, and to have been ascended by Jesus. There are two other staircases, one on either side of the Holy Stairs where people may walk up and where the worshipers descend. We *walked* up and entered a small Gothic chapel, formerly the private chapel of the Pope. I pitied those two old ladies, and felt so indignant at the priest who sat at the bottom, that if I could have spoken Italian I know I should have told them that Christ was not pleased by their torturing their bodies in that manner. Each person who visits the Holy Stairs may purchase a copy of the following tract of the priest; and I give it that you may see how they mislead the ignorant, viz:

"One of the most sacred remembrances of the Passion of our Lord Jesus Christ is certainly the Holy Stairs, worthy of the veneration of all Christians, since they were mounted so many times by our Divine Redeemer, and sanctified by his precious blood during the last hours of his life."

"These stairs, brought from Jerusalem to Rome, under the protection of the Empress Helena, about the year 326, and placed in the chapel called Santa Sanctorum, universally celebrated, have at all times been much frequented by both sexes, of every class, who mount the steps on their knees." "To engage more particularly Christians to accomplish this act of devotion, so precious and useful to the soul of the devout, St. Leo IV., towards the year 850, and Pascal II., by his bull of the 5th of August, 1100, first year of his election (the original bull is conserved in the archives of the Basilica of St. John the Lateran) granted nine years of indulgence for each of the twenty-eight steps of the aforesaid Holy Stairs, once of the Prætor's house of Pontius Pilate, when it will be mounted on the knee, with a contrite heart, praying or meditating on the Passion of our Lord Jesus Christ."

"Pius VII., by a Decree of the Holy Congregation of Indulgence, September 2, 1817, renewed this indulgence, but perpetually, and declared that it may be applied also to souls in Purgatory. *"Rome, 1866—with approbation."*

In 1510 Martin Luther was wearily climbing these stairs on his knees to obtain an indulgence promised by the pope, with rosary in hand, repeating his prayers, when his conscience whispered to him, "The just shall live by faith," and rising from his knees he descended. This was the decisive turning point in his life. In a few years after he nailed the ninety-five theses to the church door at Wittenberg, which was the dawn of the Reformation.

Just across the square we entered the church of S. Giovanni in Laterano (St. John Lateran). This is the fourth church erected on this site. The first was destroyed by an earthquake, and the second and third by fire. This one was erected in the fifteenth century. It is the church of the pope as bishop of Rome, and here his coronation takes place. On the façade is the following inscription—"The mother and head of the state, and of all the ecclesiastical world." On each side of the nave are magnificent colossal statues in white marble of the twelve apostles. The high altar is said to contain the heads of St. Peter and St. Paul; a table of wood upon which St. Paul officiated; and behind the altar the table of the Last Supper.

There are most beautiful chapels on either side of the nave. A family is said to have spent more than three hundred thousand dollars on one of these chapels. The chapel of S. Andrea Corsini is without a parallel in Rome. It is composed of the finest marble, with a beautiful vaulting, ancient columns, and the walls extravagantly inland with precious stones. A large vessel of porphyry, from the portico of the Pantheon, stands in front of the bronze figure of Clement XII. Below this chapel, down a winding stair case, is the burial vault of the Corsini, with an exquisite Pieta. The custodian lit a lamp which hung in front of it and gave us a fine view of this touching and beautiful piece of statuary—Mary holding the dead body of Christ upon her lap. The expression of grief and tenderness on the mother's face and the limp body in her arms shows the wonderful skill of the artist Bernini to chisel the attitude of life and death out of one solid block of marble. It far surpasses Michael Angelo's Pieta, in St. Peter's, to my mind. Another chapel belonging to the Torlonia family, richly ornamented with marble and gilding, has a magnificent marble relief by Tenerani —the Descent from the Cross. A man is coming down the ladder which rests against the cross, with the body of Jesus in his arms; Mary, the mother of Jesus, lovingly throws her arms about his neck, while Mary Magdalene supports his feet. The expression on all the faces is remarkable. Attached to this church is the Museum Gregorianum Lateranense. It was set apart for a museum in 1843 on account of not having any more space in the Vatican and Capitol. Here we saw, among other ancient sculptures, fine statues of Mars, Sophocles, Poseidon and Cato, numerous architectural fragments from the excavations of the Roman Forum, relics found at Ostia, a large collection of ancient Christian sarcophagi of the fourth and fifth centuries, with reliefs representing scenes from the Old and New Testament, and one representing the story of Orestes. A mosaic pavement, by Heraclitus, provokes a smile the moment you look upon it. It represents an unswept dining-room. Scattered everywhere in pretty mosaic work are cherries on the stems, chicken and fish bones, shells, slices of lemon, and there runs a mouse! It all looks so natural that a neat housekeeper immediately wants to get the dust-pan and brush and "sweep up." We ascended a flight of stairs leading to a gallery, where we looked down upon the floor or mosaic pavement representing twenty-eight pugilists, which was found in the baths of Caracalla in 1824.

At a short distance from here is the church of S. Clemente, beneath which are three different layers of masonry of Christian, imperial and republican origin. In 1857 Father Mulloony, an Irish priest, began to repair the church, and in excavating, came upon a wall covered with very ancient paintings. He continued to excavate and found an underground church dating back to 392. We descended a broad marble staircase with inscriptions on the wall and reached the vestibule of the lower church. Aided by the dim light of tapers we groped our way about. In places the ancient marble floor is quite well preserved, and here and there are frescoes on the walls, of the fourth century, some of them very perfect, and others are dim. Among the frescoes are Christ represented as beardless; Daniel in the Lion's Den; Christ blessing in the Greek mode, *i. e.*, with first, middle, and third fingers extended. Looking down a staircase we were convinced that there is still another story below the lower church. From all appearances this lower church was formerly much grander than the upper church, which is quite ordinary, as compared with other places of worship.

> With carriage and driver engaged for the day,
> We soon were traveling on the Appian Way.

The same broad, grand road, paved with blocks of volcanic stone, over which Paul was brought as a prisoner to Rome.

We alighted at the Catacombs of St. Callistus. More than forty different catacombs have been discovered, extending around the city of Rome; but this is the only one that has been thoroughly excavated. These catacombs combined cover a space of six hundred and fifteen acres. The sacristan provided us with little wax-tapers twisted up in a comical manner, which we had to untwist as they burned down. Following the sacristan, single file, we reached the dark, narrow, subterranean passages fifty feet deep and two and a half feet wide, with niches in the side walls of the length of the body to be interred, from infants to adults. These niches rise in seven tiers, one above another. After the bodies were placed in, they were closed with tablets of marble. We saw a few skeletons lying in these niches which were well preserved, but in many of them the bones were lying in disorder, and the majority had turned to dust. These monotonous passages are occasionally broken by larger chambers, one of which contains the tombs of popes on the left, and those of Anteros, Lucius, Fabianus, and Eutychianus on the right, and on the centre that of Sixtus II., who died as a martyr in the catacombs in 258. Another of these chambers, which is open above, once contained the tomb of St. Cecilia. On the walls are dim paintings of the seventh and eighth centuries, such as St. Urban and the head of Christ. Holding my little taper high, I followed close on the heels of the others, for I was afraid of getting lost in these dark, seemingly never-ending passages, running out in every direction, with dead people's bones on either side, and I imagined I could smell putrefaction, although they had been free from anything of the kind for many centuries.

Again seated in carriages, we rode for miles over the Appian Way, passing the celebrated tomb of Cecilia Metella. Here it has stood, gazed at and admired, for about two thousand years. It is a circular tower, built of lava and brick, and it is so strong that it has often been used as a fortress. It is seventy feet in diameter, and although the marble has been stripped from the outside, yet it is very picturesque in its ruin.

On we went, past monuments and tombs, till we were on the broad Campagna, and the guide pointed out the line of ruined arches, which mark where the aqueduct once conveyed the water from the distant Sabine Hills (over yonder, wrapt in a bluish haze) to the Eternal City.

Striking off in another direction, we reached at last St. Paul's Cathedral, which is about a mile and a half outside the city walls. The exterior is very plain, but the interior is rich with splendor. St. Paul is supposed to have been buried here. The interior is three hundred and ninety feet long, one hundred and ninety-five feet wide, and two hundred and twenty-five feet in height, with double aisles and transepts, borne by eighty grand columns of granite from the Simplon Pass. The ceiling of the nave is richly gilded, and the floor of the finest polished marble. It was built in 1854, so it is quite modern. Two yellowish columns of oriental alabaster at the entrance, and four which support the golden canopy of the high altar were presented by the Viceroy of Egypt, and the malachite pedestals by the Emperor of Russia. The confessio, with its half-circle of burning lamps, is richly decorated with marble from the ancient quarries in Greece, and before it are two colossal statues of St. Peter and St. Paul. There is a long series of portrait medallions in mosaic of all the popes down to the present, extending all around the church. They are five feet in diameter. The windows in the aisles are of stained glass, with representations of the apostles and fathers of the church. There are several chapels, which looked meagre, however, after seeing those at St. John Lateran, and a fine lot of paintings.

Once more we stepped into the carriage, and were soon passing through the gate of S. Paulo into Old Rome again. Near this gate is the tomb of Caius Cestius. It is a brick pyramid, cased with marble, one hundred and twenty-five feet high, and its base is a hundred feet square.

We rode on to the Baths of Caracalla. They are now a huge mass of ruins, but were once unparalleled in luxuriance. They were begun in 212 by Caracalla, and completed by Alexander Severus, and could accommodate one thousand six hundred bathers at once. The size of these grounds was one thousand and eighty feet square. The floors are of beautiful mosaic marble, from which I picked a few tiny green pieces as a souvenir. We saw the remains of a large saloon for cold baths, one for tepid baths, another for hot-air baths, and a perfuming and anointing room. At one place the wall is perfect, and is one hundred and fifty feet high and twenty feet thick. And besides all these comforts for bathing to suit the whims of the most fastidious, there were lovely gardens, fountains, refreshment shops, fancy bazaars, libraries, and games; so that it was quite a fashionable resort. *Now* it is only pretty to look at as a picture of grand ruins. Many handsome things, statuary, vases, mosaics, etc., which we have seen in different museums, come from this place; among them the Farnese Bull, Hercules, and Flora, at Naples.

While driving, we passed the Column of Trajan, and went through the Jews' quarters (misery, filth, and beggars,) near which are the House of Rienzi, the Theatre with the workshops under it, the Temple of Fortuna, and the Temple of Vesta.

The Corso, which I have before mentioned as being the principal street of Rome, is much broader than the others, and the pavement is respectably wide. Many of the streets are so narrow that they have no pavement for foot passengers, and others have them raised about a foot above the street, but so narrow that if two persons meet, one must step off in order to pass. This is the prevailing style of sidewalks in most of the old European cities. It was quite a treat therefore to take a walk down the Corso, enlivened with its gay shops, and look at the pretty Roman mosaic jewelry, the genuine article, of which we had seen so many wax imitations, retailed on the street. But it was not so much of a treat to have a small boy follow us for two squares, unfolding yards of views of Rome, and crying in a sing-song tone, "All of Rome for 'alf a franc, O——ô, that is very cheap, all of Rome for 'alf a franc!" It becomes monotonous after one has heard it ninety-nine times; and the different orders of monks, with their black, gray, or brown cowls, the priests, sisters of charity, and the young men who are studying for the priesthood, with their long cloaks and broad-brimmed hats, also became monotonous, as we were continually coming in contact with some of them. I don't enjoy seeing everybody dressed alike—"Variety is the spice of life."

One morning we went to a hotel on the Via Nazionale, where were acquaintances, and from a balcony, with them, watched a grand military parade, celebrating the Festa Della Statuto, or Festival of the Constitution. A long line of well-drilled soldiers passed, accompanied by a large and excellent band of music. Then in her carriage, with driver, footman and maid, gracefully rode the Queen, dressed in cameo pink satin, with a profusion of point lace, bowing and smiling graciously to the people on either side. She is a great favorite among her subjects. Surely if her life is as beautiful as her face, one could not help but be drawn toward her. Next came a superb array of cavalry, and then King Humbert on horseback with dignified demeanor, his long white feather floating in the breeze. By his side rode his son twelve years of age, also gayly attired; and another long line of cavalry brought up the rear.

We visited the Borghese Palace. The picture gallery here is considered the next finest to that of the Vatican, and the best private collection in the city; arranged according to schools in twelve rooms. Among the master-pieces are the Holy Family, a work of the highest rank, of large size. An artist had made a very small copy of it, about eight inches across, in water colors, a perfect little gem. Its price was one hundred and eighty dollars. Raphael's Entombment, Correggio's Danæ, Titian's

Earthly and Heavenly Love (one of his best works); and Domenichino's Cumæan Sibyl, are all charming. In the centre of one of the rooms is a very large and extravagantly beautiful table of irregular mosaic, composed of a great variety of very precious stones.

From here we went to the Palace of Barberini, a magnificent building, with fine grounds. We were anxious to see a small private gallery which it contained, consisting of three rooms. The gems are Durer's "Christ among the Doctors," painted in five days, at Venice in 1506; Raphael's portrait of the Fornarina, a most beautiful woman, with dark eyes and hair; and Guido Reni's Beatrice Cenci. The latter is the picture of which we so often see copies in American homes. Beatrice has become almost a household word. It is said that the artist painted it in the prison the night before her execution. Her sad, sweet, innocent face; her large, lustrous, hazel eyes; the wavy, auburn tresses stealing from the graceful drapery about the head; and the full ruby lips so captivated me that I purchased a copy on porcelain at my earliest opportunity.

One of the curiosities which we felt determined to see, was the church of S. Maria della Concezione, beneath which are five burial vaults and a small chapel, where services are held on November 2d, when the vaults are also illuminated. The walls of these vaults are completely covered in a ghastly manner with the bones of four thousand monks. Grinning skulls meet your gaze which ever way you turn. The bones are arranged in the shape of arches; and under each arch lies a mummy with his dried skin, dead hair, horrible teeth, and dressed in a long black robe, holding a black crucifix in his arms. And some of these mummies are standing up like sentinels dressed in the same manner. Their eyeless sockets and grinning jaws make them seem as though they were laughing at their own ridiculous appearance. The vertebræ are strung on wire, and are arranged in fantastic figures on the ceiling. They also hang in graceful festoons wherever appropriate. In front of each vault, suspended from the ceiling, is a fantastic arrangement made of human bones, strung together, making quite a fancy hanging lamp. Thigh, leg, and arm bones, finger and toe joints, shoulder blades, vertebrae, skulls, in fact every bone in the body is utilized in forming this horrible spectacle. In each vault there is a tomb filled with earth from Jerusalem. When a Capuchin monk dies, they take up the bones which have been buried the longest and use them for decoration; and the lately deceased takes possession of the tomb. So you see the grave is not to them a final resting place, as we sometimes term it.

We next visited the church of S. Maria Maggiore on the Esquiline Hill. It is very handsome, both externally and internally. It has two superb domes and a spire, and is one of the oldest churches in Rome. It was built in the fifth century, but of course has undergone many changes since then. It is one of the five patriarchal churches. Its elegant mosaic pavement seems almost too pretty to walk upon. The flat-panelled ceiling is very handsome, and the architrave, adorned with fine pictures in mosaic, is supported by forty-two Ionic columns of white marble, excepting four, which are of granite. The arches and domes are beautifully painted. The high altar consists of an ancient sarcophagus of porphyry, said to contain the remains of St. Matthew and other relics. The canopy is borne by four columns of porphyry, and the confessio in front of the high altar is perfectly exquisite, consisting of an endless variety of pretty colored marbles. There are fine chapels in the right and left aisles. One of them is *said* to contain five boards from the manger of the infant Christ. In the left transept is the Borghese chapel, with its handsome dome and altar sumptuously decorated with lapis lazuli and agate. In the right transept is also a chapel with a dome, gorgeously decorated.

As there are three hundred and sixty-five churches in Rome, one for every day in the year, we were not foolish enough to attempt to even peep into them all, but were content to examine pretty thoroughly ten of the most important.

The palace of the Cæsars, which covers the Palatine Hill, is situated just south of the Roman Forum. This mass of ruins was brought to light by excavations begun in 1861 by Napoleon III. The Palatine Hill, which is five thousand two hundred feet in circumference, is the original site of the city of Romulus and Remus. We were shown a grotto by the guide, which is supposed to be the Lupercal where the she-wolf went for safety when driven from the twins by the shepherds. A small museum has been erected, which contains many interesting fragments. We followed our guide through these ruins for two hours, as he pointed out the buildings of Caligula and Tiberius, the Palace of the Flavii, which was the chief seat of the Roman Government; the Pædagogium, or school for the imperial slaves; and the Stadium, which lies between the buildings of Septimus Severus and the old Palace of Augustus. It was interesting to us to know that Cicero and Catiline used to live on this hill; and I thought that if I could live over my college days again, I should read Cicero's orations with considerable vim. Some of the walls of the houses are in quite good preservation, and also the mosaic pavements, and here and there may be seen mural paintings, consisting of garlands of flowers, fruit, etc.

This hill is covered with beautiful foliage; trees loaded with little green oranges and figs. The day was very warm, and wearied with over-exertion, I sat down on a friendly stone to rest, while the gentlemen clambered about with their heads full of Roman history. To atone for their long absence they brought me a peace-offering of flowers—a nosegay of olive twigs, oleander blossoms, beautiful roses, tiny lavender flowers, and pomegranate buds.

One warm pleasant evening, after selecting the finest-looking horse from the large number standing in front of our hotel, with their drivers on the *qui vive* for passengers, we took a most enjoyable drive to the top of Mont Pincio, or Hill of Gardens as it is termed, a much frequented and fashionable resort towards evening. The carriage drive winds back and forth until it reaches the summit, one hundred and fifty-one feet high; where we had a magnificent view of modern Rome lit up by a glorious sunset. We also had a very distinct view of the bridge and Castle of St.

Angelo. Immediately at the foot of the hill is the Piazza del Popolo, in the centre of which is an obelisk from Egypt, the oldest thing in Rome. In this piazza is the monastery of Augustine, where Martin Luther resided when in Rome. The Pincio is the place to see fine turn-outs, coachmen and footmen clad in handsome livery, and richly attired ladies. Here are cafés, trapeziums, circular swings; diminutive street cars drawn by goats, which will carry eight children; charming walks, flowers, statuary and fountains. One particularly beautiful fountain represents Moses in the bulrushes. In the centre of the great circular basin which receives the water, rises a marble statue of the mother of Moses half kneeling, her eyes raised imploringly to heaven, with one hand pressed to her heart and the other resting upon the head of her infant, who lies at her feet in his little cradle of bulrushes, as if committing him to the care of the Heavenly Parent before launching his frail boat. The moving throng is constantly reminded of the passing time by a large clock, which is kept in motion by hydraulic power. And that all the senses may be gratified, the air is made to resound with strains of sweet music, which the Italians know so well how to produce. The shadows of night began to creep about us, and so we had to leave this delightful spot and seek our place of shelter and repose.

On the morning of our last day in Rome, we went to see king Humbert's palace, situated on the Quirinal Hill. The popes used to occupy it during the summer season, on account of its healthy location. But in 1870 the Italian government took possession of it, and it is now the residence of the king. Here is a small chapel for the royal family to worship in, richly gilded and decorated with beautiful tapestry of recent date. We passed through the king's private apartments: drawing-room, reception-room, ball-room, dining-room, breakfast-room, etc., fifteen in all, sumptuously furnished. The walls of the throne-room were covered more than half-way up with scarlet brocaded satin, and the upholstered furniture was of the same; the carpet of rich scarlet velvet, and the superb throne of the same bright hue.

There were three large rooms furnished in this manner in old gold, also two in blue, and one in green brocaded satin; and all had magnificent chandeliers, beautiful paintings and statuary. Life size oil paintings of the king and queen (Marguerite) grace one of the apartments. She, fair and lovely, is robed in white satin embroidered with gold, with twelve strings of real pearls about her neck, and an elegant bracelet encircling her well-formed arm. The statuary here and there is exquisite. One piece called "On Sunday," particularly attracted our attention. It is a lady gracefully reclining in a rocking chair, reading her Bible; the position, hands, arms, delicate slippered foot, loose flowing robe, all are perfect. The mosaics on the floor of one of the rooms came from Hadrian's villa, and one of the ceiling paintings, by Overbeck, commemorates the flight of Pius IX. in 1848.

From here we rode to the Villa Albani, founded in 1760, by Albani. It now belongs to Prince Torlonia, but he only spends a small part of his time here. It is quite a picturesque place. Three walks bordered with handsomely trimmed hedges diverge from the entrance gate. The middle path leads to a column in the centre of a circular space, and at a little distance is a pretty fountain and flower beds bordered with box. On the right is a café in the form of a semi-circle, and on the left is the casino or large mansion with galleries on each side. In the vestibule are niches filled with statuary, beautiful mosaic, marble tables and porphyry basins. We ascended the staircase and entered the gallery; here were elegantly furnished apartments—nineteen rooms in all—lavishly decorated with rare ancient sculptures. The finest pieces are Cupid bending his bow, Mercury bringing Eurydice back from the infernal regions (a relief), also the relief of Antinous, from the villa of Hadrian, and the statue of Æsop with his deformed body, so painfully true to life, and fine-shaped head, wonderfully executed. We could find no clew to the names of the artists. Many of the pieces are badly mutilated, testifying that they are ancient and of superior workmanship.

At half-past ten o'clock next morning, we bade adieu to old

Rome, feeling grateful that we had been permitted to look upon these relics of the past. A missionary and his wife from India occupied an apartment with us in the railway car, and we chatted so gayly together that seven hours pleasantly slipped by, and we were in Florence.

CHAPTER V.

FLORENCE is situated in a pretty valley on both sides of the river Arno, and is picturesquely surrounded by spurs of the Apennines. It has one hundred and twenty-three thousand inhabitants. The streets are much wider than in Rome, and the shop windows are gay and attractive, especially the mosaic jewelry shops, presenting a most tempting display of delicate flowered mosaics, so much prettier to my mind than the Roman mosaics. Then there are pretty fountains every now and then, monuments, and numerous memorial tablets, recording important events in the history of Florence. A large fountain, with Neptune seated in his car, drawn by sea-horses, and tritons sporting in the basin, occupies the site of the stake at which Savonarola and two other Dominican monks were burned on the twenty-third of May, 1498. During the study of theology, Savonarola was awakened to the corruption of doctrine that prevailed in the Romish church, and he began earnestly to expose the evils in the city of Florence; but in a few years he was judged by papal power to be guilty of heresy, and was burned to death on this spot, and his ashes thrown into the river Arno. This city has the honor of being the birthplace of Dante in 1265. Galileo died here, and Michael Angelo resided here for a time. We saw the exterior of each of their houses; they are all exceedingly plain stone buildings. A bust of Michael Angelo is over the door of the house where he lived.

We visited the famous Uffizi Gallery by wearily climbing up one hundred and twenty-six steps, and upon entering the second vestibule were greeted by two dogs and a wild boar, so perfectly formed by the sculptor's chisel that we smiled aloud at their comical appearance. We hastened on to the Tribune, an octagonal room lighted from the top, which contains the choicest gems of the whole collection, master-pieces of ancient sculpture found at different places in the sixteenth century (the names of the artists are unknown), and also modern paintings. The five following exquisite pieces of sculpture are ranged around the room: "A Satyr," playing on the cymbal and also playing a stringed instrument by the pressure of his foot; the "Wrestlers," representing two men in a desperate struggle, one holding the other down, with their heads bent nearly to the ground, and the blood vessels of the faces nearly ready to burst from exertion. The anatomy of the bodies is perfectly wonderful as delineated in the straining sinews, and swollen, distended muscles; "The Grinder," a man kneeling down, sharpening or grinding a sickle on a stone; "The Apollino," or young Apollo, is another beautiful figure; but the Venus de Medici, found in the Villa of Hadrian, outstrips them all in beauty and gracefulness of form. I think, I can truthfully say, that it surpasses any statute we saw while abroad, in its easy grace of attitude. It scarcely seems possible that cold, stiff marble, could be brought to appear so flexible. Among the finest paintings in the Tribune are the Madonna and Child, by Raphael; Venus of Urbino, by Titian; and Adoration of the Magi, by A. Durer. In another room we were delighted with the charming picture of Mary visiting Elizabeth, and also a fine picture of St. Sebastian, pierced with arrows, by Sodoma.

We were informed that the Santa Croce is the most noted church in Florence, and were somewhat disappointed at its exceedingly plain interior. It is paved with brick, and there are a great many memorial tablets on the floor, with the figures of persons on them in bass-relief, so if one is not careful he will fall down and make another *bass-relief* on the pavement. I stumbled over the head of somebody's image. The frescoes on the walls are faded and dim, having been discovered during the last twenty years under the whitewash. This church is to Florence what Westminster Abbey is to London. There are many distinguished people buried here—historians, naturalists, and other scholars. The remains of Michael Angelo rest beneath a fine monument, with a female figure weeping over it. He died at Rome in 1564, and was brought here for burial. Directly opposite, in the left aisle, is the monument of Galileo, who died in 1642. The philosopher is represented as sitting on the sarcophagus, with the world in one hand and a telescope in the other. A monument to Dante is also here, but he is buried at Ravenna.

Owing to the extreme heat we were compelled to cut our stay short at Florence, and seek the more congenial atmosphere of Venice, with its cool refreshing breezes from the Adriatic. For I felt that if I remained there long, I might also become a subject for the Santa Croce. The facts in the case are that I had overworked in Rome, and my loss of appetite, unstrung nerves, and general debility, made me a fit subject for a hospital rather than an enthusisatic tourist. But at the rate of five dollars a day one cannot afford to be sick, so I pressed on.

We left Florence at seven o'clock in the morning, and reached Venice at half-past four in the afternoon. Our train entered Venice (one of the most famous and singular cities in the world), over a bridge more than two miles long and fourteen feet wide, which spans the lagoon, and is supported by two hundred and twenty-two arches. We almost shouted for joy as we approached this city of our dreams, which had always seemed to us more like the haunt of fairies than a real, practical dwelling place. Upon alighting from the train, everything was new and strange to us. Instead of a long line of omnibuses and carriages waiting for passengers, as in other cities, there was on the canal a row of gondolas, long, light crafts, painted black, according to a law of the fifteenth century, nicely cushioned and carpeted. Some of them have a low, black canopy or cabin made of leather, and others of some light material, as a protection from the sun and rain. They are about thirty feet long and four feet wide. The prow and stern terminate in a point, and curve out of the water to a height of five feet. The rowers always stand. The porter from the Beau Rivage hotel, which we had selected, and the gondolier, placed our valises in one of these long black boats, politely seated us, and then we glided gently along, charmed with this peaceful mode of traveling; no clattering of horses' hoofs, no noise of wheels, no dust from this highway. It was amusing to watch the gondoliers ingeniously turn the corners, or dexterously pick their way through a crowd of gondolas. They throw themselves gracefully over their tremendous oars, which splash in the water with the regularity of a pendulum. We passed under the celebrated Bridge of Sighs, which connects the Doge's Palace with the prison. It is a covered gallery, and prisoners, when led to execution, passed from their cells across this bridge to the palace to hear their sentence of death. This is why it was called the Bridge of Sighs. It has two passages in it, one for the political criminals who received their sentence from the Council of Three, to pass through, and the other for the papal criminals who received their sentence from the Council of Ten. The great marble palaces on either side, which seemed to rise vision-like from the edge of the water, and the pretty bridges which connect the islands, were so fascinating that we were sorry when our first gondola ride was ended, and we stopped in front of our hotel.

The next morning after our arrival, my husband sent for Dr. Ricchetti who declared that I had not Roman fever, but that my nervous system was greatly exhausted. He toned me up so that I was confined to my room but two days, and was then able to recline in the luxurious gondola and dreamily float about through the different canals, fanned by the delicious sea-breezes, so smoothly, quietly, and lazily that I almost fell asleep. The landlord and all the servants were exceedingly kind and humored every whim during our stay of five days. I do not think it was kindness begotten of policy, but genuine sympathy. History tells us that the culminating point of the glory of Venice was at the close of the fifteenth century. It was then the grand focus of the entire commerce of Europe, and numbered two hundred thousand inhabitants. But the population has been reduced to one hundred and twenty-eight thousand, and one-fourth of them are beggars, which beset you on all sides. One writer says of them, "They lie in the sunshine; they dabble in the sea; they wear bright rags; they fall into attitudes and harmonies." The drinking water is brought from Padua, a distance of twenty-three miles, and is consequently very warm unless made palatable with ice, which they manufacture in Italy. Men sell water by the glass on the streets. Venice is built on three large, and one hundred and fourteen small islands, which are connected by three hundred and seventy-eight bridges; and one hundred and fifty canals form the streets or thoroughfares. Many of the islands are too marshy to form a good foundation for buildings and so the most of the city is built upon artificial foundations of piles or stone. The buildings rise immediately from the canals, or are separated by very narrow streets. Our hotel had a street in front of it and every evening a man gathered a crowd about him, just under our window, and there practice dall sorts of sleight-of-hand performances. And one holiday the people kept up a perfect bedlam all night long. We were not kept awake, however by the noise of carriages rumbling past, as there is not a horse in Venice. But there are two on the island called Lido, some little distance away, and the Venetians think it quite a treat to be drawn for a short distance by these wonderful creatures. The trip to Lido usually takes only about half an hour, but the wind was against us and we had but one rower, so were two hours and a half; but we were in no hurry and enjoyed it immensely. It is a pretty island and has good sea baths and a very fine restaurant. On our return we were able to form a more correct idea of the situation of Venice.

One morning we went to the beautiful Piazza of St. Mark's, the great centre of business and amusement; it is one hundred and ninety-two yards in length but only about half as wide. It is paved with blocks of marble and trachyte. On three sides it is inclosed with massive, marble buildings, with arcades; on the ground floor of which, are the most attractive shops in Venice; one filled entirely with shells, of all shapes, sizes and colors, which is enough to set a lover of conchology wild; others for the sale of photographs, lace, jewelry, and everything tempting. Here and there are brilliant cafés.

The east side of the piazza is occupied by St. Mark's church, and in front of it at some distance, is the square Campanile, or bell tower, which is three hundred and twenty-two feet high. We were wise enough not to expend our strength in ascending to its summit although it affords a fine view of the city. On the right of the church is the clock tower, rising over a gateway resembling a triumphal arch, with a splendid dial in blue and gold. This tower is adorned with statuary, and on the top is a huge bell, beside which stand two bronze figures which strike the hours on the bell with a hammer. The exterior of St. Mark's is the most beautiful, in my opinion, of any church I have ever seen, not excepting even the Cathedral of Milan. It is built in the Romanesque Byzantine style, and lavishly decorated with different colored marbles. It was begun in 976, and is in the form of a Greek cross (with equal arms), with a magnificent dome in the centre, and one at the extremity of each arm, making five domes in all. Inside and outside there are five hundred marble columns with many styles of capitals. There are five great arched doorways, and over the principal one are four horses in bronze, which were captured by Napoleon in 1797 and taken to Paris; but eighteen years after they were brought back and put in their old place. On the façade are grand mosaic pictures in the arches, eight or nine in all, representing the Last Judgment, Descent from the Cross, Resurrection, Ascension, etc. The vaulting of the entrance hall, which extends the whole breadth of the church, is mosaic work representing Old Testament subjects. The interior of the cathedral is two hundred and fifty-eight feet long, and two hundred and ten feet wide. The pavement is mosaic work in the form of all sorts of animals, even peacocks, and is very uneven, bulged up in some places and sunken down in others. On either side of the high altar is a pulpit of colored marble, supported by seven columns. On the screen in front of the high altar are fourteen marble statues, representing the apostles and two others, and in the centre is a gilded crucifix. The cathedral has a grand but sombre appearance inside. We were shown the treasury by an old monk.

Here we saw the covers of the books of the gospels (from Constantinople), lavishly decorated with gold and jewels, a crystal vase with a little red spot in it, which the old monk claimed was a drop of the Saviour's blood; a small wooden cross set in gold, made from a piece of the true cross; a cup of agate, with a piece of St. John's skull; and St. Mark's throne. Of course we could not believe these lies, but it gave us a better insight of the horrible deceptions practised in the Romish church. One of the sights of Venice is to see the pigeons fed in the piazza of St. Mark's. Just as the two bronze figures struck the hour of two on the bell in the clock tower, the large flock of pigeons started up from the ground and flew three times around the square and then lit on the window-sills of the second story on the west side of the piazza, where corn was thrown out to them. It was a pretty sight. According to tradition, "Admiral Dandolo, while besieging Candia, at the beginning of the thirteenth century, received intelligence from the island by means of carrier pigeons, which greatly facilitated its conquest. He then dispatched the birds to Venice with the news of his success, and since that period their descendants have been carefully tended and highly revered by the citizens."

The Palace of the Doges is close by St. Mark's, and is entered by a long flight of steps, at the top of which the Doges used to be crowned. The walls and ceilings of this magnificent palace are frescoed by Tintoretto, Paolo Veronese, Palma Giovane, and other famous artists. In the large hall which contains the library, on the east wall, is Tintoretto's Paradise, said to be the largest oil painting in the world, seventy-eight feet by forty-seven feet, filled with multitudes of angelic heads; the little children—cherubs—are placed nearest the Saviour. On the frieze are the pictures of seventy-six Doges. The upper floor contains the rooms in which the authorities of the Republic used to hold their meetings. In the ante-chamber of the Three Inquisitors of the Republic there is a narrow slit in the wall, resembling the aperture of a letter box, formerly ornamented with a lion's head, into the mouth of which secret documents were cast. The Chamber for the Council of Ten is a large, handsome room. The Senate Chamber contains many beautiful paintings. The one over the throne represents the Descent from the Cross, by Tintoretto. In the Voting Hall are the portraits of thirty-nine Doges. There are many other rooms in this palace, richly decorated with paintings. And in the apartments where the Doges used to reside are many Greek and Roman sculptures, brought home as booty by the Venetians.

Again we were seated in a gondola, and taken to the Academy of Fine Arts. It is situated on the Grand Canal, and was once an Augustine Convent. It contains about six hundred pictures, most of them by Venetian masters. The Assumption, Titian's master-piece, is the finest picture in the whole collection. The winged cherubs, some playing, some singing, others praying, crowd around the Virgin as she ascends the clouds, her face radiant with joy and loving trust. Her hands are reaching out towards heaven and God, who is looking down upon her. The Apostles below are gazing upwards, their faces filled with rapture, wonder and fear; the coloring is exquisite! The Entombment, by the same master, is also beautiful. He was engaged in this at the time of his death, at the age of ninety-nine years. The Madonna and Child, by Bellini; the Banquet of Dives, by Bonifacio, and many, many other grand pictures, were a rich treat for us.

Mr. Culler visited the Dungeons, the famous Rialto Bridge, with its rows of shops, filled with fruits, vegetables, dry goods, ornaments, and in fact almost everything, and the Frari church, where he saw the handsome Mausoleum of Canova.

At a lace manufactory, just back of St. Mark's, we went into the working-rooms and saw girls making lace on pillows; some using a needle, and others using bobbins. We also went into the exhibition-rooms, three or four in number, and saw thirty-two different kinds of Venetian lace, of elegant patterns and delicate workmanship. They told us they had two thousand girls at work, making lace in another factory, but only forty-five here.

Our departure from Venice was quite romantic. Night had

drawn her silvery curtains over the earth—shadows crept into the nooks and corners of the buildings; the grand old clock in the Piazza of St. Mark's had struck the hour of nine, when accompanied by the servants of the hotel, each carrying some trifling article belonging to us, we stepped into a gondola and were about to launch forth, when our landlord rushed down to the water's edge with hand extended to bid us good-bye, and shower us with kind wishes. I cannot forget that night in June: it comes back to me like a pleasant dream—as we reclined on our cushioned seats, the starry heavens above, the moonbeams sparkling in the water beneath; at the right the lovely picture of the Ducal Palace, the five domes of St. Mark's and the Campanile, varied with silvery light and shadow, with its background of deep blue sky, and the soft balmy air, lending enchantment to the whole. After many skillful strokes of the oar, our long, slender, black boat was brought up close against the great steamer which lay at anchor in the sea. Cautiously climbing up the steps to the deck of the vessel, we turned to say good-night to Venice and the moon and stars, and sought our state-room below. At eleven o'clock we started on our journey across the Adriatic Sea.

The next morning we were dressed and on deck before six o'clock, as we were anxious to see as much of the Adriatic as possible. The waves were quite feeble compared with those of old Ocean.

We landed at Trieste, Austria, at seven o'clock, and took the first train for Vienna. We passed through the town of Adelsberg, just three-quarters of a mile from the celebrated stalactite caverns. After leaving this point, for two hours we traversed a dreary, inhospitable plain, covered with blocks of limestone, a seeming wilderness of stones. A man and his wife and three small children occupied the same apartment with us. At lunch time they produced a bottle of wine, which was freely partaken of by the children, even the wee baby. Mr. Culler felt like delivering a temperance lecture, but feared lest his German might fail him. We stepped out of the car to procure a lunch, when lo! the overhanging clouds burst, and the rain descended in torrents. It seemed that all the water from the ocean had been drawn up into the clouds and was now being returned in anger. Even the train had to wait until its fury was spent, to allow the passengers to reach the cars in safety. Being wearied with our day of constant travel, we stopped off at Gratz for the night. Waking up in the morning, we were surprised to find that we had overslept and could not continue our journey until four o'clock in the afternoon. By that time the clouds had lifted and old Sol brightened up everything with his golden light. The bold mountain scenery was so different to that of the previous day. We traversed what is called the Semmering railway. For a distance of twenty-five miles it is carried along the face of precipices by means of tunnels, fifteen in number, and as many bridges, presenting a great variety of picturesque scenery. The scenery in our car was also picturesque, certainly very verdant, for directly facing us sat a loving couple, whose kisses, caresses and fond glances would have been a sufficient emetic for a bilious person—outstripping anything of the kind in America.

We reached the great, busy, bustling city of Vienna, with its population of one million twenty thousand seven hundred and seventy, late in the evening, and took up our abode for a few days at the hotel Holler, where we had the poorest accommodations in all our experience. Our room was facing a small open court, from which arose all the fumes of the kitchen, predominant among which were those of onions. This vile odor penetrated everything.

People talk about the beggars and fleas of Rome, but they are as nothing compared with the onions of Vienna. My little single bed had two feathers in it, but I failed to locate either of them. The meals were good and well prepared, but who could enjoy them after being steeped in an atmosphere of onions? Aside from the onions, however, Vienna is a beautiful city, with broad streets (such a luxury after being accustomed to the narrow streets of Italy!) flanked with high, massive, handsome buildings and palatial dwelling houses, with plate-glass windows. To be sure the most ancient part of the city has narrow, uninviting streets. We strolled through the Outer Burgplatz, where we saw the handsome equestrian statues of Archduke Charles, and that of Prince Eugene; and through the Joseph Platz, which contains the bronze equestrian statue of Emperor Joseph II. Close at hand is the lovely Volksgarten, in the centre of which is the Temple of Theseus, an imitation of the one at Athens. It contains a fine marble group by Canova called The Victory of Theseus over the Minotaur. Theseus with giant power is choking this fabulous monster whose back he has already broken, and with a huge club raised in the other hand is prepared to deal the deadly blow. Anatomically the bodies of each are wonderful! We visited the Imperial Library, which occupies a fine large hall beautifully ornamented with columns and statuary, and contains many valuable relics, among which are purple parchment with gold and silver letters of the sixth century; palm leaf manuscripts; cotton, linen, and mulberry paper; an illustrated work on medicinal herbs, of the fifth century; parts of the book of Genesis, of the fourth century, on purple parchment; fragments of the Roman History of Livy, brought from Scotland in the seventh century; illustrated French Bible; Dante's Divine Comedy, of the fourteenth century; a Chinese manuscript, on blue paper with golden letters, and a much worn prayer book of Charles V. with colored pictures.

St. Stephen's church, considered the most important building in Vienna, is a handsome Gothic structure of solid limestone, in the form of a Latin cross. The handsome groined vaulting is supported by eighteen huge pillars, which are lavishly decorated with statuettes. It has two ancient and three modern stained-glass windows of rich coloring. In the nave is a handsome Gothic stone pulpit, adorned with reliefs of four Fathers of the church, in quaint old hats. On one of the walls is a statue of the architect of the church, looking through a window as if watching the expression of visitors' faces to see how they liked his work. In his hand he holds a rule and pair of compasses. The exterior of the church is magnificent, but the interior seems almost barren when compared with the wealth of the Roman churches.

We took a drive to the Prater, the great, grand park of Vienna, four thousand two hundred and seventy acres in extent. Running through this are two spacious avenues miles in length. Of course we took the principal one, called the Haupt Allee, for a mile or two, and then turned and drove past the Aquarium, cafés and places of amusement. It was here in the Prater that the International Exhibition was held in 1873, and we were much interested in looking at the Machinery Hall and handsome rotunda, which are the only buildings that have been allowed to remain standing.

On our return we stopped at a small new Gothic church, a perfect gem of architecture, called the Votive church, built to commemorate the Emperor's escape from assassination in 1853. The church was completed in 1879. It has a beautiful façade, and two slender, open towers, three hundred and forty-five feet high, handsomely decorated with statues. The interior is fresh and new, finished in excellent taste, and has no less than seventy-eight richly colored stained-glass windows. The high altar is also in good taste, the pulpit graceful and unique, and the pipe-organ over the entrance door, large and handsome. The gilded vaulting, fine architecture and beautiful windows lit up by the kindly sunbeams, gave it the most cosy and inviting appearance.

At half-past six o'clock on the morning of the Fourth of July, we were conveyed by a small steamer through the Danube canal (as the broader arm of the river does not touch the capital), to the Danube river, where we boarded a large steamer and rode all the day long and until twelve o'clock at night, on the historical, beautiful, blue Danube, of which we had so often sung in America, to the tune sol, sol, mi, mi, fa, mi, re, re, mi, fa, fa, mi, re, do, mi, etc. Unfortunately, however, owing to the previous rain it was quite roily, giving it a yellowish tinge instead of blue, which took away half of the poetry for me.

We were just comfortably seated on deck when we heard American tongues behind us. We immediately faced about and extended our hands, feeling that the only introduction necessary was to say we were from America. We chatted gayly together, and soon learned enough of their history to know that they were both physicians from Illinois, who had been attending medical lectures in Berlin and Vienna. As we had no flags or fire crackers, and an oration might have been out of place, even if it could have been understood, we could think of no other way of celebrating the anniversary of America's Independence than by feasting together on a good dinner, prepared on the steamer.

The scenery along the Danube is perfectly charming. Lofty rugged mountains rise on either side, some in bare baldness and others covered with gigantic pines. Here and there are pretty, quaint villages scattered along its banks. The wealthy Benedictine Abbey of Gottweih, on a hill seven hundred and twenty-six feet high, presents an imposing appearance.

We passed the picturesque village of Dürrenstein, where Duke Leopold VI. kept his enemy Cœur de Lion a prisoner for fifteen months.

On a vine-clad hill is built the town of Spitz with a ruined castle and an ancient church. On the roof of the latter are six clay hares represented as running, placed there to commemorate a snowdrift that completely covered the church so that the hares ran over it.

Then we passed a once dreaded robber's castle. Its owner is *said* to have thrown his prisoners from the top of the dizzy rock into the abyss below. Many other castles situated on the projecting points of mountain heights, add much to the beauty of the scenery. The river is divided in one place by a large island, on the north side of which, it descends in rapids, which used to be very dangerous to vessels. But the rocks in the bottom of the river were blasted for the last time in 1853, and the passage is now quite safe; but they still continue to fire a cannon at this point every day, so as to prevent a collision with another vessel which might be approaching the bend from the other side. We enjoyed this trip to the full, and were sorry when the shades of night gathered about us and shut out the lovely landscape from our view. We stopped off at Linz for the night and the next morning we partook of a delicious breakfast of Danube fish, on a vine-clad verandah overlooking the river. Everybody who can afford it ought to have just such a place to eat breakfast during warm summer weather; I believe it would put them in a good humor for all day. I'm sure it had that effect upon us.

Once more we were being whirled along on the railway train, passing through Salzburg, where Mozart, the great musician was born, and towards evening found ourselves in Munich, and were soon settled in the handsome, commodious hotel Belle Vue, which is centrally located, where we were initiated into the German custom of sleeping between two feather beds. Of course the upper one was made of swan's down, consequently very light, and could easily be thrown off if desired. We found it quite a luxury. Our readers must remember that July at this altitude in Germany calls for winter clothing at night. Munich, the capital of Bavaria, is situated one thousand seven hundred and three feet above the level of the sea, making a cool summer resort. It has nearly one hundred and seventy thousand inhabitants, and its wide beautiful streets are well built up with massive but not ornamental structures.

The Bavarian National Museum contains objects of art of every variety, from the Roman period down to the present day. Here we saw very old, carved bedsteads, with a canopy over each, beautiful carvings in mother of pearl, ivory and wood. A large basket of flowers, exquisitely carved out of wood, was a rare curiosity to us, consisting of blossoms and leaves of many varieties, arranged so artistically that it appeared almost impossible to be the work of man; full blown roses, with petals so thin and delicate that it seemed the wind might blow them away. Here are the celebrated parchment prayer-books, with paintings by Memling. One room is filled with instruments of torture, among which were two chairs completely covered with sharp spikes—seat, back, arms, and even the foot-rest. I think I would stand a long time before I would try to rest in a chair of this description. But what interested me most was the little, old fashioned piano, used and owned by Mozart when he was learning to play when a boy, with only three and a half octaves.

and legs like those of my kitchen table. There is a large collection of musical instruments of all varieties, from the fourteenth to the nineteenth century; a queer-shaped violin of the sixteenth century; a drum of the seventeenth century, and a piano of 1780. Several rooms contain costumes of great elegance of the Bavarian sovereigns—Max. Joseph I., Lewis I. and his wife, Theresa, Max. II., King of Greece, and his wife, and others; among which were gentlemen's coats, beautifully embroidered with wreaths of flowers wrought in silk; hats, shoes, crowns, babies' caps, ornaments, etc., of odd shapes and styles. We also especially noticed two colossal vases of blue and white glass, exceedingly delicate and beautiful; a silver-gilt hammer, executed from the design by Michael Angelo for the use of the Pope Julius III., at the opening of the great Jubilee Festival in 1550; and here is even a *boudoir* (a ladies' private-room) of a Countess Fugger, from the Chateau at Donanwörth, preserved in all its parts and appointments.

The Old Pinakothek is a picture gallery in the shape of the letter I, containing more than fourteen hundred pictures, arranged according to schools, viz., the Upper and Lower German; Flemish and Dutch; Netherlandish; French; Spanish; and Italian schools. Of course we can mention only a few of the most important; a panel picture by Albert Durer, representing St. Paul and St. Mark standing together, is very fine. St. Paul stands up majestically in the famous bluish-white robe, admirably shaded and falling in graceful folds, with an eye expressive of undaunted courage and firmness; a triptych, in the centre, Adoration of the Magi, at the sides, the Annunciation and the Presentation in the Temple, by Roger Vander Weyden the elder, the coloring perfect and beautiful throughout; the Seven Joys of Mary by Memling; five wonderful pictures by Murillo, viz., two beggar boys eating grapes and melons; two beggar boys gambling; two beggar boys with a puppy; two girls counting the price of their fruit; and an old woman cleansing the head of a boy, who is engaged in eating a slice of bread. The artists favorite number appears to be two, and his subjects—

beggar boys. But indeed they are strikingly true to life. At a little distance one might take them for real bits of humanity if they were not hung against the wall. One large apartment is filled with paintings by Rubens. The six following are the most remarkable, The Lion Hunt, Perdition of Lost Souls, The Last Judgment, Conversion of Saul, Battle of the Amazons, at the Bridge of Thermodon ; and the Massacre of the Innocents, a picture that makes one's blood run cold to look upon. The mothers have such looks of agony and desperation on their faces as they try to save their babies from the savage, brutal men, who would tear them from their arms and slay them before their eyes.

The Basilica is not handsome, but is built like the Italian churches of the fifth and sixth century. The arches are supported by sixty-six columns of gray marble, with capitals and bases of white marble. The walls are decorated with fine paintings by Hess, and there are thirty-four medallion portraits of the popes above the columns. The sarcophagus of Lewis I. and his queen, Theresa, is at the right of the entrance. There was a funeral service at the church while we were there. The coffin was covered with lighted candles, and the priest burnt incense over it. The double quartette choir sang most beautifully, accompanied by the rich-toned organ, which was of peculiar shape, being in four separate, upright sections, without any ornamentation whatever.

Our next excursion in sight-seeing took us to the English Garden. This, after an hour's drive through its labyrinth of trees, we found to be a very extensive park, beautifully laid out in carriage-drives and foot-paths. It is watered by two arms of the Isar river, which has a very picturesque little water-fall, and nestled among the leafy trees is a pretty little lake which is used for boating, signified by the many bright-colored boats which lay at anchor. Another important ornament to the grounds is a small Grecian temple built of marble, consisting of a canopy supported by ten columns, erected by Lewis I. and situated on the summit of a fresh, green, closely-shaven knoll. Then there is a Chinese tower, a café, restaurant, and also an enclosed deer park.

Our coachman then took us to the king's palace, where with a large party of others, we were piloted through the various apartments (by the custodian); a ball room of great splendor and magnificence; two card rooms, with portraits around the wall of thirty-six remarkably handsome ladies in elegant costumes, painted so delicately that the beautiful gauzy lace looked too real for the painter's brush; the battle-saloon, containing twelve large paintings of battle scenes from 1805 to 1815; the Hall of Charlemagne, representing this king in seventeen different scenes; the Barbarossa Hall, of the same nature; the Hapsburg Saloon, and the Throne Saloon, with six superb bronze statues, more than life-size, on either side, and at the end a gold and garnet throne. The furniture of these apartments is upholstered in various tints of satin. Next came five rooms containing twenty-seven large pictures, completely covering the four walls of each room, telling the story of a German poem, with Sigfried and Chriemhild as the hero and heroine. These frescoes are by Schnorr. We were not acquainted with the poem, and so could not fully appreciate it. I wanted very much to see the treasury of this palace, which is said to contain a splendid blue diamond, a pearl half-black and half-white, and several other rare and beautiful precious stones. But it was the wrong day for that exhibition, so we had to submit to "the powers that be."

From here we went to the Allerheiligen Hofkirche or Court Chapel, comparatively small, but elegant in taste and design in the interior. The walls are covered with a variety of marbles, and the arches are supported by columns of mottled marble. The vaulting and arches are ornamented with frescoes by Hess. Everything shines with splendor about it. Many of the squares of Munich are adorned with fine monuments, one to Schiller; that of king Maxmilhan II., erected by his devoted people in 1875. The king (in bronze), dressed in his coronation robes, stands on a red granite pedestal. He holds the constitution in his right hand and in his left a sword. At the base of the pedestal are figures representing Enlightenment, Strength, Justice and

Peace. Above are children bearing the Bavarian coat-of-arms, and wreaths of laurels. An obelisk one hundred and five feet high, cast of the metal of guns captured in war, was erected to the memory of thirty thousand Bavarians who perished in the Russian war. These monuments were cast at Miller's foundry, and after receiving that information, of course we immediately started off to see these celebrated Bronze Works.

We first entered the Museum, which contains the original models of all the statues cast in the foundry; among which are the equestrian statue of George Washington, which is erected in Richmond, Virginia; and the statue called Emancipation— Abraham Lincoln, standing with the roll of the Constitution in one hand, and the other outstretched towards the negro, who kneels at his feet with his fetters broken. This is erected at Washington and Boston. We were much interested in seeing how the work of moulding and casting is done in the foundry, and watching the men at the different processes, from the liquid metal to the finishing touches of the artist's file. They were casting a bronze statue which is to be called Germania, and will be one hundred feet high—a female figure—to be erected at Bingen on the Rhine. It is so large that it had to be cast in several pieces. The feet and garments up to the waist was in one piece, the body in another, the head in another, etc.

We visited the Academy of Arts and Sciences, where we were exceedingly delighted with the collection of minerals, which are rare and beautiful, and the collection of fossils, considered the most comprehensive in Europe. The quartz crystals are very fine. One is certainly more than two feet long, and two large pieces, each more than a foot in length, consisted of myriads of crystals promiscuously grouped together, but each slender and perfect, about the size of a lady's finger. Here are beautiful amethysts, clear and brilliant; rubies, topaz, serpentine, and many lovely stones of which I do not know the name—room after room filled with these treasures. In other apartments there were several skeletons of animals belonging to the early periods. The fossils of some of the larger animals are still imbedded in the slate in which they were found. There are petrified fish, shells and corals of all descriptions from all parts of the globe, some from Cincinnati, Ohio, some from Florida, and other parts of the United States.

Our fourth and last day in Munich was the Sabbath. At the court church of St. Michael, which is about three hundred years old, we listened to very fine, classical music for an hour, male and female voices, accompanied by an organ and orchestra; the church was packed, there being scarcely standing room. After the audience had dispersed, soldiers came in, hundreds of them, and filled every seat so that other people had to stand. The priest preached to them about half an hour, and at the tap of the bell every soldier dropped on his knees, making the sign of the cross on his face and breast, and remained kneeling until the signal to arise, when with one accord they changed their position with the same dexterity and uniformity as if on drill. The services closed with several pieces of soul-stirring, sacred music, rendered by the brass band.

Early Monday morning we left Munich. We passed through Augsburg, where Charles V. held his illustrious diets; that of 1530, at which the Protestant Princes presented to the Emperor and the Estates the Augsburg Confession—the reformed creed framed by Melanchthon. We reached Friedrichshafen soon after noon. At this depot, instead of using trucks to convey the luggage from the depot to the steamboat-landing, a tall, wiry woman performed this menial duty. A large, portly, muscular man weighed her down with budgets until she had two enormous valises in each hand, any one of which a woman of ordinary strength could not have managed, and a good sized shawl-case under each arm! I was wondering if he would not set one on her head, when off she started at such a brisk pace that we with difficulty kept up with her.

We crossed Lake Constance to the town of Constance. For some time it rained pretty hard, but we stayed on deck under our umbrellas to enjoy the scenery. This lake is forty miles long and seven and a half wide; and the depth of water where we crossed is about nine hundred feet. It is of a dark green color, and forms the boundary of three different countries—Germany, Austria and Switzerland. The scenery is not considered as fine as on the other Swiss lakes, although it is very pretty with its banks of green hillsides dotted with villages and the Alps mountains in the distance. When we reached Constance we immediately took another steamer down the Rhine river to Schaffhausen, where we arrived early in the evening, and stayed over night.

Soon after leaving Lake Constance the steamer entered the Untersee, the greatest width of which (five miles) is at Berlingen. Not far distant from this point the scenery is very picturesque. The handsome chateau of Salenstein stands on a lofty pinnacle, and this pyramid is so completely covered with trees from base to summit that it looks as though the chateau rests on the top of the trees. On an adjacent hill, with beautiful grounds, is the chateau of Arenaberg, formerly the residence of Queen Hortense, the mother of Napoleon III. At Stein the river becomes much narrower. The loveliest rainbow spanned the Rhine—one end rested in a soft, velvety, green meadow, freshened by the shower, and the other in a quiet, little village, built of white stone, with its church spires pointing heavenward, looking for all the world like a pretty picture from a book of poems; the violet, indigo, blue, green, yellow, orange and red of the bow, so distinctly visible that it appeared like a fairy suspension bridge, far exceeding the one at Niagara, or that marvel of wonder which connects Brooklyn with New York. Yes, it surpasses them in beauty and strength and endurance; it is everlasting—its maker and builder is God.

Early next morning we went by train to the little village of Newhausen, a distance of but two miles, and remained there four hours to view the Falls of Schaffhausen, the finest in Europe. They are indeed very grand, but nothing to compare with our own Niagara. From the station we followed a winding, shady path down a sloping hill, and crossed over a bridge to the Schlosschen Worth (a restaurant), situated on an island opposite to the falls. It is a sort of tower shaped stone building, with a balcony or verandah around it, from which we had a fine general view of the falls. The Rhine river, three hundred and seventy-five feet in width above the falls, is precipitated in three leaps over a rocky ledge. The rapids, the whirlpool, and the falls, taken together, are about one hundred feet in height. Here we sat for some time, gazing at this grand beauty of nature. Two gigantic rocks, and two of smaller dimensions, rise above the falls, just where the water comes tumbling down with frantic madness. The middle and highest rock is visited by fearless tourists by means of a row-boat. I thought I should like to go, but concluded to watch another party, consisting of a gentleman and his two daughters, make the trip first. As they neared the rock, the little boat was tossed like a feather on the foaming billows, or as a tiny shell on the ocean wave. My heart stood still. The boat was whirled round and round, hither and thither, while the oarsmen with their strong arms battled for the mastery, and at last anchored; and the party, drenched with the spray, ascended the rock by a path, protected by an iron railing, to the little pavilion on the summit, where they waved their handkerchiefs to us across the Rhine. I turned to my husband and said I would not go to the rock under any consideration. He laughed at the sudden change of mind, and we stepped into a boat, and crossed the river to what is called the Fischet, an iron platform projecting over the foaming abyss, with a pavilion. This is considered the grandest view of all. The water comes leaping down in a terrific manner, deafening the ear with its sound; and the spray gives the beholder a gratuitous shower-bath, making it necessary for him to be protected by a rubber cloak which the custodian of the grounds provides. We followed the path a little higher up the hill, and passed through a romantic rocky gallery, where the water dashing over the rocks sounded like the thumping made by the revolutions of a mighty water-wheel. We emerged upon a wooden platform which commanded a view several feet higher than the Fischet. Still ascending the hill, we reached an iron pavilion, where we could look down upon the cataract.

On the summit of this wooded hill we reached the Schlöss Laufen, a picturesque castle, the proprietor of which owns the beautiful grounds on this side the Rhine and charges a small admittance. Close to this mansion is a very pretty pavilion with stained-glass windows, furnished with a centre table and chairs, where we obtained still a different view of the falls, and the bridge called the Rheinfallbrücke, six hundred and thirty feet long, directly above the falls, which is both a railroad and foot-bridge.

We walked over it to the other side, and followed the shady, romantic path skirting the edge of the precipice leading through the village, where we shortly took the train for Lucerne, by way of Bale and Olten. We passed through the Hanenstein tunnel, twenty-nine hundred and seventy yards long, and as the German trains creep along very slowly, it seemed much longer. In 1857, when this tunnel was being made, sixty-three workmen were buried alive by a fall of earth. The train skirted the bank of Lake Sempach for several miles.

Upon arriving at Lucerne we found we should just have time to get our tea before going to the Organ Concert at the Hofkirche, which began at half-past six o'clock in the evening. This famous organ is so constructed that it can be made to produce the sound of nearly every other musical instrument. We were rapt with wonder and admiration during the entire hour. The organist, an elderly gentleman, seemed to control this giant monster as if by magic, instantly subduing the loudest peals to the sweetest strains, at other times gradually diminishing from the most powerful swells of which the organ was capable to the softest notes of a music-box, then ceasing entirely until we had heard the faint echo. We were unable to determine whether this echo was produced by the organist or by the reverberations in the church. We heard a choir of voices, accompanied by an orchestra, each part clear and distinct, but on turning around we saw no one but the old man touching the keys with his fairy fingers, causing us to wonder if we were in the land of dreams. Solos by the Alpine horn, violin, flute, etc., attended with magnificent choruses, all came from the keys of this wonderful organ. But the grandest effort of all was a thunder-storm amid the Alps. At first the mutterings of the thunder were heard in the distance, then it came rolling on in its power and grandeur, until it fairly shook the windows of the church, filling the hearers with reverential awe, as when it comes in reality; then came the rain-drops upon the roof, first a gentle patter, then a steady, heavy shower; and instinctively every eye in the audience was cast towards the windows, as if expecting to see a genuine storm. And when all was over, and the audience began to disperse, I remained spell-bound for a moment, scarcely realizing where I was, wondering at what the brain and fingers of one man had accomplished. On returning to our hotel, we crossed over a curious old bridge, covered with a roof, in the inner compartments of which are one hundred and fifty-four paintings, representing historical events in Switzerland.

The next morning we awoke to welcome in the fifth anniversary of our wedding day, the memorable twelfth of July, and thought a delightful way to celebrate it would be by a sail across the beautiful lake Lucerne, the most charming and picturesque of the Swiss lakes. It has so many promontories extending into it that its banks are very irregular. When pictured on a map it looks like a spider with its legs stretched in every direction, or like the species of mollusks denominated Octopus Vulgaris. It is twenty-three miles long, from one to two miles wide, and its greatest depth five hundred and ten feet. After being comfortably seated on deck we took a backward look at Lucerne, with its towers and battlements, which indeed formed a lovely picture. Immediately to the left rises the lofty Rigi, four thousand four hundred and seventy-two feet above the level of the lake, the highest point of a group of mountains, twenty-five miles in circumference, so often ascended by tourists, stopping at Lucerne, by means of the new railway. Near the base of this mountain are groves of almond, fig and chestnut trees, and higher up terraced slopes covered with verdure, affording pasture for more than four thousand head of cattle. On the opposite side of the lake looms up, to the height of six thousand nine hundred and ninety-eight feet, the wild, barren, serrated cliffs of Pilatus, festooned with clouds from which it is reputed scarcely ever to be free. Facing the traveler in the distance the scenery is magnificent!—one mountain rising above another, of different shades and hues. Every variety is seen on this lake—the purest snow-white mountains, all tints of green, from the lightest to the darkest shades, and brown, barren rocky peaks, lending variety and charm to the whole.

Perhaps my readers all remember the story of Gessler compelling William Tell to shoot an apple from the head of his son, and after it was skillfully achieved, Gessler asked him what he meant to do with a second arrow in his girdle: " To have shot you, if it had slain my son," was the reply; whereupon Tell was seized, bound and thrown into a boat on Lake Lucerne, to be imprisoned in a castle. But a sudden storm arose; Tell was the only one on board who knew the shore, and could safely guide the helm; entrusted with this, he ran the boat near a rocky ledge, seized his bow and arrows, sprang on shore, and thus gained his freedom.

We reached Alpnach a little before noon, and there took a carriage (as the diligence was full), and crossed the Alps by the Brunig Pass, a distance of twenty-five miles, to Brienz, where we arrived about five o'clock in the afternoon. It rained nearly all the way, but as we were dressed warmly and well protected, we did not suffer. This Pass, although not so bold and wonderful as the Simplon, is pleasing and picturesque. The road winds easily up the mountain, requiring only two horses for a carriage, except for a distance of about two miles, where a third horse was called into service. A tall, strong woman, with no outside wraps, not even a bonnet, with her back hair braided with white ribbon (a style peculiar to the Swiss women along these lake shores) walked this whole distance through the cold, driving rain, and at the end of the two miles led the horse back to the hotel. Many Swiss and German women do the work of men, ploughing, sowing, and reaping in the fields with their husbands and brothers. We rode along the bank of the little Lake Sarner, only about four miles long, and after a distance of a few miles, when, at quite a high elevation, we looked down into the peaceful bosom of Lake Lungern nestled among the mountains. It was a pretty sight, and although we could see it for a mile or two it was far too short a time. Our road wound through pine forests, with pretty views of the green valleys below and the lofty mountains around and above us, with charming cascades spirting and dashing down their sides. The delicate blue harebells springing up in the crevices of the rocks filled their tiny cups with rain drops, and laughed at us poor travelers who were trying to keep out the rain with gossamers and blankets. As we neared Brienz the scenery became more bold, the road passing under projecting rocks and skirting precipices. We were glad to seek shelter for the night at the White Cross hotel.

Next morning—

> "When the mists had rolled in splendor,
> From the beauty of the hills,
> And the sunshine warm and tender,
> Fell in kisses on the rills"—

we stepped on board a small steamer on Lake Brienz, which is situated very much like Lake Lucerne, with lofty mountains on either side rising immediately from the lake; but is much smaller, being only nine miles long. We passed the lowest fall of the Giessbach, which empties its volume of water into the lake. It consists of a series of seven cascades, leaping over the rocks from a height of more than a thousand feet above the lake. And there are two pretty little islands covered with trees, from one of which peeps out a beautiful Swiss cottage. This lake, with its shores dotted with pretty villages and ruined castles, sheltered by lofty mountains, is a sight long to be remembered.

We left the steamer at Bönigen, and went by train, a ten minutes trip, to Interlaken. The cars on this train had two stories; of course for novelty we took seats in the upper story. Arriving at Interlaken we went to the Du Pont hotel, where from the windows of our room we could see the Jungfrau (young wife) mountain. Interlaken is a town romantically situated between Lake Brienz and Lake Thun, and hemmed in on the other two sides by towering ranges of mountains; this strip of land is two miles long. There are two small villages adjoining Interlaken, called Unterseen and Aarmühle; the population of the three together being four thousand and eighty. This is a very fashionable summer resort, from whence many interesting excursions are made to Grindelwald, Lauterbrunnen, etc. We found many Germans, English, and Americans spending a few weeks in this delightful place. There are forty-five hotels in these three villages, and many of them, especially on the Hoheweg, are grand establishments with lovely grounds, flowers in abundance, fountains, pretty rustic arbors, and everything more like elegant private mansions than hotels. There are a few pretty Swiss cottages decorated profusely with wood carvings, and having so many nooks and corners, verandahs and queer-shaped roofs, so light and airy that they look more fit to be the homes of fairies than those of romping boys and girls. While many of the structures are of fine design, and of new and stylish construction, the village is not wanting in many quaint old Swiss buildings with projecting roofs, and made of hewn logs, such as we see in every picture of Alpine scenery. The lion of the place is the Jungfrau, towering up to the majestic height of thirteen thousand six hundred and seventy-one feet, covered with her mantle of perpetual snow, pyramidal in shape, surrounded by other mountains arrayed in living green. It is a sight of which the eye never tires.

Retracing our steps to the station of Aarmühle, from thence following a most romantic path, with here and there a guideboard pointing out the way, we soon reached the foot of the Heimweh Fluh (homesick mountain), which is quite easy of ascent, as wooden steps have been constructed in places to assist the traveler, and occasionally there are rustic seats, where one may rest and gather strength for the onward march. We had soon reached the restaurant, and from the Terrace, which commands a fine view of the lakes Brienz and Thun, we looked down upon these lovely sheets of water far beneath us—such near neighbors, and yet each minding its own business: no envy, no rivalry here. Ascending a little higher to the small belvedere, we beheld the Jungfrau, Mönch, and Eiger in all their magnificent splendor, each lifting his snowy head as if to pierce the sunlight of heaven. The Hoheweg is *the* street of Interlaken, a delightful avenue of walnuts, lined with shops displaying the most exquisite wood carving and charming Swiss landscapes in oil painting. Wood carving is carried on here quite extensively, and in other towns along the lakes Brienz and Thun. They ship it to Geneva and other cities. Here we saw almost everything beautifully carved out of wood—delicate vases, paper knives, handsome fans, pen-holders, crumb-pans and brushes, nut crackers, brackets, animals large and small, horses, cows, deer, lions, bears, and dogs, busts, and so on, as natural as life. Oh, the most tempting things! but too bulky to carry in a tourist's satchel. One shop had a superb collection of oil paintings on porcelain. I could not leave without purchasing a copy of Raphael's blue Madonna and Guido Reni's Beatrice. We walked through the grounds of the Kursaal, a lovely Swiss cottage with tasty garden, clean, neat walks, flowers and foliage, where there was a fine concert, illumination, and fire-works, in the evening. Still further up the Hoheweg we reached the monastery and nunnery, now suppressed. A part of the monastery is used as a hospital, and the rest for government buildings. The nunnery has been changed into a prison. Four different denominations now worship in the old Monastery church, viz., Episcopal, French Protestant, Scotch Presbyterian, and Catholic. It is a very queer old church, barnlike and uninviting in the interior. At one point in the beautiful street I have described, there are no buildings on the side towards the Jungfrau, as it would be considered almost sacrilegious to cut off the view of so grand a spectacle. But rather, under the spreading branches of the stately walnuts, are comfortable seats, where on a warm day one may sit and be revived by the cool breezes from this mountain of snow. I must say I fell in love with Interlaken. It is the most fascinating little village to one of a poetical turn of mind. I say of it what Horace did of Sabinum, "Ille terrarum noter praeter, omnes angulus ridet"—this piece of earth has pleased me more than any other; and if I ever live to be an old lady with cap and spectacles, too feeble to be of any service to mankind, I could ask for no more enchanting spot to spend my latter days than in one of these snug Swiss cottages, where I could gaze upon the Jungfrau, this majestic pile of purity sparkling in God's sunlight—this matchless picture from the brush of the Almighty.

We enjoyed a sail of eleven miles on Lake Thun, its entire length. It is very similar to its neighboring lake, having precipitous mountains on either side, some snow-capped, others green and brown, the most distinguished being the Niesen, a regular-shaped pyramid seven thousand seven hundred and sixty-three feet high—the Jungfrau, Mönch, Eiger, Schreckhorn, and Wetterhorn. This lake is remarkably deep, measuring eighteen hundred and thirty-seven feet. On its bank is the town of Spiez, where there is a grand old chateau which has belonged to one family for three hundred years. The water of all these lakes in this part of Switzerland is emerald green, so bright that the foliage looks dingy when compared with it.

At the town of Thun, we took the first train for Strassburg, stopping at Berne (the city of which the bear is the heraldic emblem) for dinner, and at Bale over night, where we found a budget of news awaiting us from America, among which was a long, newsy letter from one of our church elders.

CHAPTER VI.

STRASSBURG, Germany, is a city of one hundred thousand inhabitants. It is situated two miles from the river Rhine, with which it is connected by two canals. It was founded by the Romans in the sixth century, and is mostly made up of ancient buildings. The streets are very narrow and crooked, some of them barely wide enough for a carriage to pass through, and darkened by the roofs of houses, almost touching each other, in the same manner as in Genoa, which I have before described. In 1681, Louis XIV. of France seized the city of Strassburg, but in 1871 the Germans regained possession of it. It is fortified by a belt of thirteen strong outworks, some of them four or five miles from the town. Goethe was educated here.

Although Strassburg is very ancient, and has narrow, uninviting streets, yet it has many attractions. Fine monuments are to be seen here and there, among which is that of Gutenberg, the inventor of printing in the year 1436; it is in bronze. Gutenberg stands with a printed manuscript in his hand, and by his side is a primitive printing press. The four bass-reliefs on the pedestal represent the gratitude of the nations from the four quarters of the globe. The one representing America, contains the figures of George Washington, Franklin, John Quincy Adams, and others.

The magnificent cathedral, containing the wonderful, world-renowned clock, is of Gothic architecture, and the exterior is almost as beautiful as the cathedral of Milan. From the opposite side of the street we stopped to admire its splendid façade, rich with ornamentation; three grand arched portals—one mass of sculpture; hundreds of statues—among the finest Gothic works in existence. It has two great square towers, from one of which rises the light open-work steeple to the dizzy height of four hundred and sixty-five feet, being higher than St. Peter's at Rome, or St. Paul's at London. The interior is lighted with stained-glass windows, of the fifteenth century, of extraordinary size and rich colors—golden, purple, crimson, and blue, blending harmoniously. The large rose window, forty-two feet in diameter, over the portals, is peculiarly lovely. Fourteen massive cluster-pillars support the lofty arched roof. There are two large organs, one in the choir and the other in the nave, projecting over an arch, making people philosophize how the performer could get to it. It looks like a double organ—a small one in front of a large one. Then the pulpit of delicately carved stone is superb! so beautifully wrought that some parts of it look like lace or embroidery. The baptismal font is similar, though not so fine. In the south transept is the large astronomical clock, which took several years to construct it, made by Schwilgné, of Strassburg. Its exterior is of different colored marble and bronze. It looks like an immense high altar at first sight, perhaps thirty feet high. At the base is a large globe, "showing the precession of the equinoxes, solar and lunar equations for calculating geocentric ascension and declination of the sun and moon at true times and places." Back of this is a large dial, showing the day of the month, and the difference of time between certain localities. A female figure stands by the side of this dial, and with an arrow points to the day of the month. Then this dial has the hours and minutes on it, and several hands pointing to the time at New York, London, etc. At the right is the mechanism by which the mean tropical revolution of each planet, visible to the naked eye, is shown, and at the left that indicating the ecclesiastical year. Just above, and immediately under the first gallery, the symbolic deity of each day comes out of the niche, and at the close of the day passes out of sight through another niche—Apollo on Sunday, Diana on Monday, etc. This being Saturday, Saturn was on exhibition—a man in a chariot, with a scythe over his shoulder, drawn by a mythical steed, with a cock's head and feet, and the body that of a serpent. On the front of the first gallery is the dial proper of the clock, to the left of which sits an angel which strikes the quarters of the hour on a bell in his hand, and to the right another angel reverses an hour-glass, which he holds in his hands, when the sand has all run through. Back of this is a large dial indicating the signs of the zodiac and the planetary system. Above this is a globe representing the moon. The dark side was turned out, as it was the time in the month when the moon did not shine. Above is the second gallery, where stands a skeleton which strikes the hours on a bell with a leg bone. He raises his arm painfully slow, as if he had rheumatism, but strikes with a good deal of force when his club comes down. At the first quarter a figure representing Boyhood comes out of a niche, and with a wand strikes one on a bell, then passing in front of the skeleton he skips out through another niche on the other side. Next comes Youth, and strikes the second quarter in a sprightly manner with his shepherd's staff; Manhood, a soldier bold, with his weapon of war, strikes the third quarter, and at the end of the hour decrepit Old Age hobbles out, and with quite an effort raises his crutch and gives the bell four strokes, then slowly totters out of sight. In the third gallery stands a figure of the Saviour, and at twelve o'clock the twelve Apostles move around him. At the right of the clock is a winding staircase reaching to the top of the clock. At the left is a tower containing the weights, on the top of which is a rooster which stretches his neck, flaps his wings, and crows at twelve o'clock. This remarkable clock regulates itself. We were interested in watching its performances for nearly two hours.

This is the city where the storks build their nests on large, flat-topped chimneys, apparently of brushwood. They make a very pretty ornament to a house, standing on the top of the chimney with their long, slender legs, long bills, and white breasts. One nest had three young ones in it, stretching their necks and opening their mouths wide for food.

Of course we went to see the Lutheran church of St. Thomas, a plain Gothic structure of the thirteenth century. The choir contains a very fine marble monument to Marshal Saxe. Pigalle labored twenty years on this piece of sculpture. The Marshal, in a calm, resolute manner, is going down the steps which lead to his grave; a skeleton figure, wrapt in a winding sheet, representing Death, is holding open the lid of the sarcophagus with one hand, and in the other holds an hour-glass, telling him that his time has come; while a female figure, representing France, strives to hold him back with one hand, and to drive away Death with the other. Hercules with sorrowful countenance supports himself with his club at the foot of the tomb. On the left is the Austrian eagle (lying upon its back); the English leopard, stretched helpless upon the ground; and the Dutch lion held at bay, gnashing his teeth, with the broken flags beneath them. On the opposite side, the flags of the victorious party are waving in the breeze, the whole representing the Marshal's victories over these countries in the Flemish wars. Near by is the sarcophagus of Bishop Adeloch. There are double aisles on each side of the nave, and the large organ is over the entrance. In the right transept, in a metallic coffin, is a mummy, the Duke of Nassau, a general killed on the field of battle in the thirty years' war, dressed in the clothes he used to wear; also a mummy dressed in steel-colored silk, with handsome, wide, real lace in her sleeves and about her neck, and a diamond ring on her finger. Here is also the tomb of James Oberlin, Professor of Ancient Literature and Antiquities, who died in 1806. I wonder if my Alma Mater in Ohio was not named after him. We were shown a large shell which fell at a distance of thirty feet from the monument without bursting, just two days before the surrender of the town in 1870.

On Sabbath, we attended services in this church. The civil service began at nine o'clock and the military service at eleven. We were belated a little by having to wait for our breakfast, and so were not there on time. And behold! as in the case of the foolish virgins, the door was shut, and locked. We went to another door, but gained no admittance; so we went back to the principal entrance, and looking up, I spied a sort of wooden handle dangling from a long, slender wire, and said, "I believe that's a door-bell." "A door-bell on a church!" said my husband, derisively. "Yes; you pull it, and see if it isn't." Immediately upon so doing, the door was unlocked, and we were told that the services had begun and we could not enter. We tried to step in, and just as the man was about to shut us out, the sacristan, with whom we talked the day before, poked his head out at the door, and then said to the doorkeeper, "Let them in. The gentleman is a Lutheran clergyman from America." On tiptoe he took us to the first seat, where we listened a full hour to a German sermon. As I could only understand a word now and then, I fell to moralizing thus: "Well, if American church-goers knew that the doors would be locked at the beginning of the service, they would always be in their seats to hear the first note of the organ, and if those who complain when the sermon is half an hour long, would go to Germany and receive treatment for awhile, they might be cured." The singing by the congregation was soul-stirring. Between this and the military service several persons remained for communion. Precisely at eleven o'clock the second service began. It was a beautiful sight to look over that vast audience of soldiers, dressed in their uniforms, with their swords at their sides, listening attentively through the lengthy discourse. It seemed so fitting and right that they should be permitted to lay aside their duties, and come up to the house of the Lord to worship Him in spirit and in truth; and who more than they need the prayers and admonitions from the sacred desk, for are they not called to face death every day? A few of the soldiers constituted a choir, and rendered all four parts in rich harmony, standing in front of Marshal Saxe's monument; the whole army, accompanied by the powerful organ, swelled the grand choruses till the vaulted arches caught up the strain, and sent the echo back again.

The next morning we were off for Heidelberg, where we arrived in about five hours by train, and selected the Schloss hotel, away up on a hill near the castle. The drive from the station to the hotel, which occupied twenty minutes, was charming. At first we passed through the Leopold street, to the right of which is a beautiful park, displaying great taste in its arrangement and ornamentation; then we began to wind up the hill, back and forth, until the town rested far beneath us on the banks of the river Neckar. We were given a room at the very tip-top of the hotel, it being much crowded during "the season;" but we did not complain, as it commanded a most excellent view of the castle, the one thing we came to see. After walking for some little distance through a shady, romantic path, we found ourselves in the castle garden; passing along the great terrace, and by the restaurant, then crossing the bridge over the moat, we came to the gateway with its formidable portcullis, under the square watch-tower, by which we entered the court.

Heidelberg Castle is an immense structure, surrounded with massive stone walls and a deep, wide moat. It was founded in the thirteenth century, but has undergone many alterations since then. It was nearly all burned down, rebuilt, struck by lightning, and partly blown up by the French; so it is now in a very ruinous condition. The part directly facing us is called the Friedrichsbau, consisting of four stories, Doric, Tuscan, Ionic, and Corinthian, with the façade completely covered with ornamentation, life-size statues in niches, rich tracery, etc. Within, on the second floor, is a small museum, containing several pictures of princes, former occupants of the castle, very ancient documents, a model of the castle, two handsome sets of porcelain China, used by the kings, a curious clock, two hundred years old, a case filled with coins, Carl Theodor's cradle, Luther's wedding-ring—a broad, chased band of gold with a small garnet set—and other relics. An arched passage leads under this part of the castle to the Great Balcony, a broad stone platform, perhaps eighty feet long, with a heavy cut-stone railing; and at either end, a small stone pavilion, from which you can look down upon the town of Heidelberg, three hundred and thirty feet below, with its celebrated university building and its grand old bridge across the Neckar. In the corner, to the left of the Friedrichsbau, is the entrance to the wine-cellar, containing the celebrated Heidelberg Tun, an immense cask holding fifty thou-

sand gallons; and just think of it, it has been filled with wine and
emptied three times during its existence. Imagine a barrel thirty-
two feet long, twenty-six feet high, and the diameter of the head
twenty-two feet, with a staircase on either side leading to a platform on the top. Of course, our whole party mounted it. Opposite to the Tun stands a wooden figure of Perkeo, the court
jester of Elector Charles Philip, with a wine-cup in his hand.
It is reported as a fact that he used to drink eighteen bottles of
wine in a day. There is also another Tun in this cellar, which
holds ten thousand gallons. Above the cellar is the Ruprecht's
Halle, further back is the Alte Bau, and beyond this, towards
the Watch-tower, is the Ruprechtsbau. The large apartments
inside were once used as banquet halls. Between the Dicke
Thurm or Thick Tower (which we ascended), of which only one
semicircular half now remains, and the Friedrichsbau, is the
Elizabethenbau, which was erected by Frederick V., King of
Bohemia, in honor of his consort Elizabeth, daughter of James
I. of England. At the right of the Friedrichsbau is the Otto
Heinrichsbau, with a very fine façade ornamented with statues.
In the corner between these two buildings rises the Octagonal
Tower, which we ascended; and while surveying the city below,
we were accosted by a lady and her daughter, with whom we became acquainted in Paris; romantic, indeed, was our place of
meeting. At the other end of the Heinrichsbau, in the corner,
is the Gesprengte Thurm, or blown-up tower, which is ninety-
three feet in diameter. The walls are twenty-one feet thick, and
so solidly constructed that when the French tried to blow it up,
one huge part separated, and fell in an unbroken mass into the
moat, where we looked down upon it from the top of what now
remains. This tower is the most picturesque part of the structure to my mind, with its jagged, mutilated top, cavernous holes,
and broken arches completely overrun with the kindly ivy
which seeks to hide its wounds with its clinging terdrils. One of
these sympathizing nurses is two hundred years old, its stems near
the ground being as large as the trunk of an ordinary-sized tree;
its leaves large, fresh, and green. There are two old chapels

in this castle; one has a few shabby oil paintings, the best preserved of which is a portrait of the man by whose direction the Great Tun was made; and the other has a ground floor, with nothing remaining but the bare walls and some iron chandeliers. We were taken through dark, subterranean passages, which in days past resounded with the tread of armed soldiers. After passing out under the Watch Tower we turned to the right, and entered a delightful garden filled with large shade trees, with pleasant seats from which the exterior of the castle could be viewed.

After resting here we crossed the bridge, and once more were in the Schloss Garten, where we listened to a fine concert given by an orchestra. Then from the great terrace we took another parting look at this splendid pile of ruins, unrivalled anywhere in Germany, and I doubt if in Europe:

> "'Tis with the thankful glance of parting praise;
> More mighty spots may rise—more glaring shine,
> But none unite in one attaching maze,
> The brilliant, fair, and soft—the glories of old days."

The next morning my husband ascended the mountain back of the castle on foot to the Molkencur, which is one hundred and ninety feet above the castle; then climbing still higher to the König's Stuhl (King's Chair), nine hundred and five feet above the castle, and more than eighteen hundred feet above the sea level. There is a tower ninety-three feet high on the top of this mountain (which is a spur of the Geisberg), and of course he was not satisfied until he had reached the summit of this, where he had a grand view of the Castle, the Neckar, the Rhine, and the old Black Forest of legendary tales. Looking directly east from the top of the tower, a most remarkable sight presented itself—a dividing line, as straight as an arrow, in the forest separated the oak from the pine.

An hour's ride on the train brought us to Worms, and we were soon in the Luther Platz, which is tastily ornamented with parterres of beautiful, blooming roses of all colors, from the most delicate tints to the rich, deep hues, and shady trees with inviting seats beneath. In the centre is the imposing monument of Martin Luther, the great Reformer. A platform forty-eight feet square has a large pedestal of granite in the centre, surrounded by one of bronze ornamented with reliefs, representing scenes in the life of Luther, and medallion portraits of others who assisted in the Reformation. On this stands the majestic figure of Luther in bronze, eleven feet in height; he holds a Bible in his hand, and his noble face full of courage and faith is lifted heavenward. At the corners of the pedestal are seated Huss, Savonarola, Wyckliffe, and Petrus Waldus. On the four corners of the platform are granite pedestals surmounted by statues of Philip the Generous of Hessen, Frederick the Wise of Saxony, Melanchthon and Reuchlin, each nine feet high. Between these on smaller pedestals are allegorical figures of towns, representing Magdeburg (mourning), Augsburg (making confession), and Speyer (protesting). Between these figures are the coats of arms of the twenty-four towns of Germany which first received the Protestant religion.

From here we walked to the Cathedral, and took a good look at its exterior. It is a very large edifice, with four towers. It was in front of this church that the quarrel between Brunhilde and Chriemhilde occurred, which is spoken of in the Nibelungen, and which we saw portrayed in painting at Munich. A short distance from this cathedral, where the fine Heyl'sche Haus now stands, was formerly the Episcopal Palace, in which Luther made his defense before Emperor Charles V., and a large audience, in 1521, closing with these words: "Here I stand; I cannot act otherwise: God help me! Amen." These words are on his monument. The garden surrounding this mansion, which now belongs to an English gentleman, is open to the public, and is very attractive.

Again we entered the railway train, and reaching Frankfort soon after sunset, took up our abode at the Frankfurter Hof, a very fine hotel, with all the modern improvements, elevator, etc., and lavishly ornamented with granite columns, accommodating hundreds of guests. Our first sight was the Ariadneum, a round stone building in which is exhibited an exquisite piece of sculpture "Ariadne on the Panther," the masterpiece of Dannecker. It revolves on a pedestal, and every part seems perfect. The light falling from the stained glass window above upon the crimson curtain which encloses it, gives the white marble a flesh tint. This, together with the perfect form of the limbs arms and body, give it a very life-like appearance. She is the embodiment of grace from the tip of her delicately-formed foot to the crown of her beautiful head. If I say it is magnificent, that does but half express it. Go and gaze upon it yourself, and there drink in the wondrous beauty from the sculptor's chisel.

From here we went to the Zoological Garden, and found it to be on quite a large scale. The grounds are extensive, affording sufficient room for the large collection of animals, birds and reptiles to move about freely. Here we saw an immense elephant, the largest in Europe, now that Jumbo has been transferred from the Zoological Gardens in London to Barnum's Menagerie in America. The keeper performed all sorts of tricks with him for our amusement. It was indeed comical to see this great, clumsy, ugly animal attempt to dance, and ever since, when I hear a person trying to play a waltz or some quick piece, adapted to the piano, on a cabinet organ, I am reminded of his awkward attempts. We were shown (as a special favor) a cute little zebra only three days old, all legs and head; but with the characteristic stripes distinctly marked. There is also a very good sea-water aquarium in connection with these gardens.

The Städel Art Institute next claimed our attention. On the ground floor are a great many casts of celebrated pieces of sculpture which we had seen in other cities; and on the upper floor, the Picture Gallery, consisting of twenty-three rooms and several cabinets containing works from the early Italian, Flemish, early German, and modern German masters; among the latter, A Storm at Sea, by Achenbach; John Huss at the Council at Constance, in his long cloak trimmed with mink, by Lessing; Hardanger by Evening Light, by Saal; and a Ruin on a Lake by Morning Light, by Funk, particularly attracted our attention.

We saw the house in which Goethe was born in 1749, and a monument erected to his memory not far from it. In the largest Platz in the city is a monument to Gutenberg; and in another a statue of Schiller, in bronze. There are seven Lutheran churches in Frankfort, dating back to the thirteenth century; but they are not open on week days, so we could see nothing but the exteriors. The house at which Luther preached on his return from the Council at Worms, is a quaint old building. Frankfort is built on both sides of the River Main, and has one hundred and eighteen thousand inhabitants. The Zeil, the principal street, is a broad, handsome thoroughfare, with elegant shops reminding one of Vienna; but the Jews' quarters present an ancient and uninviting appearance.

We went to Mayence by train, and from there took a delightful trip of seven and a half hours down the Rhine River, as far as Cologne. This is considered the most interesting part of the river. The Rhine is quite crooked, taking very sharp turns, so that it often appeared as though we had reached its terminus. The most picturesque part of the trip is between the vine-clad hills of Bingen—"Fair Bingen on the Rhine—" so touchingly referred to in that beautiful poem about the dying soldier, and Coblentz, it being the narrowest part of the valley of the Rhine. Between these two places are no less than twenty-one castles, charmingly situated high up on its rocky banks, most of them ruins which have been destroyed by the French. Marksburg Castle, four hundred and eighty-five feet above the river, is the only old fortress which has remained uninjured; and Rheinfels Castle is considered the most imposing and magnificent ruin on the river. The scenery is bewitching! You do not lose sight of one castle before another comes in view. On a rock in the middle of the stream, opposite to the Castle of Ehrenfels, is the Mouse Tower, which derives its name from an old legend, and indeed nearly all these castles along the Rhine have some legend connected with them. For instance, the Sterrenberg and Liebenstein Castles, often called the Brothers, have the following legend: "Conrad and Heinrich, sons of the Knight Bayer von Boppard, the Lord of Liebenstein, were both in love with their handsome adopted sister Hildegarde. Heinrich, the more generous of the two, left home, and joined the crusades, leaving his brother to win her love. That his son and the fair bride might still be near him, the old Knight built the Castle of Sterrenberg for their reception; but his death occurring before its completion, the nuptials were postponed. Meanwhile, Conrad's heart grew cold towards Hildegarde. Hearing of the valiant deeds of his absent brother, his soul burned to share his honors, and weary of an inactive life, he joined the crusades. Hildegarde now passed her days in the lonely castle of Liebenstein, brooding over her sad lot; not doubting the affection of Conrad, but weeping over the uncertainty of his return. Suddenly Conrad returned to Sterrenberg with a lovely Grecian bride, and the outraged Hildegarde, stunned by the blow, shut herself up in the loneliest chamber of her dreary abode, and refused to see any one but her attendant. Late one evening a stranger knight demanded the hospitality of the castle. He proved to be the chivalrous Heinrich, who, hearing of his brother's perfidy, resolved to avenge his foster-sister's wrongs. He accordingly challenged Conrad to single combat, but before the brothers' swords had crossed, Hildegarde's figure interposed between them, and insisted on a reconciliation, to which they reluctantly consented. Hildegarde then retired to the convent of Bornhofen, at the base of the rock on which the castles stand. Conrad's Grecian bride soon proved faithless, and he, overcome with shame and remorse, threw himself on his generous brother's breast, exclaiming that no consolation was now left him but his friendship. Thus their estrangement ended, and the brothers thenceforth lived together in harmony and retirement at Liebenstein, while Sterrenberg was forever deserted."

Opposite to Coblentz is the strong and imposing fortress of Ehrenbreitstein, three hundred and seventy eight feet above the river, only accessible on one side. This fortress has never but twice yielded to an enemy. It is often called the Gibraltar of the Rhine. Among the passengers, we met Miss Camp, who stopped off at Coblentz, it having been several weeks since she parted company with us.

Cologne is one of the most important commercial cities in Germany, and has a population of more than one hundred and thirty-five thousand. Most of the old narrow streets have given place to seventy new ones, with modern, substantial, handsome buildings. This is the city where the veritable Eau de Cologne is manufactured; and the shop-windows are filled with bottles of this delicate perfumery. Of course, our object in stopping at Cologne was to see its celebrated cathedral; and certainly it is grand, with its two massive yet ornamental towers rising majestically to the height of five hundred and eleven feet (but recently completed), even exceeding the tower of Strassburg cathedral. It has also a central tower, three hundred and fifty-seven feet high, and a great profusion of ornamental turrets, flying buttresses, arches, canopies, cornices, tracery, and statues—a huge mass of sculpture. There are several bells in the towers, the largest of which was cast from the metal of French guns, and weighs twenty-five tons. The foundation stone of this cathedral was laid in 1248, and it is not all finished yet. Actually, many of the oldest parts have so crumbled with decay that they have had to be repaired before the entire edifice is completed. The portals are handsomely decorated with sculpture; the centre, or principal one, is ninety-three feet in height and thirty feet in width. The nave has double aisles on either side, and is three hundred and ninety feet long and one hundred and forty-five feet high. The stained-glass windows are very beautiful, especially the rose window over the central door. The church is quite plain in the interior when compared with the exterior; but it has fifty-six handsome pillars, and the choir is flanked with seven chapels, containing quite a number of sarcophagi and monuments.

Just back of the cathedral is the iron bridge which crosses the Rhine. It has two stone towers at each end, and over the entrance on the Cologne side, is an equestrian statue of Frederick William IV., and at the other end an equestrian statue of William

1. We went to the Church of St. Ursula to see the bones of eleven thousand virgins, a sight which a gentleman in Paris said we must not fail to see; and were somewhat surprised to find them in glass cases around the walls, perhaps twenty feet from the floor—the skulls all on one side by themselves. There are also several old paintings on the walls illustrating the legend that "St. Ursula, an English princess, when on her return from a pilgrimage to Rome, was barbarously murdered at Cologne with her eleven thousand virgin attendants." There is also a monument to this saint in the church.

After a ride of eight hours, we arrived at Brussels late in the evening, and were soon snugly quartered at the Vienne Hotel. The broad streets, with their gay shops brilliantly lighted, gave us at once a favorable impression of the capital of Belgium, which is about the same size as Munich. It is a beautiful city, a Paris in miniature; the residence of the king and queen. It is divided into the upper and lower city. The former has fine, broad streets, boulevards, palatial dwellings, handsome squares, public gardens, and is the abode of the wealthier classes; the latter is more ancient and crowded and where the laboring classes dwell. French is spoken by the upper, and Flemish by the lower classes. From the fine display of elegant lace in the shop-windows, we soon began to realize that we were in the lace country. Yes, it may well be called the lace country, for this little kingdom of Belgium has one hundred and thirty thousand women employed in the manufacture of it. There are many establishments where it is made in the city, but the most of the girls engaged in this work are out in the country towns, as it is too expensive to board them in Brussels. And these poor creatures work for the meagre pittance of one franc (twenty cents) a day. We were told by the proprietor of a shop, where for some little time we watched these girls (some of them almost too old to go by that name) making beautiful point lace with their deft fingers, that this extremely delicate work is so trying to the eyes that in eight or nine years those who follow it go entirely blind—and all for twenty cents a day! It is almost martyrdom for a lady to enter one of these shops filled with this tempting luxury of apparel, unless she has a pocket full of money. One piece of exquisite point lace, about a quarter of a yard wide, had been made to order to trim a wedding dress, and it only cost sixty dollars a yard!

The Wiertz Picture Gallery consists of two small rooms of designs and sketches, and a large room filled with paintings. The artist Wiertz could never be induced to sell any of his productions. But when he died in 1865 the government purchased this collection, and it can now be visited by the public. The artist was very eccentric, as his pictures show, but strictly original and very talented. In the principal saloon are seven very large pictures, some of them representing giant's arms and limbs, etc., very coarse and uninteresting to me; but the life-size paintings, and those of less dimensions, possess a certain charm which rivets your attention. One is entitled Napoleon in Hell. There he stands enveloped in flames, with a look of sullen firmness upon his face; while women who have become widows through the cruel wars waged for his selfish glory, are thrusting into his face mutilated arms and limbs severed in battle; one holds up an apron filled with arms, hands, feet, head, etc.; on the other side of Napoleon is a widow, supporting in her arms the dead body of her husband, and pointing to Napoleon as the cause of her great grief; while the innocent baby caresses the father, and two small boys stand behind with their fists clenched at Napoleon, as if they were ready to avenge their mother's wrongs. It is a most thrilling picture! Another painting, called Curiosity, is of a woman peeping through a half-open door; and so natural is it that when you first catch sight of it you instinctively start, as you think a real person is watching your movements. There are three other pictures of the same style, viz., two ladies leaning out of a window (I could not believe that this was a painting until I went close up to it); a dog in his kennel, as natural as life; and a Concierge sitting by an open window. Two corners of the room are partitioned off, and seeing others go up to these screens, and look through small holes about as large as an old-fashioned copper penny, we followed suit, whereupon the most horrible sight presented itself. The picture, for I suppose it was a picture, was placed at some distance from the eye, and so finely executed that it looked like life. It is called Hunger, Madness, and Crime. By a fireplace sits a woman on a stool, with her murdered baby upon her lap, partly covered up in a cloth; her face is that of a maniac; tears are in her eyes, yet a fiendish smile plays around her mouth. She has built a fire in the fireplace with the dear little stockings and shoes and garments of her child, and above it hangs the iron pot, with one limb and foot of the baby in it. Extreme poverty and hunger produced madness, and the result was this horrible crime. I became so intensely interested in it that I forgot where I was, and imagined that I had accidentally discovered a woman doing this very thing. She has taken every precaution not to be discovered, for the windows are shaded, and even the key-hole covered. When I turned away my gaze with sickening horror, and remembered that I was in a picture gallery, I laughed at my credulity; but I could have paid no better compliment to the artist.

Looking through another of these small openings, we saw the picture called "Resuscitation of a Person Buried Alive." This is a person in a coffin, holding up the lid with one arm, and looking out upon the surrounding skeletons. One of these openings, large enough to put your whole face in, made every body laugh. A bust was painted with the head fantastically draped, and all perfect except that the face was missing. When you pressed your face against the opening, by some ingenious reflection of a mirror, your own face completed the picture, making it a very handsome or homely painting, according to the physiognomy of of the spectator. I considered it the plainest portrait painting I had seen in all my travels. We went away much pleased with this little gem of a gallery, wondering at the strange conceptions and highly gifted talent of the artist.

In the Park, which is the fashionable resort of Brussels, handsomely adorned with statuary and fountains, we sat on penny chairs and listened to a concert given by the orchestra of the Royal Theatre, one of the most excellent bands anywhere to be found in the world. The music was simply grand!

The cathedral, which is a Gothic structure, is very handsome. It was begun nearly seven hundred years ago, and the two towers are not more than half completed yet. The splendid stained-glass windows date from the thirteenth century to the present. There are statues of the twelve apostles on the pillars in the nave. The pulpit is very peculiar, yet very beautiful. It is a representation in carved wood of Adam and Eve being driven out of Paradise by an angel. Among the the foliage is a peacock, dove, squirrel, monkey, bear, fox, an eagle, and an owl. On top of the sounding-board is the figure of the Virgin crushing the head of the serpent with the cross. The king has a beautiful throne, or seat, in the choir, with garnet-velvet curtains, trimmed with gold fringe, and a garnet and gold canopy. The queen also has a seat in one of the aisles near the entrance; but she being the "weaker vessel," painted carved wood is considered sufficiently elegant for *her*.

Directing our steps to the Place de l'Hotel de Ville, or market place, we saw an unusually fine display of blooming plants and cut flowers for sale. This is considerered one of the finest mediæval squares in existence. In the year 1568 twenty-five nobles of Netherlands were beheaded here by order of the Duke of Alva. The Hotel de Ville and several old guild houses surround this square, all elegant, and especially the Hotel de Ville, which has a magnificent façade, profusely decorated with sculpture. It has a very handsome open tower, three hundred and seventy feet high, which is surmounted with a gilded metal figure, representing the Archangel Michael, sixteen feet in height.

We went up into the Salle des Marriages, and saw a couple joined together in the holy ties of matrimony; another pair who had but just been yoked together; and still another couple, who with palpitating hearts were awaiting their turn; so we came to the conclusion that they had quite a flourishing business there.

Congress Column, erected to commemorate the Congress of

June 4, 1831, when the present constitution of Belgium was established, is one hundred and forty-seven feet high, and is surmounted by a statue of the king in bronze. There is a female figure also in bronze at each corner of the base, and nine figures in relief on the lower part of the column, representing the different provinces in Belgium; also two immense bronze lions are lying one on either side of the entrance to the tower.

We went to the Musée de Peinture. This picture gallery is now considered the finest collection in Belgium. Those which pleased me most were, Abdication of Emperor Charles V., by Louis Gallait; Adoration of the Magi, by Rubens; The Miraculous Draft of Fishes, one of De Crayer's best works; The Compromise, or Petition of the Netherlandish Nobles in 1565; a picture by Verboeckhoven, of a shepherd carrying a lamb in his arms and driving home his flock of sheep, while the heavens are black with the gathering storm; and Judas After the Condemnation of Jesus, by A. Thomas. The latter is thus portrayed: Two men who have been constructing the cross, which is on the ground with the tools scattered around it, have grown weary, and one is lying down to rest by a rude fire, while the other, in a sitting posture with head bent forward resting on his hand, is sleeping. Judas approaches them, with cautious, stealthy tread, with his bag of gold in his hand, when his restless eye suddenly catches sight of the cross. The red glare of the open fire lights up the faces of the sleepers, while the pale moonbeams reveal the look of condemnation and fear on the face of Judas. It is a most striking picture! One of Ruben's most repulsive pictures is the Martyrdom of Saint Livinus, whose tongue the executioner has torn out and offers to a hungry dog.

On the ground floor is a natural history collection, stuffed animals of all kinds and descriptions from the elephant, giraffe, buffalo, lion, yak, hippopotamus, bears, tigers, elks, etc., down to the tiny canary bird and mouse, the birds in a gallery above the animals. The work is done so adroitly that they look exactly like living animals. Another apartment was filled with skeletons of a great variety of animals.

On our way to church on Sabbath, we saw the shops open just as on any other day, and people at work just the same.

In going to Antwerp, we passed through the village of Vilvorde, where William Tyndale, the English reformer and translator of the Bible, was chained to a stake, strangled, and finally burnt to death in 1536.

Antwerp is the principal seaport of Belgium, with about the same population as Brussels, and carries on an extensive trade with Great Britain and Germany. It is noted for its splendid docks, with their walls of solid masonry five feet thick. My husband explored the dock yards, and also an extensive fish market, which was a novel sight to him; but as I did not go I will not attempt to tell you what I saw there. The cathedral was founded in 1352. It is to have two towers something like those of the Cologne cathedral, but only one is finished. It has a chime of ninety-nine bells. There are several small shops built up against the side of the church which detract very much from its exterior beauty. The interior is quite plain, the pillars by which it is supported are without ornamentation; but the stained-glass windows of the sixteenth century are splendid. The pulpit of carved wood is similar to the one at Brussels, and the carved wood stalls in the choir are wonderfully beautiful. The chief attractions, however, are the three grand pictures by Rubens, which adorn the walls and are covered with heavy, green rep curtains, only unveiled at certain hours of the day. The Descent from the Cross, Rubens' masterpiece, is, I believe, the grandest picture I ever looked upon. Five men, among whom is Joseph of Arimathea, are letting down the limp body of the Saviour from the cross, upon a white linen sheet which is grasped by the teeth of one of the men at the top to keep it in its place. This white drapery gives a very fine effect to the picture. Mary Magdalene, Mary the mother of Jesus, and the other Mary, are at the foot of the cross waiting to receive him. Each figure and face is wonderfully expressive; but one must see it to form any idea of its grandeur. The Elevation of the Cross is magnificent, and the Assumption is also a famous picture, but not so attractive as Titian's Assumption. One painting in the Cathedral by L. Francken the elder, is Christ Among the Doctors, in which Luther, Calvin and Erasmus represent three of the doctors of divinity.

Not far from the Cathedral is a monument to Rubens. A figure of this master thirteen feet high stands on a pedestal twenty feet high. At his feet are scrolls and books with brush and palette, showing that he was a statesman as well as an artist. We also visited the house which belonged to him, containing some of his early paintings.

We had heard so much about the Zoölogical Garden at Antwerp, that we went to see it at our earliest opportunity. The grounds are not so extensive as at Frankfort, but they are much more beautiful, being laid out in great taste, ornamented with lovely flower-beds, trees, etc. Some of the animals' cages are bordered with beds of delicate, blooming roses. There are a great many handsome stone buildings, some of them quite ornamental, for the animals. The lion-house has a very wide promenade between the cages, with a marble floor and stands of blooming plants down the centre; and just think of it! even large, elegant mirrors grace the walls. I could not satisfy myself as to whether these looking-glasses were placed here to make the promenade more attractive for the visitors, or to satisfy the vanity of the lions—perhaps for both. The goats have very fine artificial rocky heights upon which to clamber; the bears have rocky caves or dens; and the surroundings of all the animals seem to be in accordance with their habits and mode of life. One building contains a natural history collection—stuffed birds mostly—but there were two monstrosities which I will mention; a pig with two heads, and a young fawn with two bodies uniting into one, and having but one head. Where the two bodies united on the back, two legs stood straight up. It must have had the advantage over most animals, for it could walk either side up.

The Bourse, or Exchange, corresponding to our Board of Trade, is a very fine structure, having an entrance on each of the four sides. It is one hundred and sixty-eight feet long, and one hundred and thirty-two feet wide. The glass roof is supported by a handsome iron frame-work wrought in the form of clusters and leaves of grapes and other fruits. It is surrounded by a double arcade, supported by sixty-eight columns, opening towards the centre in Moorish-Gothic trefoil arches, with a gallery above. A great variety of armorial bearings ornament the walls. We afterwards saw it filled with men, buying and selling and making bargains.

The walls of the entrance hall of the Picture Gallery are covered with paintings representing the assembly of the Antwerp masters—one hundred and thirty-six in all. Antwerpia, seated in a chair, is distributing wreaths to them. Among the number are Rubens, Van Dyke, Teniers, Massys, De Crayer and Snyder. Ascending the stairs we passed through five large rooms containing six hundred and fifty pictures, mostly by Flemish masters, sixteen of which are by Rubens. In the first room is Rubens' old chair in a glass case. The seat and back are of leather. The gems of the gallery are the Annunciation by Roger Van der Wyden; two heads, one of Christ and the other of Mary, by Quinten Massys; Christ Crucified Between the two Thieves, by Rubens, and also Christ on the Cross by the same master; and then, at last, after having seen so many matchless pictures by this master, we looked upon one most striking and beautiful representing himself—the Death of Rubens, by Van Brée.

During our long journey of eight hours from Antwerp to Amsterdam, the train creeping along at a snail's pace, and stopping, seemingly to rest, altogether too frequently, we had a rare opportunity of viewing the landscape, in which innumerable windmills figured; these giants constituting one of the most picturesque features of Dutch scenery. They are massive stone towers, with immense flyers. Some of them are used in saw mills, others in grinding corn, manufacturing paper, etc.; but their principal use is to pump up the water from the low ground to the canals, which conduct it to the sea. Each sail, or flyer, is about sixty feet long. Holland is said to be the lowest country in the world, the most of it lying several feet below the sea level. It is protected from being flooded by the sea by embankments called dykes. The surface of the embankments is covered with branches of willows, intertwined and filled in with clay so as to make it compact, or strengthened with walls of masonry. Canals intersect the country everywhere. We saw orchards, gardens, pasture fields and houses surrounded by canals, which take the place of fences. Every once in a while you see little foot-bridges across these canals, which are constructed on the trap-door system; so that if a farmer wishes to go to his pasture field he throws down the little bridge, passes over, and then throws it in a perpendicular position again, so that cattle and sheep cannot cross. There are seventy-three canals in the city of Amsterdam, three of which are very large, dividing the city into ninety islands, which are connected by three hundred bridges. The buildings are mostly of red brick. They are very high and narrow, and many of them are so far out of the perpendicular that they look as though they were tipsy; they are all built on piles, and when the piles at one end of a house sink a little deeper into the mud, it somewhat resembles the Leaning Tower of Pisa. Baedeker tells us that in 1822 the great Corn Magazine literally sank into the mud, the piles having been inadequate to support the weight of thirty-five hundred tons of grain which were therein stored at the time. The drinking water is brought to Amsterdam by means of pipes, a distance of thirteen and a half miles.

The Dutch are proverbial for their cleanliness. Every bit of brass or metal in the house must shine so you can see your face in it. Women are everywhere, and at all times, scrubbing and cleaning; they get down on their knees and wash the pavements of the streets, the courts of the houses, floors, and halls in hotels, and the waiting-rooms in depots, until a stranger almost becomes impatient at having to walk through so much slop.

The Rijks Museum contains five hundred and thirty-eight pictures, almost all belonging to the Dutch schools of the seventeenth and eighteenth centuries. Rembrandt, the greatest of all the Dutch masters, died in 1669 almost penniless; but he left the world a rich legacy in valuable pictures. His masterpiece, called the Night Watch, represents a captain with his company of arquebusiers emerging from their Guild-hall. The peculiar lights and shadows, the attitude and appearance of the men, and the harmony of the whole, is most striking and beautiful. Another by the same master entitled the Stamp Masters, represents four of the directors of the guild of the cloth-makers seated at a table, with faces so natural that you almost expect them to speak. Then there are eight admirable pictures by Hondecoeter. His forte is painting the feathered tribe, chickens, ducks, birds. etc. He does it to perfection ; the picture called the Floating Feather, is considered the most famous ; Paul Potter is the chief among animal painters, and Snyder is also excellent; Van Dyke is one of the most beautiful portrait painters; and Teniers has always some jolly social, or home scene. The latter are usually confined to the kitchen ; and almost invariably you discover somewhere in the apartment a brass kettle, which he undoubtedly knew he could paint to perfection. From here we went to a little gem of a gallery called Van der Hoop, containing only about two hundred pictures, many of them beautiful landscapes, sea pieces, and snow scenes, so dainty and pretty and natural that one could almost imagine that it was nature herself adorned in her robe of green, or wrapped in her mantle of white. A very small picture only six inches square, of a hermit, by Gerard Dow, is exquisitely done. A Sick Girl and a Physician, by Jan Steen, is also good.

We next went to the King's Palace, the finest edifice in Amsterdam. It was built for a town hall, but was presented to Louis Napoleon for a King's Palace in 1808. The interior is very beautiful. The walls of the apartments are ornamented with sculptures in white marble. Over the door to the room where cases of bankruptcy were settled, when it was a town hall, is a large piece of sculpture representing " The Fall of Icarus ;" and the moulding above the door, in marble relief, is made up of rats and mice gnawing boxes and papers. The rooms are all furnished extravagantly, but the reception room is the most elaborate of all. It is one hundred and seventeen feet long, fifty-seven feet wide, and one hundred feet high, and unsupported by pillars. The walls are entirely of white marble adorned with bass-reliefs. The King of Holland, who resides at the Hague, only spends one week every year at this palace. It is built on thirteen thousand six hundred and fifty-nine piles. We ascended to the top of its tower, where we had a good view of this queer old city, intersected with canals bordered with trees; its multitude of bridges, innumerable housetops, church spires, rustic looking windmills, the docks with their forests of masts, the Zuyderzee, and away in the distance, the concierge pointed out to us the large church at Haarlem.

We stopped while in Amsterdam at the Bible Hotel—an open Bible carved out of marble, over the entrance door, serves as a sign. The owner has the first Dutch Bible printed in 1542, and this fact gave the name to the hotel. Amsterdam has a population of about three hundred and seventeen thousand.

We had but one more city on the Continent which we intended to visit, and that was the Hague, and in two hours after entering the cars we were there. It is a very pretty place, having broad, handsome streets, large squares, and spacious houses. It is quite an aristocratic city, of one hundred and two thousand inhabitants. The king and many nobles reside here. In the centre of the city is a sheet of water, with a small island called the Vijver. It is surrounded by shady trees, and is inhabited by ducks and swans, making it quite a fashionable resort for the citizens. It, like other Dutch towns, has many canals. We came here chiefly to see two celebrated pictures, viz., Paul Potter's Bull and Rembrandt's School of Anatomy. These we found upon visiting the picture gallery, and felt that they repaid us for our trouble and expense to see them. Paul Potter's "Bull" is so natural from the tips of his horns to the point of his tail that you are almost persuaded that one of these animals has stepped behind an immense picture frame. Less prominent in the picture are a cow, ram, sheep, lamb, and shepherd in the background. Rembrandt's School of Anatomy represents a scholarly anatomist, dressed in a black cloak, with a lace collar and a broad-brimmed felt hat, explaining the anatomy of the arm of a corpse lying on a table before him. The skin has been removed from the arm, and with a pair of scissors he is cutting a sinew. His left hand half raised, and the expression of his face tell us that he has paused to make some explanation. Seven men, members of the Guild at Amsterdam, are gathered about the corpse, watching the operation attentively, each with a different expression on his face. If you take a seat, as we did, and study this picture carefully, you will become so absorbed in it that you will imagine you are in the very presence of this company. The characters look like true living men, and the corpse like a true dead man. Several other pictures by Hondecoeter, Girard Dow, Jan Steen, Albert Dürer, Rubens, Van Dyke, and Holbein, are also very fine. From here we went to a small Museum, where chief among its treasures was a top to a large circular table, which surpassed anything of the kind that we saw at Rome. It was of ebony, inlaid with pearl in the form of a wreath of flowers. There are no two buds, leaves, or blossoms, alike. Its arrangement is most graceful in form, and the tints of pearl, yellow, pink, blue, drab, and green, are distributed with the greatest taste.

In the evening we left the Hague for Flushing, where we immediately took a steamer to cross the North Sea. We had a nice state-room and slept well until morning, but were delayed from landing about two hours, on account of fog. It was so dense that it was necessary to weigh anchor and wait until it had lifted. The different vessels in and near the harbor, blew the fog horns, whistled and rang bells as signals of their whereabouts, to avoid collision. We landed at Queensborough at about eight o'clock in the morning, boarded a train for London, and in two hours were in Mr. Burr's private boarding house once more, where we found precious letters awaiting us from my mother and one of my many sisters, and also from one of our Newton Deacons, and the Miss Grieblings.

CHAPTER VII.

I can not tell you what a thrill of pleasure it gave us to once more set foot in "Old England," a Christian nation, whose Sabbaths are kept holy, after being in so many places on the Continent where the Lord's Day is not used as a day of rest and worship. England! "that pretty island which," says Franklin, "compared to America, is but a stepping-stone in a brook, scarcely enough of it above water to keep one's shoes dry." Yet this little island has for two centuries been the mistress of the seas, with all the consequences of that opportunity. It is the centre of the wealth of the world, and the heart of this centre is London. If you would feel the throbbings of the pulse of the world, press your finger on the Bank of England. One writer says, "There is not an occurrence, not a conquest or a defeat, a revolution, a panic, a famine, an abundance, not a change in value of money or material, no depression or stoppage in trade, no recovery, no political and scarcely any religious movement, that does not report itself instantly at this sensitive spot. Other capitals feel a local influence; this feels *all* the local influences. Put your ear at the Bank, or Stock Exchange near by, and you hear the roar of the world." London, the largest city in the world, with its population of three and a half millions, covers an area of seventy-eight thousand acres, and is situated on both sides of the river Thames, about fifty miles from its mouth. Its massive buildings of brick or stone, have magnificent edifices among them, but the majority are plain substantial looking structures blackened by smoke. Its broad handsome thoroughfares, gorged by carriages, cabs, hansoms, carts, street-cars, omnibuses and hundreds of pedestrians; together with its narrow, crooked, dim streets, form such a labyrinth, that if a stranger does not lose his way many times, he may consider himself most fortunate. The streets and roads patrolled by the Metropolitan police extend over six thousand, six hundred miles. The main thoroughfares are traversed by fifteen hundred omnibuses and tram-cars (street-cars), and eight thousand five hundred cabs, (besides private carriages and carts) employing forty thousand horses. Then besides all this, the river Thames is continually traversed by steamboats, having more than twenty landing places. Why just think of it; the London Bridge, which is nine hundred and twenty-eight feet long, and fifty-four feet wide, built of granite, is crossed daily by no less than twenty thousand vehicles, and one hundred and seven thousand foot passengers!

The shops of London contain everything that can be bought anywhere in the wide world. This is the great centre of trade. It is not necessary to go to Rome or Florence to buy mosaics, to Switzerland for wood carving, or to China or Japan for their wares, for they are here.

The London fogs, of which everybody has heard, occur in the fall and winter, especially in November, and are thought to be caused by the water of the Thames being warmer than the air, and giving forth vapor until the atmosphere is densely charged; then this overhanging vapor absorbs the smoke from thousands of chimneys, forming a cloud of such thick blackness as to turn noonday into midnight. This can be easily comprehended when we consider that London consumes eight million tons of coal annually. Perhaps it would be of interest here to mention the fact that in 1407 the plague of London carried off forty thousand inhabitants, and in 1349 the pestilence destroyed sixty thousand.

The day after our arrival being the Sabbath we went to the "City Temple" to hear Dr. Joseph Parker. He preached a very eloquent sermon, one of a series on the book of Acts. He is quite a handsome man, with dark hair and side-whiskers, and is an earnest, fluent speaker, but I did not like his manner at all —he seemed too self-conscious and conceited. Those who have heard him frequently, however, say that one soon gets accustomed to his manner and becomes so absorbed in his flow of eloquence and depth of thought that this seeming pomposity is not noticed.

In the evening we went to old Westminster Abbey to hear Canon Farrar. Although we were there a long time before the services begun, yet the iron gates were closed; locked; and a placard placed on the front of the church, "Abbey full." We inquired of the police and found that sitting and standing room was all occupied, but that the gates would be opened in the course of time, and if we chose to wait, we could take our chance of getting in. So we with a vast crowd of others stood outside the iron fence, for one solid half hour. After several who had become wearied with standing came out, we gained an entrance. Mr. Culler stood through the whole service and I sat on a projection of a marble monument, about six inches wide. I *saw* the Rev. gentleman, but was so far removed that I don't suppose I should know him from Adam if I should see him again. Could only catch a word occasionally, but distinctly heard the singing, which was grand! especially the hallelujah chorus at the close. We almost thought that this stirring music in the brilliantly-lighted old Abbey must awaken some of the dead, who sleep in such vast numbers beneath this roof, and whose monuments are crowded into every nook and corner.

We spent an entire day in wandering through this immense building, looking at its beautiful monuments, and reading epitaphs. It is an imposing Gothic structure, blackened with smoke and age, having two huge square towers of mixed Grecian and Gothic style, two hundred and twenty-five feet high. The building, including the chapel of Henry VII., is five hundred and eleven feet long, the breadth at the transepts is two hundred and three feet, and the height of the roof from the mosaic pavement is one hundred and one feet. It is more than six hundred years old. The moment we entered we were struck with amazement at the profusion of elegant monuments, rich in statues, reliefs, and tracery, towering above us on either side. "It is the only national place of sepulture in the world--the only spot whose monuments epitomize a people's history." King and queens, statesmen, poets, musicians, divines, lawyers, philosophers, and historians, lie buried here. This is considered the greatest honor which the nation can bestow upon the dead. All the coronations have taken place here, from the time of Edward the Confessor to Queen Victoria, and more than twenty of them lie buried here. Among the number are Edward the Confessor, Edward I., III. and VI., Henry V. and VII., Mary I. and II., James I., Charles II., William III., George II., Queen Anne, Elizabeth, and Mary, Queen of Scots.

Here and there, hanging against the walls are placards with bits of prose and poetry concerning Westminster Abbey. We will give you two, which we copied verbatim, that you may have an idea what they are like, viz.: "Where our kings are crowned there our ancestors lie interred, and they must walk over their grandsire's head to take his crown. There is an acre sown with royal seed, the copy of the greatest change, from rich to naked, from ceiled roof to arched coffins, from living like gods to die like men. There the warlike and the peaceful, the fortunate and the miserable, the beloved and the despised, will mingle their dust, and pay down their symbol of mortality, and tell all the world that when we die our ashes shall be equal to kings', and our accounts easier, our pains for our crimes shall be less."

Another reads thus:

> " Mortality, behold and fear!
> What a change of flesh is here;
> Think how many royal bones
> Sleep within these heaps of stones!
> Here they lie—had realms and lands,
> Who now want strength to lift their hands,
> Where, from their pulpit, sealed with dust
> They preach, ' In greatness is no trust.'
> Here's an acre, sown, indeed,
> With the richest royal seed
> That the earth did e'er suck in,
> Since the first man died for sin.
> Here the bones of birth have cried
> Though gods they were, as men they died."

The beautiful tomb of Mary, Queen of Scots, who was beheaded in 1587, is surmounted by an alabaster effigy, the face of which is very handsome, and is now generally admitted to be a genuine likeness of the queen. The tomb of Queen Elizabeth, who died in 1603, bears the effigy of this "lion-hearted queen" and her sister Queen Mary or "Bloody Mary," who burned two hundred and eighty persons at the stake in four years of her reign, is buried in the same grave. Here are two children of James I. one a baby in a cradle, upon which an American lady has written a beautiful poem. In a white marble sarcophagus are two skeletons, accidentally found in a wooden box under the stairs which formerly led to what is called the Bloody Tower in the London Tower, and supposed to be the remains of Edward V. and his brother Richard, Duke of York, murdered by the order of their uncle, Richard III. The tomb of Henry VII. and Elizabeth his queen, is magnificent!

The Poets' Corner is in the south transept, and here we saw the names of John Gay, Robert Southey, Shakespeare, Milton, Gray, Spencer, Ben Johnson, Dryden, Addison, Chaucer, Campbell, Thompson, Oliver Goldsmith, Isaac Watts, Wordsworth, Mason. Of course there are many monuments here to persons who are buried elsewhere.

We pass on, and the names of learned men of all professions, whom we have reverenced from childhood, confront us on every hand. Here are John and Charles Wesley, Sir Isaac Newton, John Herschel, James Watt, Charles Dickens, William Pitt, Warren Hastings, Bulwer Lytton, John Russell, Mrs. Scott Siddons, Lord Macaulay the historian, John Blow, doctor in music. Under the tablet is a canon in four parts, which I sang—my first experience in singing from a marble book. I will mention but one more, the monument of Handel, which represents the great musician standing with his left arm resting on a group of musical instruments, his attitude and countenance expressing great attention to the music of an angel, playing on a harp in the clouds above. Before it is the celebrated Messiah, open to that soul-stirring air, so universally admired, and so often sung at Easter services, "I know that my Redeemer liveth."

Close by the Abbey are the Houses of Parliament, or Westminster Palace, a magnificent Gothic edifice, built of hard magnesian limestone, and occupying eight acres of ground. It is in the form of a parallelogram, more than nine hundred feet long and three hundred feet wide. There are large square towers at each end: the one at the southwest corner, called the Victoria Tower, is three hundred and forty-six feet high and seventy-five feet square, and is entered by a gigantic archway appropriated to the sole use of the Sovereign; at the northwest corner is the Clock Tower, three hundred and twenty feet high, having a dial on every side, each twenty-two feet in diameter. The clock strikes the hours and chimes the quarters on eight bells. Midway between these towers, above the octagonal hall, rises the Central Tower, three hundred feet high. Then there are numerous other subordinate towers, and hexagonal, open-worked pinnacles, bearing gilt vanes and handsomely carved decorations, which produce a very picturesque effect, especially from the river side. The roofs of the entire building are of iron-framing, and the covering plates are also iron. The windows are of stained-glass. It was begun in 1840, and is considered the most magnificent building that has been erected in England for centuries, having cost nearly ten million dollars. It contains no less than five hundred rooms, and there are four hundred and fifty statues in and about the building. The walls of the interior are beautifully frescoed.

We first entered the Queen's robing-room, the walls adorned with fine fresco-paintings, below which is a handsome panelled dado, six feet high; the upper compartments consisting of exquisite wood carvings, illustrating the life of King Arthur, from his birth to his death. The ceiling, doors, and fire-place, are all elaborate. At one end of the room is the Queen's seat, under the canopy of carved oak, enriched with the Rose, Thistle, and Shamrock, as the badges of England, Scotland, and Ireland. After the Queen has here arrayed herself in her royal robes, she passes through the Royal Gallery, and the Prince's Chamber, into the House of Lords. The Royal Gallery is one hundred and ten feet long and forty-five feet in width and height. The ceiling is splendidly panelled and decorated. In the niches of the doorways and bay-window are statues of English kings and queens. There are two large paintings on the opposite walls, each forty-five feet long and twelve feet high, composed of life-sized figures. One is an admirable picture, representing the interview between Wellington and Blucher after the "Battle of Waterloo," the central figures of which are the Duke and Blucher, mounted upon their faithful steeds, fervently clasping each others hands. It has been settled between them that the Prussians should pursue the enemy, while the war-worn English rested on the battlefield. On either side of the Generals is grouped the staff of each. The great variety of horses, with their different attitudes, is wonderful! Some of them are snuffing at the dead bodies which are stretched about them on the ground. The wounded are being cared for; some are just expiring, and the broken musical instruments, scattered weapons, and shattered shell, help to complete the confused mass. The other picture, called the "Death of Nelson," represents a naval battle, the central figure of which is the wounded Nelson, half raised from the deck, supported in the arms of the captain, surrounded by an anxious group of soldiers. All the bustle and uproar of a battle at sea is portrayed in a vivid and striking manner.

The Prince's Chamber, a sort of ante-room to the House of Lords, where the Queen is received by the chief of the nobility, has beautiful arches at either end. Beneath the one on the north wall is the statue of Her Majesty, Queen Victoria, with a statue representing Justice on one side and Clemency on the other— all of white marble. The dado is divided into square spaces, filled with bass-reliefs in bronze, representing important events in the lives of the queens of England: such as the Escape of Mary, Queen of Scots, the Murder of Rizzio, Queen Elizabeth Knighting Drake, Raleigh spreading his cloak as a carpet for Queen Elizabeth. The ceiling is also rich in ornamentation.

The House of Lords is ninety feet in length, forty-five in

breadth, and of the same height. It is lighted with twelve lofty stained-glass windows, upon which are represented all the kings and queens from the time of William the Conqueror. Its pavement is of handsome mosaic work, and its walls are beautifully frescoed. The ceiling is flat, and is divided into eighteen large compartments by massive tie-beams, apparently of solid gold; these are each again divided by smaller beams into four, and in each centre are different colored devices and symbols, producing a rich and gorgeous effect. This is the grandest room in the building, and whichever way you turn something rare and splendid meets your gaze. At one end is the throne, elevated on steps, covered with scarlet velvet carpet, bordered with gold-colored fringe. The canopy to the throne is divided into three compartments; beneath the central one is Her Majesty's state-chair, which she occupies when she opens, prorogues or dissolves parliament. It is one mass of exquisite carving, and the straight back is bordered with a row of large brilliant, egg-shaped pieces of rock crystal. On either side are state-chairs, one for the Prince of Wales and the other formerly occupied by the late Prince Consort, both alike and somewhat plainer than the Queen's. At the opposite end of the room is the reporter's gallery, and immediately above it the stranger's gallery, beautifully panelled and decorated. The Lord Chancellor sits in the centre of the room, on a scarlet seat without back or arms, called the "woolsack." The seats for the Peers, or Lords, are on either side, rising in tiers one above another, comfortably upholstered.

The House of Commons is not quite as large, and is more plainly decorated. We also passed through the Peers' Lobby, Peers' Robing Room, the Central Hall, the House of Commons, Lobby, St. Stephen's Hall, St. Stephen's Crypt, in which there is a magnificent chapel, and lastly into the Court of Appeals, where we saw the old fellows in curled and powdered wigs and black robes. The top part of the wig is frizzed; then there are three rows of curls, seven in a row; below this, one row of four curls; and below, one row of two curls; and then two little hair tassels.

The British Museum is an immense affair, covering seven acres of ground, containing printed books and manuscripts; ancient and mediæval sculptures and antiquities; gold ornaments and gems; coins and medals, dating from 700 B. C.; zoölogical specimens; fossils, minerals, and botanical specimens. The library is perfectly wonderful, comprising one million, three hundred thousand volumes, and fifty thousand manuscripts. Here we found Lady Jane Grey's manual of prayers, used by her on the scaffold; the Mazarine Bible—the oldest complete printed edition known, printed by Gutenberg and Faust in 1455; the original manuscript of Walter Scott's Kenilworth, and also that of Macaulay's History of England; Luther's ninety-five theses; Mary Queen of Scots' will, in her own hand-writing; the autographs of George Washington, Benjamin Franklin, Napoleon Bonaparte, Martin Luther, Calvin, John Knox, Charles Dickens, and scores of other distinguished men, badly written of course. The Egyptian galleries are crowded with old and interesting relics, including a large collection of mummies and antiquities of all sorts; colossal heads, obelisks, sphynxes, sarcophagi, statues, lions, and winged bulls. There is also a fine collection from Assyria and Babylonia. One room contains gold ornaments and gems from Egypt, Etruria, Greece, Rome, and also modern jewelry. One gold snuff-box is set with twenty-eight diamonds. Think of that vile stuff being deposited in such a beautiful jeweled casket! Then there are large exhibitions of pottery, majolica, china, glass, etc., rooms of vases, bronzes, beautiful specimens of Elgin and Hellenic marbles. Here is the finest natural history collection we have ever seen anywhere without any exception, consisting of a magnificent variety of stuffed birds, with nests and eggs; innumerable humming-birds, birds of paradise, with their handsome plumage; animals of all kinds from every clime. Three large rooms of sea-fish, from the whale and shark to the small round fish, covered with prickly horns; a room of turtles, one gigantic tortoise, which lived to the age of eighty years, weighed eight hundred and seventy pounds; heads of two orang-outangs, preserved in oil; a frilled

lizard, having a long tail, with a spike at the end; all sorts of
reptiles, including a gigantic anaconda throttling a wild pig,
with his tail wound around the branches of an artificial tree
(the tail of the snake, not that of the pig); skeletons of all sizes
and varieties. Then there are several rooms filled with the finest
assortment of shells in the world (so declared in the catalogue)
of innumerable varieties, shapes and colors, a most gorgeous display! Then there are the most beautiful specimens of coral and
sponges; one large piece of brain-stone coral must have been
more than six feet in circumference. The coins and medals form
an unrivaled series of the mintages of the world. I was never
particularly fascinated with a lot of valuable coins locked in a
glass case. "A bird in the hand is worth two in the bush."
There is a very fine lunch-room on the upper floor to accommodate visitors, who are in the Museum all day; which we found
very enjoyable and convenient.

One bright morning after riding for some distance in a 'bus we
alighted at Hyde Park; this with Kensington Gardens, St-James Park and Green Park, form a continuous tract of open
ground, in all eight hundred and two acres. The last two, however, are small. This broad, open, country-like space is often
called one of the lungs of London. It is certainly a good place
to breathe plenty of fresh air. We walked diagonally through
Hyde Park (which is intersected by broad foot-paths and carriage drives, with here and there clumps of noble trees) and
crossed the pretty bridge over the Serpentine river into Kensington Gardens. This river, dotted with small pleasure boats, adds
much to the beauty of the scenery. The carriage drive along
its north bank is called the "Lady's Mile." We saw ladies
riding horseback, with costumes so similar to that of the gentlemen, (tall silk hats and tight-fitting jackets) that we had to take
a second look to distinguish them; also ladies rowing with as
much ease, apparently, as gentlemen. We were there too early
in the day to see the crowds of fashionable people who frequent
these parks. Some of the principal walks are beautifully bordered with flower-beds. At the southeast corner of Kensington

Gardens we came to the National Monument to the late Prince Albert, the husband of Queen Victoria. This excels everything in the form of a monument that we saw anywhere—the most sumptuous! It is approached by flights of gray granite steps, forty-five in number. At the four lower corners of this pyramid of steps, which is about one hundred and thirty feet square, are four colossal groups of Italian marble statuary representing Europe, Asia, Africa and America. Europe is represented by a female figure seated on a bull, with a crown upon her brow and a scepter in her hands, surrounded by four other female figures— Italy, seated on a broken column, with painter's palette and a musical instrument, tells of her fine arts—England, with her trident and shield, seated upon a rock, with the waves dashing against it, proclaims that she is mistress of the sea,—Germany, with open book upon her lap, reveals the sciences; and France, with sword and leaf of laurels, speaks of military victory. In the group called Asia, a female figure is seated on an elephant clumsily kneeling; beside the elephant stands a Persian with high cap, long robe and a shawl draped about his waist, with writing utensils, a Chinaman with specimens of pottery, one of India's dark race with barbarous weapons of war, and an Arab in a sitting posture. The African group consists of a female figure seated on a camel; an Egyptian, standing by a sphynx; a Moorish merchant with turban, pipe and bale of goods; and an Ethiopian instructed by a European. America is represented by a female figure riding a buffalo across the wild prairie. Fearlessly she rides, with spear in hand and shield to protect, attended by a female figure on either side; one representing the United States bears the stars and stripes and with a starry-tipped rod points the way; the other, with furs and snow-shoes, represents cold Canada. In the rear is a figure called Mexico, seated on the skin of a wild beast with his war-club in his hand, around which is coiled a rattlesnake; and at his right is a South American hunter with gun and lariat. The base of the monument, above the steps, is surrounded by two hundred life-sized figures, in bass-relief, of the greatest statesmen, philosophers, divines, poets, painters, and musicians the world has ever produced. Resting upon this base are four clustered columns of red and gray granite, which support a handsome Gothic canopy of gilt and elegantly wrought mosaic designs. At the corners of the platform on which these columns stand are groups of marble statuary, representing Agriculture, Manufactures, Commerce and Engineering. Beneath the canopy is the bronze gilt statue of His Royal Highness, in a sitting posture, fifteen feet high. Half way up the columns and also where they terminate at the top, are eight bronze statues in all, eight feet high, representing Astronomy, Philosophy, Medicine, Chemistry, Rhetoric, Geometry, Physiology and Geology. Rising above the canopy is an exquisite spire one hundred and seventy-five feet high, surmounted by a gold cross. This spire is also ornamented with eight bronze statues, eight feet high, representing Faith, Hope, Charity, Humility, Fortitude, Temperance, Justice and Prudence. And away up at the top, gathered around the foot of the cross, are eight figures of angels. The spire and canopy are both richly ornamented with precious stones of different varieties, which glitter in the sunlight. This splendid monument, which cost nearly six hundred thousand dollars, is marvelous in design and workmanship, elaborate, even to the smallest details, and the English people may well be proud of it. But when Queen Victoria shall have passed away, can, or will, the nation erect a *more magnificent* structure to her memory, as her position calls for? —she being the *Queen*, and he only the husband of the Queen. The dedicatory inscription on the monument reads as follows:

> " Queen Victoria and The People
> To The Memory Of Albert, Prince Consort,
> As A Tribute Of Gratitude
> For A Life Devoted To The Public Good."

Opposite to the monument is the Royal Albert Hall of Arts, a large amphitheatre which will hold ten thousand people, built something after the style of the Colosseum at Rome. It is used for musical entertainments, concerts, exhibitions of art, public meetings, balls, etc. Just south of this building is the site of the old Crystal Palace. From here we walked a short distance to the South Kensington Museum. Some people consider this even finer than the British Museum. I should say so too, if it were not for the Natural History Department at the British Museum. The building itself is much finer. The floors are of mosaic work, and the collections are admirably arranged in glass cases, with a good description of each article attached to it. Here is quite a good display of paintings, both in oil and water colors. Those which pleased me most were "The Death of Amy Robsart," by Yeams, a fine portrait of Charles Dickens, by Frith, Harmony by Dicksee, and "The Waning of the Year," by Earnest Parton. Here are departments for sculpture, jewels, enamels, carved ivories, metal work, carvings in stone and wood, china ware, porcelain, glass, terra cotta, furniture, musical instruments, laces, embroidery, tapestry, etc., etc.

It seemed like meeting old friends to see plaster casts of the "Column of Trajan," Michael Angelo's "Moses," the pulpit of the Baptistery at Pisa, the "Biga," or Roman chariot of the Vatican, and a copy in bronze gilt of the wonderful doors of the Baptistery at Florence. And think of seeing a harpsichord, more than two hundred years old, which used to belong to Handel! Among the gems is a shoulder knot—an epaulet—completely covered with diamonds, which was presented to Lord Beresford by the Portuguese army. There are elegant refreshment rooms in the building, where we obtained a good lunch.

We had heard of the Tower of London from childhood; of its threefold use as fortress, palace and prison. We had read of the torture, misery, murders and executions which its walls had witnessed; and when young in years we often looked with sorrowful eyes upon an old discolored wood-cut in an English history, portraying the execution of Anne Boleyn, the wife of Henry VIII., and mother of Queen Elizabeth. Dressed in her white robe and long-flowing veil, she approaches the execution block with firm yet graceful step, her hands uplifted and her eyes raised to heaven, commending her soul to God. The executioner, with a touch of sympathy in his downcast eyes, stands ready to give the fatal blow.

Poor Lady Jane Grey was also beheaded here, and Katherine Howard, Sir Thomas More, and scores of others—indeed, history tells us that for several hundred years the axe was seldom still; and for centuries these dungeons echoed with the groans of prisoners. No wonder then that when we beheld its many strong towers, some thirteen in number, the recollections of the past almost made us sick at heart. Its area within the walls covers a space of twelve acres, and its massive walls are fourteen feet thick. The earliest and principal portion is the White Tower, built by William the Conqueror, in the eleventh century —but there are good reasons for supposing that it was begun by Julius Cæsar. I fully indorse the following description of the Tower of London: "It is a confused mass of houses, towers, forts, batteries, ramparts, barracks, armories, store-houses and other buildings." This has always been the place of deposit for the national arms and accoutrements.

We first entered the Horse Armory, on the south side of the White Tower. It is one hundred and fifty feet long and thirty-three feet wide. A row of equestrian figures extends the whole length of the apartment, with both horses and riders fully equipped in suits of armor, showing the various styles of the different periods between the thirteenth and seventeenth centuries. Each suit, for the sake of chronology, is assigned to some king or knight, viz.: There is a gallant rider clad in steel armor from head to foot, labelled "The Earl of Leicester" (Robert Dudley); there is King Henry VI., with sleeves and skirt, back and breast plates all of chain mail, the limbs protected by jambs and the feet by long pointed sollerets. Then there are any amount of warriors standing up like sentinels, completely sheathed in steel from the helmet to the boots. Some of these coats of mail are so ingeniously wrought that they are as flexible as any garment could be—they are apparently made of innumerable fish scales; others are of steel plate with joints at the elbows, knees, etc.; and others are of chain steel. Then there is a curious collection of old, ancient weapons of war.

The department in the White Tower called Queen Elizabeth's

Armory contains the weapons and instruments of torture used during her reign. Among the latter are the thumb screws, heading block, heading axe and Lochaber axe. And there is Queen Elizabeth on horseback, dressed in a beautiful silk robe, bespangled with pearl beads, which was precisely copied from the costume she wore when she went in state to St. Paul's Cathdral to give thanks for the deliverance of England from the threatened invasion of Spain.

The Banqueting Hall and Council Chamber are now filled with sixty thousand stand of rifles, handsomely arranged, and pistols, swords and bayonets ingeniously set up so as to form different-shaped figures.

In one of the dungeons under this White Tower Sir Walter Raleigh was imprisoned for a time. We also saw the room where he wrote the history of the world, during his thirteen years of confinement in this old historic tower. He certainly had plenty of time.

In the Beauchamp Tower we saw the State Prison Room with its interesting records cut in the stone walls by those who were confined there. Some have even attempted to cut a verse of poetry on the solid walls; and John Dudley, Earl of Warwick, has rudely engraved quite an elaborate shield containing the armorial bearings of his family—the Bear and Ragged Staff.

After a good deal of manœuvering and extra feeing of one of the wardens, who wore a funny, little, low-crowned black velvet hat, with a striped red, white and blue band of ribbon, we finally gained admission to the Bloody Tower, and entered the small room in which the young princes, Edward V. and Duke of York were smothered by order of their uncle, who was afterwards Richard III., and saw the small staircase where their bodies were thrown down, and where, some time afterwards, their remains were found and respectably buried in Westminister Abbey.

But we turn from this dark picture to look upon a bright one. In the Wakefield, or Jewel Tower, as it is more commonly called, is deposited the Regalia, or Crown Jewels, with which the sovereigns of England are invested at their coronation. It consists of royal crowns covered with diamonds, pearls, emeralds, rubies, sapphires, etc., royal scepters, swords, twelve elegant salt cellars, baptismal font, sacramental plate, tankards, dishes and spoons, all of solid, brilliant gold, placed within an inclosure lined with white, and faced with beautiful plate glass, in the centre of a well-lighted room, with ample space for visitors to walk around it. The collective value is thirty million dollars. Among these gorgeous treasures is one of the largest diamonds in the world, called the Koh-i-noor, which is valued at two million pounds sterling, and is about the size of a walnut. Queen Victoria's crown is the handsomest, consisting of a cap of purple velvet, confined with hoops of silver, and surmounted by a ball and cross. It is extravagantly adorned with the following jewels :

    1 very large ruby,
    1 very large sapphire,
    4 smaller rubies,
   16 smaller sapphires,
   11 emeralds,
 1363 brilliant diamonds,
 1273 rose diamonds,
  147 table diamonds,
    4 drop-shaped pearls,
  273 round pearls.

After leaving the Tower, we walked through a circular iron-tube, about eight feet in diameter, under the bed of the river Thames, running from one side to the other, lighted with gas; for which privilige we paid one-half penny each—boats were plying the river above our heads. We reached this tube by going down a winding stair-case of one hundred and three steps, and the same number of steps brought us again to the light of day on the other side of the river. We then re-crossed in a swift passenger boat, and landed in the neighborhood of St. Paul's Cathedral.

One evening we went to see Madam Tassaud's celebrated

Wax Works; although the establishment is carried on by her sons, she having been dead for many years. This exhibition was first opened in 1772, in the Palais Royal in Paris, and was removed to London thirty years after, and has continued to be a source of entertainment to the public ever since. The apartment called the Hall of Kings contains fifty figures of kings and queens from the time of William the Conqueror down to the present. The faces are carefully modeled from portraits of the persons they represent. The hair of the head and beard is natural, the eyes of glass, and the wax of such a perfect flesh-tint as to bear very close inspection. The forms and attitudes are faultless, and they are all dressed in the richest costumes; the style of the garments corresponding with the period in which they were worn. Some of the queens are actually attired in court dresses, which were purchased after being laid aside by the owners. And so life-like did all these figures appear (which are life-size) in their magnificent apparel, in this brilliantly lighted hall, that I almost felt out of place in my short, plain, walking suit. But the consoling thought that they were nothing but wax, put me at my ease until I peered into somebody's face who grew restless under my searching gaze, and began to move. Discovering that it was a real, live, human being who was standing quietly admiring a wax figure before her, I humbly begged pardon and withdrew. Queen Victoria and her whole family are here, four sons and five daughters, viz., the Princess Royal, Victoria; Albert Edward, Prince of Wales; Princess Alice, Prince Alfred, Princess Helena, Princess Louisa, Prince Arthur, Prince Leopold, and Princess Beatrice. There are also wax representations of other distinguished personages, among which are Knox, Calvin, Luther, Wesley, Spurgeon, Abraham Lincoln, Grant, and our beloved Garfield. Then there are dear, little wax babies, dressed in the most bewitching manner, softly nestled in their cradles, with tiny hands and feet so natural— even to the delicately formed pink nails, that you feel that you must press them in your own palm. Then there is a department of curiosities and relics mostly of Napoleon Bonaparte. Here is the camp bedstead upon which he lay while an exile in St. Helena, and upon it is stretched the wax figure of the great General. And here is his carriage, which was captured at the Battle of Waterloo. I stepped into it, and sat while one of the attendants explained the drawers, table, writing-desk, and lamp for cooking, with which this wonderful carriage is furnished.

Lastly, there is a Chamber of Horrors, containing murderers, men and women, with crime written on their faces, dressed in all sorts of costumes, from that of the gentlemen to the beggar clothed in rags. Guiteau is there! A platform which has often been used for hanging, and also the real knife of the guillotine used during the Réign of Terror in Paris are here. This terrible axe beheaded over twenty thousand persons; and with a shudder I touched with my finger the cold steel that severed Marie Antoinette's head from her body. Her beautiful picture has always graced the home of my childhood, and I felt that I knew her.

Of the many outdoor monuments and public statues with which London is ornamented, perhaps the Column of Nelson, in Trafalgar Square, is among the finest. It is of Portland stone, one hundred and forty-five feet high, surmounted by a statue of Nelson, seventeen feet high. The capital of the fluted column is of bronze, made from cannon captured from the French. The pedestal is beautifully adorned with bass-reliefs; and at the four corners of its base are projections upon which crouch four noble, colossal bronze lions. On either side is a magnificent fountain, spouting up the water to be caught in its immense granite basin, the whole surrounded by statues of distinguished men.

On the north side of this square is situated the National Art Gallery, which compares very favorably with any of the Continental galleries. Although it was not founded until 1824, yet it has purchased so many valuable works of distinguished artists that the British, French, Italian, Dutch and Flemish schools are well represented, forming a collection of eleven hundred paintings, by Paul Veronese, Guido Reni, Rembrandt, Rubens, Correggio, Laurence, Landseer, Hogarth, Turner, and hundreds of others. Eight rooms are devoted to the English school of painting. In the basement is Turner's collection of water colors. Among the British collection is Hogarth's greatest work, called "Marriage a la Mode," a series of six exceedingly comical pictures, portraying scenes in married life; "Shoeing the Bay Mare," by Landseer, and the "Scanty Meal," by Herring—three horses eating, with very little in the manger, all admirably done. The "Magdalene," and also the "Madonna in Prayer," by Sassoferrato, are very fine. There are several good views of Venice, which brought back this romantic place to us with great vividness; and here is a small copy of Rembrandt's "Night Watch at Amsterdam." The "Resurrection of Lazarus," by Sebastian del Piombo, is the most important Italian painting in England. It was painted in competion with Raphael's "Transfiguration;" and "The Family of Darius at the Feet of Alexander," is considered the finest work of Paul Veronese.

From here we went to see the Egyptian obelisk, called Cleopatra's Needle, which is situated on the Thames Embankment. It is seventy-five feet high, eight feet wide at its base, and weighs two hundred tons. On either side is an immense bronze sphynx.

The Sabbath came again, and in the morning we went to hear Rev. Charles H. Spurgeon, in company with Philip Phillips and wife, who were acquainted with one of the deacons of the church, and through him we immediately obtained most desirable seats. Everybody who wants to hear this great preacher goes very early, for although the church will seat about seven thousand people, it is always crowded, we were told. All those who own pews have them reserved for them until ten minutes before the services begin; after that, if there is sufficient room, the strangers are seated. The church is not beautiful, but large, and has two galleries. In front of the pulpit is a raised platform for the deaf. It was crowded with this class of men, women and children, many of them with ear-trumpets. Mr. Spurgeon is a short, thick-set man, with black hair, small, piercing black eyes, and full beard, sprinkled with gray. He preached an eloquent, impressive sermon extemporaneously. Text: Psalm lxxxiv. 11. They have congregational singing, the chorister standing by the minister's side; and without the aid of an organ, that vast audience, provided with hymn books, made "a joyful noise unto the Lord." After the services, we were invited to commune with these Baptists. This is one of the very few Baptist churches in the world, where they invite or allow other denominations to commune with them. We were greatly mortified at the verdant audacity of an American lady (happily not of our acquaintance) who, no sooner had the benediction been pronounced, and the Amen uttered, than she was up in the pulpit, soliciting Mr. Spurgeon's autograph. Think of it! Of course she did not get it. In our own limited experience we are so bored with autograph albums, that we often wish the person who invented them had to fill them with writing. In the evening, I went to hear Rev. Dr. Newman Hall. He preached grandly from the text, "The Sword of the Lord and of Gideon." This Gothic church built in 1874, is very fine both externally and internally. The vaulting is supported by massive-stone pillars, and a gallery extends around three sides. A large pipe-organ and choir of thirty-two voices, well trained, added much to the services. When Newman Hall was in America he received large contributions towards erecting this Congregational church, amounting to about thirty-five thousand dollars, which was expended upon the handsome tower and spire.

Mr. Culler and Mr. Philip Phillips went the same evening to the Salvation Army meeting at Congress Hall, curious to learn something of its workings. It is called the Salvation Army because it is fashioned after the model of an army, warring against sin. It was originated in the east part of London in 1865 by William Booth, a Methodist minister, and its present leader. The stations of the army are in London, and the principal towns of England and Wales, in Scotland, the north of Ireland, Australia, and some places in the United States. It operates as follows:

1. By holding meetings out of doors, and marching, singing

through the streets, accompanied by martial music, dressed in a uniform of navy blue, trimmed with red braid, and marked with the letter S. on the collar. In their songs they use the language of everyday life to convey God's thoughts to all in novel and striking forms, set to popular song-tunes.

2. By visiting places where liquor is sold, prisons, private houses, speaking to and praying with all who will allow it.

3. By holding meetings in theatres, music halls, saloons, and factories, thus securing hearers who would not enter a church.

4. By making every convert a daily witness for Christ, both in public and private.

Some of its advertisements seem almost sacrilegious to a refined Christian person. However, my knowledge concerning it is too limited to speak for or against it. During the year ending April 12, 1880, the Salvation Army received and expended more than seventy thousand dollars. I wanted to purchase a silk dress, and was informed that I would do well to buy of Hitchcock and Williams in St. Paul's church-yard. This announcement struck me as being very comical. The idea of a firm expecting to sell dress goods in a grave-yard, whose occupants need no earthly apparel! But when we investigated the matter we found that the cemetery which surrounds St. Paul's cathedral was formerly much larger, including the square around it, and therefore the shops in the immediate vacinity are said to be in St. Paul's church-yard.

Approaching this majestic edifice of classic style, built of Portland stone (though sadly blackened with smoke), from Ludgate Hill, the western front presents a very fine aspect; a broad flight of gray granite steps leads to the grand entrance, under a double portico of coupled columns, the lower being of the Corinthian and the upper of the Composite order. On either side of the portico is a handsome tower, two hundred and twenty-two feet high. The clock tower has two dials, facing the west and south, each twenty feet in diameter. The minute hand is nine feet eight inches long, and weighs seventy-five pounds. The figures are more than two feet long, and the pendulum is sixteen feet long. The other tower is the belfry, in which an immense bell has just taken the place of the old one. Upon which is engraved "Vae mihi si non evangelizavero,"—Woe unto me if I preach not the Gospel. The entablature between the towers contains a representation of the Conversion of St. Paul, in bass-relief, and above are statues of St. Paul, St. Peter and St. James, each eleven feet high. The cathedral is in the form of a Latin cross, and there is also a handsome entrance at each transept. The dome with its noble proportions, one hundred and eighty-nine feet in diameter, rises from the intersection of the nave and transepts. The entire length of the church is five hundred feet, breadth at the transepts two hundred and fifty feet, and the height from the pavement to the top of the cross is three hundred and sixty feet. It is the third largest church in the world, being excelled only by the Milan Cathedral and St. Peter's at Rome. It was begun in 1675, and was completed in thirty-five years afterwards. After looking at the exterior to our satisfaction we entered, and found that around the walls are more than fifty finely-executed monuments, mostly to English naval and military heroes. Here is a monument to Major General Robert Ross, "who having undertaken and executed an enterprise against the city of Washington, the capital of the United States of America, which was crowned with success, he was killed shortly afterwards while directing a successful attack upon a superior force, near the city of Baltimore, September 12, 1814." Lord Nelson's monument records: "His splendid and unparalleled achievements during a life spent in the service of his country, and terminated at the moment of victory by a glorious death, in the memorable action off Cape Trafalgar, October 21, 1805." And here is a monument to Sir John Moore, whose burial at midnight we have so often read in our school reader, beginning:

> "Not a drum was heard, not a funeral note,
> As his corse to the rampart we hurried;
> Not a soldier discharged his farewell shot
> O'er the grave where our hero was buried."

Turner, the celebrated painter, has also a monument erected to his memory. A statue of Bishop Heber, in a kneeling posture, with one hand upon his breast and the other resting upon the Bible, is very beautiful. On the pedestal he is represented as confirming two heathen converts. He died in 1826 while a missionary in Calcutta. He was the author of that grand hymn, "From Greenland's Icy Mountains," which we so often sing in our Woman's Home and Foreign Missionary Society. The splendid pipe organ, which contains sixty stops and four manuals, is divided into three parts, the swell and choir organ being on the south side, the solo and great on the north side, and the pedal organ, which contains two stops thirty-two feet long, under one of the arches. The large bellows are in the crypt, and are blown by three powerful hydraulic machines; the air is thence brought to reservoirs in various parts of the instrument by means of zinc tubing. Although there is a great distance between the different parts of the organ, yet the touch answers instantaneously to the performer. The wood carvings in the choir stalls are of rare beauty. We descended to the crypt and saw the black marble sarcophagus which contains the remains of Lord Nelson, and stands directly beneath the dome. The porphyry sarcophagus of the Duke of Wellington is in a small apartment by itself, which is lighted by four large polished granite candelabra around the coffin. In still another part of the crypt is Wellington's splendid funeral car. Sir Christopher Wren, the architect of this cathedral, also lies buried in the crypt. We returned to the floor of the cathedral, and then proceeded to ascend to the dome. We soon came to a door which leads into the church library, and of course stopped to take a peep at it; then up we climbed again two hundred and sixty steps, and found ourselves in the Whispering Gallery. Its acoustic properties are certainly wonderful! I put my ear to the wall and distinctly heard what the guide whispered at the extreme opposite side of the circular gallery, one hundred and forty feet in diameter. Here we had a good view of the paintings in the dome, representing events in the life of St. Paul. When the artist was painting these pictures he stepped back to mark the effect of his work, and unconsciously was just on the edge of the scaffolding; another step would have cost him his life, when a person seeing his danger snatched up a brush and drew it across the picture. The artist, rushing forward to save his painting, saved his own life. We continued our climbing, and in due time reached the Stone Gallery, where we had a splendid view of London, stretching out in a grand panorama on every side, as far as the eye could reach. But the Golden Gallery was far above us, and we could not be satisfied until we had also viewed London from that standpoint; so up we went, and then ambition spurred us on until we at last gained the stone lantern which crowns the cathedral, with its ball and cross. This lantern has a small opening in it, through which we looked down three hundred feet upon the people below in the nave, who looked about as large as flies. But "what goes up must come down," and so did we.

The Zoological Gardens in Regent's Park are exceedingly interesting and instructive. They contain the largest and most complete collection of living animals in the world; five hundred quadrupeds, one thousand birds, and one hundred reptiles. This collection was opened to the public more than fifty years ago, and by constant improvements in the grounds and additions to the collection, it has become a superb and popular resort. All the animals have room to move about at their pleasure. The monkey house, in the shape of a conservatory, of iron and glass, is large, affording plenty of room for scores of these comical creatures to run, leap, swing, and perform all sorts of antics, to the infinite delight of crowds of people who gather about them. The lion house has large, roomy cages, containing several varieties of these ferocious animals. On the opposite side of the building are rows of seats, where visitors may sit and watch their movements, and see them fed at four o'clock p. m. This is quite exciting. The keeper throws in great pieces of nice fresh beef, and they instantly seize and tear it to shreds with their sharp claws and teeth, and devour it ravenously. One old fellow got a leg-bone, and it took him a little longer than the others to strip the meat from it. He laid himself out for a good dinner, and taking the bone in his fore paws, began to gnaw at it with a satisfied air. I suppose his inward gratification was in some mysterious manner communicated to his tail, for it began to wag most graciously. The lion, unconscious that he possessed this caudal appendage, and spying it, upon casting a backward glance, supposed it to be some sneaking intruder, and dropping his bone, he snapped at it most savagely. Perceiving his mistake, he again resumed his meal. But this selfish scene was enacted several times before the bone was picked. We smiled at this, but shuddered when his deafening roar resounded through the building like a heavy clap of thunder, as if proclaiming himself the King of Beasts. Here is a building containing two or three hundred parrots of the most gorgeous colors imaginable, white, pink, blue, green, yellow, black, scarlet and mottled; all talking, whistling, screaming, chattering; presenting the best illustration of confusion I ever witnessed. Then there is the reptile house, with its huge tropical snakes trying to keep themselves warm under heavy blankets, with which they are provided. The chief attraction, however, is a monstrous pair of hippopotami, presented by the Viceroy of Egypt. We watched them for some time swimming around in a large artificial pond which is connected with their stable. Two large elephants and several camels, with scarlet velvet seats upon their backs, were making themselves useful as well as ornamental, by giving the children a ride, and thus earning something for the Zoölogical Society. Each seat will accommodate six children. Among all the animals I saw I will give the palm to the rhinoceros for being the ugliest. He is a great, clumsy, awkward animal, with a skin somewhat resembling that of the elephant, only it does not fit so well. It hangs in folds around his short neck; a fold also extends between the shoulders and fore-legs, and another from the back to the thighs. He has a fearfully homely head, with funnel-shaped ears, not much larger than a donkey's, and a single black horn near the end of the nose. Here may be seen animals from all parts of the globe;

elephants, hippopotami, rhinoceroses, giraffes, camels, yaks, buffaloes, elks, reindeer, lions, zebras, bears, tigers, panthers, goats, beavers, tapirs, ant-eaters, sea-lions, kangaroos, deer, gazelle, ducks, flamingoes, pelicans, gulls, sand-pipers, parrots, ostriches, bald eagles, vultures, leopards, raccoons, foxes, wolves, alpaca sheep, bisons, boa-constrictors, rattlesnakes, alligators, crocodiles, Polar bears, monkeys, donkeys, llamas, hyenas, antelopes, innumerable birds and fishes, and many other animals which I can not now recall. The annual expense of these Gardens is one hundred and twenty-five thousand dollars.

We went to Sydenham, a thirty-minutes' ride on the train, to visit the Crystal Palace. This magnificent structure was built in 1853, and is made entirely of glass and iron. Five hundred tons of glass, and nine thousand six hundred and forty tons of iron, were used in its construction. It is one thousand three hundred and ninety-two feet long, three hundred and eighty-four feet wide, and two hundred feet high, and cost about nine million dollars. It is a permanent exposition building, erected for the purpose of furthering the education of the people, and affording innocent amusements and musical treats. In the central part of the building is an immense organ, having nearly five thousand pipes; and there are raised seats for the accommodation of the Handel orchestra, which consists of four thousand performers; and below there are seats which will accommodate eight thousand people, surrounded by beautiful tropical plants. A concert is given here every day, at two o'clock p. m. Being present at that hour, we enjoyed a rich musical feast. The palace is divided into different departments or courts, viz: the Greek court, Egyptian court, Italian court, Sheffield court, manufacturing court, china and glass court, etc., where we saw a model of the Colosseum, Pantheon, Roman Forum, plaster casts of several noted pieces of statuary that we had seen in different cities all over the Continent, a picture gallery, a department where silk ribbons are woven, another where pictures are printed on linen handkerchiefs, another where all sorts of ivory and shell ornaments and jewelry are made, a department in which candies are manufactured in every conceivable style and shape. A candy chair, large enough for a person to sit on, was made of fifty-six pounds of loaf sugar. And there were whole tea-sets made of sugar. Then there are scores of tempting stalls or booths filled with attractive articles, such as jewels of coral and gold, photographs, laces, tidies, ribbons, and fancy things of all descriptions. Refreshments can also be obtained here. The palace is surrounded by a most beautiful park of one hundred and ninety-two acres, laid out in gravel walks, handsome flower-beds, luxuriant trees, sparkling fountains, artificial lakes, elegant statues, broad terraces and rustic arbors, making it a most delightful retreat from the rush and bustle of London.

The Royal Academy of Arts is an annual exhibition, from May until August, of works of modern artists, in oil, water colors and sculpture. Thirteen large rooms are devoted to this purpose, and besides these is a spacious room where the annual banquet is held, another for lectures and the distribution of prizes, schools of art for students, and a library room. All works sent for exhibition are submitted to the judgment of a council, whose decision is final. No artist is allowed to exhibit more than eight different works. All the pictures must be in gilt frames. Works which have been already publicly exhibited in London, or copies of any kind (excepting paintings on enamel) are not admitted. There are a number of other rules, showing that the whole arrangement is very systematic. There were one thousand five hundred and forty-one pictures on exhibition this year, and all admirably executed. It was a real treat to see these fresh new pictures in modern styles after seeing so many by the old masters. One entitled "Members of the Commons," was a landscape with two jackasses and a flock of geese in the foreground. Another picture termed Romeo and Juliet consisted of a stone wall with a cat on the top and another on the ground in the next yard. And still another picture portraying young Prince Arthur with his arms around Hubert, imploring him to spare his eyesight. His young, sweet face contrasts strangely with the dark visage of the man beside him, and you seem to hear him saying,

"O spare mine eyes, though to no use but still to look on you." There were many beautiful landscapes, sea pieces, and one lovely snow scene that I should so much like to call my own. Then there were portraits exquisitely painted; one a full length of the Princess Louise (Marchioness of Lorne). "The King Drinks" represents a lion lapping water from a running brook in a forest: there he is, life size and so natural that you almost shrink upon the first glimpse, for fear he may suddenly spring upon you. Many of these pictures were already sold. It seemed a pity that they could not all be kept together as a permanent picture gallery. Among the statuary was a marble bust of Her Majesty, Queen Victoria, sculptured by her daughter, the Princess Louise.

One afternoon we went to the Charing Cross station, near the National Gallery, and took a little trip on the underground railroad to Kew Gardens. This mode of traveling is not at all pleasant. It is like going through a tunnel, only when it comes out from under the buildings, streets, etc. It passes also under the Thames river. We enjoyed the Kew Botanical Gardens more than we can tell. They are very extensive, containing two hundred and seventy acres, handsomely laid out in broad walks, rare trees, flower-beds, an artificial lake with a fountain in the centre, surrounded by the most artistic-shaped beds of blooming plants, with the flowers arranged in a special manner, so as to give regularity to the distribution of color; and a large range of hot-houses containing the plants, flowers and vegetable curiosities of every clime. Here we found a vast variety of cactuses, and the most extraordinary fuchsias, like running vines, and literally covered with blossoms. There are six hundred species of ferns, including tree and tropical ferns. The palm house, quite a palace of glass, is three hundred and sixty-two feet long, one hundred feet wide, and sixty-four feet high. Some of the palms reach to the roof. Here is the cocoanut palm, with the nut growing directly in the centre; the banana with its immense leaves and clusters of fruit; coffee, nutmeg and clove trees, each bearing fruit, but in a green state, and the "deadly Upas tree," from Java. One of the water-lily houses has, in a large hot water tank, the wonderful Victoria lily. Its leaves are circular, about six or seven feet in diameter, and they rest on the surface of the water. The edge of the leaf is turned up, resembling a pie-pan. There was a large white bud in the centre, but no full blown lily. There were perhaps eight or ten of these immense leaves; one was dead and had been turned over, so we were permitted to see the very strong net-work of ribs on the under side.

Our last day in London was the Sabbath. In the morning we went to Whitefield's Tabernacle; in the afternoon to St. Paul's Cathedral and heard Canon Liddon very indistinctly, as the building is so immense that it seems to swallow up the sound, the music being exceptionally fine; and in the evening Mr. Culler went to hear Stopford Brooke, a brilliant writer and thinker, but not of the orthodox faith. We left London at noon on Monday from the Paddington station. The hackman tried to extort more money from us than his fare, and when he found we were sharp enough to attend to our own affairs, remarked, in his rough, burly manner: "We are quite as clever as you are on the other side of the water."

CHAPTER VIII.

Reaching Windsor, we proceeded immediately to the Castle, leaving our baggage at the station. It scarcely seemed possible as I looked at this huge structure, with its magnificent Round Tower and more than half a dozen others rising in their majesty and strength, that I was really beholding Windsor Castle, one of the Queen's residences. We were admitted to all the State apartments except the Waterloo Chamber (which contains portraits of sovereigns, statesmen and generals concerned in the war against Bonaparte) which was not shown on account of the great crowd of visitors from London, it being Bank Holiday. These apartments are the Queen's Audience Chamber, the Queen's Presence Chamber, the Guard Chamber, St. George's Hall, the Grand Reception Room, the Waterloo Chamber, the Grand Vestibule, the State Ante-room, the Zuccarelli Room and the Vandyke Room. The walls of the first two rooms are embellished with Gobelin tapestry, representing the history of Queen Esther in seven scenes. They are very beautiful, the figures standing out like life. Over the doors and mantel-pieces are also large portraits of distinguished persons. One represents Mary, Queen of Scots, life size, in a mourning habit with a crucifix in her hand; and in the background is a representation of her execution at Fotheringay. There are also Latin inscriptions on the picture, giving a brief history of her life and death. The Guard Chamber contains a collection of arms and armor and many interesting relics, among which is the fore-mast of the vessel Victory, which was completely perforated by a cannon ball at the battle of Trafalgar; two historical chairs, one made from an oak beam taken from "Alloway's auld haunted kirk" and the other from an elm tree which grew on the battle field of Waterloo.

We next entered St. George's Hall, a room two hundred feet long, where the Queen confers the Order of the Garter, which was here instituted in 1349, by Edward III. Its ceiling is decorated with the coat of arms of the Knights of the Garter, and the walls ornamented with the portraits of the sovereigns, from James I. to George IV. At each end is a music gallery with pipe organ. In front of one of these galleries is the sovereign's throne, and on the wall behind it are twenty-four shields, with the coat of arms of each sovereign of the order, from Edward III. to William IV. The names of the several knights are printed on the side walls.

The Grand Reception Room has a large blue and gilt vase standing on either side of each door. The walls are hung with handsome Gobelin tapestry, representing the story of Jason and Medea. At one end of the room is a magnificent green malachite vase, presented to the Queen by the Emperor of Russia; and on either side of it a beautiful granite tazza, presented to King William IV. by the King of Prussia.

The Grand Vestibule is a large apartment, lighted from above by an octagonal lantern of rich design. Here are ancient suits of armor, military trophies, etc., and at one end is a fine marble statue of Queen Victoria seated on her throne, accompanied by her favorite dog "Sharp."

The frescoed ceiling of the State Ante-Room represents a banquet of the gods. There are six pieces of Gobelin tapestry in this apartment, and some of the most delicate wood-carving wrought into fish and fowl, and festooned wreaths of flowers and fruit. Let into the wall over the fire-place is the stained glass portrait of King George III. in his coronation robes. The light coming through the colored glass gives a fine effect to the picture.

The Zuccarelli Room contains nine large paintings by that master, and the Vandyke Room contains twenty-two pictures by Vandyke. In one of the apartments is an ivory throne, carved in the most exquisite and lavish manner.

On one side of the Castle is a beautiful green terrace, ornamented fantastically with brilliant flowers. On another side is an extensive deer park of five hundred acres, for the British Royalty, and it is connected with another immense park of eighteen hundred acres by the "Long Walk," a superb avenue three miles long, flanked with graceful elms.

Belonging to the Castle is St. George's Chapel, and adjoining it Prince Albert's Chapel. They are said to be very sumptuous in the interior, but Bank holiday is not the time to see them.

The quaint old city of Oxford has twenty colleges and only forty thousand inhabitants. It is fairly crammed with literature and literary people. History stares at you from every standpoint, even the very atmosphere seems freighted with the breath of knowledge. We first visited the Bodleian Library, a large quadrangular building with an open court in the centre. The Divinity School occupies a beautiful room on the ground floor, with elaborately groined ceiling, richly carved with heraldic bearings and monograms. It is used for exercises for the University degrees of B. D. and D. D. From this room we entered what is called the Convocation House, used for conferring degrees upon students who have passed the requisite public examinations; and also for the transaction of general business. We were taken into a small room adjoining this, where we were shown a variety of black robes, differing in the cut of the sleeve, or shape of the hood; worn to indicate the degree of scholarship attained. We then ascended the stairs to the famous Bodleian Library, which contains more than two hundred and fifty thousand volumes and twenty thousand manuscripts. It has a right to a copy of every book published in England. Through the centre are glass cases containing many relics, and models of ancient buildings; among which were the exercise books used by Edward VI and Queen Elizabeth when they were children; various specimens of illuminated books, made by monks, between the eighth and tenth centuries, the letters all perfectly made by hand, upon fine, thin parchment, with beautiful, bright-colored illustrations and gold blazonry, which must have taken the patience of Job to execute; the very lantern taken from Guy Fawkes, when he was about to blow up the Houses of Parliament, in the reign of King James I; Sir Thomas Bodley's iron chest, with a lock covering the whole interior of the lid; a German Bible, printed in 1541, with Martin Luther's and Melanchthon's signatures on the fly leaf; the original manuscript of Robert Burns, containing verses on a louse; an old map of England, made in the fourteenth century; a picture of Robert Dudley; a beautiful model of Calcutta Cathedral, in white marble; and a chair made out of Drake's ship, bearing the following inscription by the poet Cowley, in 1662:

> "To this great Ship, which round the Globe has run,
> And matched in race the Chariot of the Sun,
> This Pythagorean Ship (for it may claim
> Without presumption, so deserved a name)
> By knowledge once, and transformation now
> In her new shape this sacred port allow.
> Drake and his Ship could not have wished from fate
> A happier station or more blest estate,
> For lo! A seat of endless rest is given
> To *her* in Oxford and to *him* in Heaven."

We next went to the Sheldonian theatre, which is very near by. We were told that at the annual commemoration the galleries and parquet, which will seat about four thousand persons, are crowded to listen to the Creweian Latin oration in commemoration of founders and benefactors; and also prize compositions recited by their authors. It is here that degrees of honor are conferred upon distinguished men. A candidate for the degree of Bachelor of Music or Doctor of Music must compose an oratorio, and conduct its rendering under the baton. We ascended to the cupola, where a gentlemen pointed out the different colleges and other buildings of interest. The names of the colleges are Magdalen, Corpus Christi (Christ Church College), Wadham, Keble, Hertford, New College, Queens, University, All Souls, Brasenose, Oriel, Merton, Pembroke, Worcester, Balliol, Trinity, Exeter, Jesus, Lincoln, and St. John's. Each college is built with an open court or quadrangle in the centre, and each has its chapel connected with it, in which the students are expected to attend divine worship. Some of these chapels are very handsome, yet they are all different. These colleges all belong to the Church of England, but have been endowed by different men, and each has its own library.

After passing through the great stone archway, and crossing the court of Christ Church College, we entered the Cathedral, which is the chapel for the college, and also the chief church of the diocese of Oxford. Its spire is one of the most ancient in England. The choir has a superb groined roof, and is profusely embellished with wood carving. This church was erected in the twelfth century, and the college with which it is combined was founded by Cardinal Wolsey, in 1525. Under the Belfry Tower, which is situated at one corner of the quadrangle, we ascended the dining-hall staircase, the elegant fan tracery of the stone roof being supported by a single slender column. This dining-hall, where the students come to take their dinner at seven p. m., is a grand room. The ceiling is of Irish oak, decorated with armorial bearings. The stained glass windows give it a richness, and the walls are ornamented with seventy portrait paintings of men who have graduated from this institution, and have afterwards gained distinction. The Prince of Wales and also Prince Leopold graduated here. The portraits of Queen Elizabeth, Henry VIII. and Cardinal Wolsey, the two latter by Holbein, hang at one end of the room. We were told that in 1533 a banquet was given to Henry VIII. in this room, and that Elizabeth, James I. and Charles I. had witnessed dramatic representations here. In the centre of the room were long dining tables and benches. We explored the kitchen where the meals are prepared, and saw a monstrous gridiron on wheels, which was formerly used for broiling the "chops." Hanging against the wall was a list of students' names and the number of their rooms. They have all their meals taken to their own private apartments except the dinner. We were somewhat surprised to learn that every one of these colleges have their provisions sent from London, and in fact all their necessaries. So the colleges are no benefit to the commercial interests of Oxford. It being vacation, the students were away rusticating, so we did not have the pleasure of seeing them in their long black gowns and peculiar caps. The quadrangle is two hundred and sixty-four by two hundred and sixty-one feet, being larger than that of any of the other colleges. Its lovely greensward, closely shaven, looked as soft and rich as a velvet carpet. To the north is the Library, a handsome edifice, having a picture gallery on the lower floor, and the books and manuscripts of historic interest on the upper floor. At the south of the quadrangle are the New Buildings, which contain fifty sets of rooms for students' lodgings. As a special favor, we were permitted to visit some of these apartments. The undergraduates each have a sitting-room and bedroom, which they furnish themselves, according to their taste and means. One gentleman, whose apartments were furnished handsomely, had his walls ornamented with no less than eight deer heads (stuffed). I think when he gets through college, and has a real, live dear of his own he will not be so fond of these. A Bachelor of Arts has four rooms to himself: two bedrooms, an extra one to accommodate a friend or visitor, a private sitting-room, and a room in which he may lecture to a few students or listen to their recitations. Each student rooms alone. On the west side of the quadrangle, above the grand entrance gateway, rises the splendid tower which contains the celebrated "Great Tom," a bell weighing eighteen thousand pounds. We climbed to its summit; and, after admiring the giant bell on the exterior, we thought we would stand inside, as it was plenty high enough, and hung a sufficient distance from the floor to admit of our crawling under. While standing up inside, I said to my husband, "What if this bell should ring!" No sooner had the words escaped my lips than the monstrous iron hammer, regulated by the machinery of the clock in the tower, struck the hour of four, on the outside of the bell. I crawled out pretty lively, but Mr. Culler got the full benefit of the four strokes. Every night, at five minutes past nine, "Old Tom" tolls one hundred and one strokes, as a signal for the closing of the college gates, which are immense iron structures, and all the stores of Oxford close when they hear the "mighty Tom" We were told that an old sexton, who had rung the bell for twenty-five years, one night made a mistake, and rang it an hour too soon. Every shop closed, and the next day the old man was discharged for his carelessness.

In front of that portion of the college termed the New Buildings, is a lovely avenue of elms, called the broad walk. This communicates with a beautiful shaded river walk, a mile or more in length, which encloses a large grassy meadow. Some of these venerable elms have been standing since the time of the Reformation. Great care is taken to preserve them. They are of gigantic size, and their spreading branches meeting overhead, form a complete leafy canopy. One of the oldest trees had evidently met with some accident, for the mutilated part of the trunk is walled up with brick and mortar, to prevent its decay. On the same principle as filling teeth, it was much better to preserve it in this manner, than to pull it up by the roots and throw it away. We followed this shady path down to the Thames river, where the shore was lined with barges belonging to the College Rowing Club. During the summer term, the eight-oar races take place, when some twenty crews compete for the glory of heading the river.

An elderly English gentleman, a bachelor, who owns a large estate called the Manor House, Hampton Gay, nine miles from Oxford, by the name of R. Langton Pearson, was stopping for a few days at our hotel, and kindly offered to accompany us and render us all the assistance which his familiarity with the place afforded. We found him to be a gentleman of superior taste and culture, and most companionable. Since returning home, we received a letter from him, from which we quote the following: "I have not forgotten our argument concerning Byzantine architecture, when in Exeter College Chapel, August 9. Since that time I have been reading up on the subject of the course and current of architecture, its origin, successive and simultaneous developments, relations, periods, and characteristics of its various known styles, more especially in its progress from the East to the West; beginning with Ancient Egyptians, whose origin is lost in the night of time, beyond the ken of historic or monumental record—Assyrian—Babylonian—Persian—Greek—Roman—Christian—Romanesque—Byzantine—Saracenic—Norman Sicilian—Norman, or more correctly, Round Gothic, Pointed Gothic, *i. e.* the style known as early English, Geometrical, the Decorated and the Perpendicular—the Italian Renaissance and its treatment in England, France, Spain, etc. For instance: St. Peter's, at Rome, is an example of the Italian Renaissance, as St. Paul's in London is an example of the English Renaissance. I have had access to the reference library at the Bodleian, which contains grand works upon the subject, with magnificent illustrations of the various examples. The study of the Egyptian and Assyrian is to me vastly interesting in relation to the history in the Old Testament."

Having so thoroughly "done" Christ Church College, we did not care to enter into the details of the others, as they are all similar in their operations and arrangements.

Just here let me state that Oxford is the birthplace of Methodism, founded by John Wesley, and a beautiful Methodist church stands as a memorial of his work.

Instead of each college having its own apparatus, there is an Institution called the University Museum, for the teaching and study of the natural sciences, provided with everything which is necessary for the perfection of knowledge in Mathematics, Chemistry, Mineralogy, Geology, Zoölogy, Anatomy, Physiology and Medicine.

We walked through the Botanic Gardens, which occupy five acres, furnished with herbaceous and aquatic plants, indigenous and exotic, containing several conservatories, also a library and lecture-room for the Professors of Botany. Magdalen College was founded in 1458, and is considered the finest in architectural beauty. It, like most of the other colleges, is over-run with ivy, giving it a most picturesque appearance. Its buildings form three quadrangles, covering an area of eleven acres, and its grounds occupy one hundred acres. Here, in green meadows, adorned with graceful elms, were great numbers of tame deer. We took a stroll down "Addison's walk," a romantic, shady avenue, so called, because when he was a member of this college he so often frequented this delightful, winding path, which appears to have no end. Returning to the chapel, we were told that every May-day morning at five o'clock, a Latin hymn is sung by the well trained choir of the chapel on the summit of the tower; a custom which has been kept up for centuries.

We visited the chapel of New College, and were much pleased with it, especially the stained glass windows. The large West window, painted in 1777, delighted me more than any stained glass I had seen anywhere. The chief picture represents the Nativity, and the lower range of figures, the cardinal and Christian virtues. The latter are life-sized female figures in the most graceful and expressive attitudes, beautiful in form and feature; and the windows on one side of the choir, designed by the scholars of Rubens, are exquisitely rich in coloring. The figures are clad in robes of the most gorgeous hues, garnet, gold, blue, and rich olive green, yet all blending harmoniously.

The greatest attraction of All Souls College chapel is the singularly beautiful reredos. It comprises thirty-six large, and nearly one hundred small statues, under profusely carved canopies, surrounding the principal subject, the Crucifixion. It completely covers the end of the chapel, and is much finer than a similar one in New College Chapel.

We also visited the chapels of Trinity, Exeter and Worcester Colleges. The latter is sumptuously decorated in the Romanesque style, with marbles, mosaics, gildings, paintings, and is considered by many to be the handsomest of all the chapels of Oxford.

In St. Mary's Church there is a marble slab in the floor, upon which are the following words: "In a vault of brick, at the upper end of the choir of this church, lies Amy Robsart, the ill-fated heroine of Sir Walter Scott's Kenilworth. Her body was conveyed to Oxford from Cumnor Hall, some three or four miles distant."

Allow me to quote what another says about the view from Queen's College up High street: "The visitor here beholds the finest sweep of street architecture which Europe can exhibit. Antwerp may have quainter pieces, Edinburgh more striking blendings of art with nature, Paris and London may show grander coups d' oeil (prospects), and there is architecture more picturesque in Nuremberg and Frankfort, but for stately beauty, that same broad curve of colleges, enhanced by many a spire and dome, and relieved by a background of rich foliage, is absolutely without a parallel."

Of course we could not leave Oxford without visiting the University Printing Office. This establishment is one of the largest and most complete anywhere. The south wing is devoted to the printing of Bibles and prayer-books, and the north wing to works of a learned and educational character. We walked through the large press-room, two hundred and ninety-three feet long by twenty-eight wide, where we saw thirty presses running by steam-power; passed through the stereotype, electrotype and type founderies, and in fact, through all the departments, and received explanations of all the different operations. The large corps of workmen were most courteous and seemed glad, to give us all the information in their power. We walked between stacks of unbound Bibles reaching from the floor to the ceiling, with only narrow passages between them. One large room, which they termed their laundry, was filled with printed matter hanging up to dry. They send their books to London to be bound, and the daily amount sent away is astonishing!

The Martyr's Memorial, a handsome carved stone monument, bears the following inscription on its base: "To the Glory of God, and in grateful commemoration of his servants, Thomas Cranmer, Nicholas Ridley, Hugh Latimer, Prelates of the Church of England, who, near this spot, yielded their bodies to be burned; bearing witness to the sacred truths which they had affirmed and maintained against the errors of the Church of Rome; and rejoicing that to them it was given not only to believe in Christ, but also to suffer for his sake. This monument was erected by public subscription in the year of our Lord, MDCCCXLI." Upon leaving Oxford, we could truly say with Hawthorne, "It is a despair to see such a place and ever to leave it; for it would take a lifetime, and more than one, to comprehend and enjoy it satisfactorily."

A ride of two and a half hours on the train brought us to Cheltenham, my birthplace. It has a population of forty-five thousand, and is a most charming city, and a fashionable watering place, picturesquely surrounded by the Cotswold range of hills, which forms a lovely background in the landscape whichever way you turn. The greatest attention is given to the cleanliness of the streets. The walks and drives in the town and suburbs are especially pleasing, presenting handsome residences, beautiful yards, and flowers in rich abundance. Here, as everywhere in England, the ivy is most luxuriant; enhancing the beauty of churches, costly edifices and private mansions, and also kindly covering up the ugliness and poverty of unsightly buildings. Passing through the streets one sees many invalids in easy chairs, or small low carriages drawn by men. The principal mineral springs are the Montpeller Spa, the Pittville Spa, and the Cambray Spa. Besides its sanitary celebrity, it is famous as an educational town. It has four colleges, grammar schools, and several private schools. Its churches and chapels are twenty-two in number. The Promenade, a broad avenue lined with stately trees, leads to the most fashionable part of the city. The principal thoroughfare is High street, which is crossed by Hales Road. Not far from where they intersect in Rose Hill street, stands the house in which I was born, thirty-four years ago. Although its present occupants were strangers, we made bold to ring the door-bell, briefly give our history, and ask to see the house. While in an upper chamber where my eyes first opened to the light of day, I thought of how eventful my life had been thus far, and my good husband declared that God sent the little English baby to America to be a wife for him. Immediately upon our arrival in the city, we learned through a cousin that we had many relatives living here, who greeted us with sunny faces and warm hearts, and during our stay of five days, did all in their power to make it pleasant for us. It seemed delightfully strange to be visiting with aunts and uncles, cousins, second cousins, and even a great-uncle, whom I had never seen before, except with unconscious baby eyes; and when on Sabbath we attended St. Mary's Church, grown gray with the breath of age, having been founded in the eighth or ninth century, my thoughts wandered from the sermon occasionally, as I found myself wondering just in what spot in this ancient church my parents were married, fifty years ago. The names of Battledown Estate, Landsdown Place, Leckampton Hill, High Street, Hales Road, Rose Hill Street, Prestbury, Cross Hands, and Hardwick, all seemed familiar from hearing my father talk about them. In an old-fashioned graveyard at Hardwick, more than half the tombstones bear the name of Yeend.

This rest of a week was a refreshing oasis in our journey. and recruited in body and mind, after many affectionate farewells and thrilling hand-shakings, we set out for Stratford on Avon, to see Shakspeare's old home. [Quite a remarkable fact that two such illustrious persons as myself and Shakspeare should be born within a distance of four hours' ride from each other.] We found his low, humble, old-fashioned stone cottage in Henley street, and as thousands of visitors go to see it every year, of course there were several others there on the same errand as ourselves. The front-room was called the kitchen, where the meals were prepared over an immense fire-place, and the floor is paved with uneven stones of various sizes. In the next room, called the best kitchen, was a large blank-book in which visitors were expected to record their names. This is quite a curiosity in itself, containing the names of rich and poor, high and low. in every language. We ascended an old, queer staircase to the room in which Shakspeare was born, so low that even a short person can touch the ceiling with the hand; and visitors have taken advantage of this by scribbling the ceiling with autographs until there is actually room for no more; the walls are in the same condition, and even the panes of glass are completely covered with the names of visitors cut with diamond rings, and among them we could legibly trace the name of Walter Scott. In an adjoining room hung a fine portrait of the poet when he was about forty years old. It is covered with glass and placed in a fire-proof frame, or safe, which is securely locked every night. A door in the front kitchen leads into the museum, an apartment formerly used by Shakspeare's father for picking wool. Here we saw the veritable desk that Shakspeare used when a boy at school; and from the manner in which it was hacked, and cut, and covered with rude initials, we concluded that the great poet resembled our modern boys in mischievous propensities. We saw his signet-ring, which he used to wear on his thumb; a handsome carved vase made from his mulberry tree; scores of manuscripts, copies of the first second and third editions of his works, his library, and other relics. We then turned our steps to the church where Shakspeare is buried. On the stone in the floor which covers his remains, are the following lines, said to have been written by himself:

> "Good Friend, for Jesus' sake forbear
> To dig the dust enclosed here.
> Blessed be the man that spares these stones,
> And cursed be he that moves my bones."

Near him are buried his wife and family. On the wall, within an ornamental arch, is the bust of Shakspeare holding a pen in one hand and a scroll in the other; and beneath is this inscription:

> "Stay, passenger; why goest thou by so fast?
> Read if thou canst, whom envious death hath placed
> Within this monument: Shakspeare, with whom
> Quick nature died; whose name doth deck this tomb
> Far more than cost, since all that he hath writ,
> Leaves living art but page to serve his wit,"
> Died in 1616, aged fifty-three.

That same evening we went to Warwick, and next morning started out to see the Castle. Arriving at the gates before time for opening, the porter advised us to view the Castle from the bridge across the Avon River. We were admiring its stately grandeur, when whom should we see approaching but a brother minister, Rev. G. W. Halderman, his wife and little boy, from America. It was a happy meeting on this historic spot, and we spent the day together. Passing through an embattled gateway, we approached the Castle by a broad road cut through the solid rocks, which are entirely covered with the most luxuriant ivies; and spreading branches form a lovely canopy overhead. We were soon in the outer court, where looms up the Castle in all its sublimity. On the right is Guy's Tower, thirty feet in diamter, and one hundred and twenty-eight feet high, with walls ten feet thick. On the left of this tower, and connected with it by a strong embattled wall, is Cæsar's Tower, which is eight hundred years old. The whole structure is simply immense! It suffered severely from fire in 1871, but has been thoroughly restored. It is owned by Earl George Guy Greville, and as the family came home the day before, many of the apartments were not open to visitors. We, however, were shown the great hall, containing a collection of armor, with the Bear and Ragged Staff of Robert Dudley's crest carved on the Gothic vaulting; the red drawing-room, the cedar drawing-room, the gilt drawing-room, the State bed-room, and the boudoir. These apartments are all furnished in the most sumptuous manner; the walls decorated with costly paintings, among which is the celebrated picture of Ignatius Loyola, the founder of the Order of the Jesuits, a portrait of Mrs. Scott Siddons, one of Henry VIII., by Holbein, and a life-size portrait of Charles I., by Vandyke. Prominent among the statuary, is the bust of the goddess Proserpina, by our American sculptor, Hiram Powers, and a magnificent bust of the Black Prince, son of Edward III., by Chantrey. The pure antique furniture throughout the whole suite of State rooms is matchless; handsome mosaic tables, one valued at fifty thousand dollars, superb cabinets, Etruscan vases, rare and beautiful clocks, one with twelve curious and highly-finished pink enamels, one to each hour, set in silver, representing events in the life of Christ; precious caskets, rare chinas and crystals, and antiques of all descriptions scattered everywhere, yet displaying the greatest taste in arrangement. The bed and furniture in the State bedroom are of crimson velvet, and formerly belonged to Queen Anne; her full-length portrait also adorns the room.

The chapel where the family assembles every morning for prayers is rich but plain. The altar piece is of carved oak; and the windows are of stained glass. From here we walked to St. Mary's church, where in the Beauchamp chapel is a monument to Robert Dudley, Earl of Leicester and his Countess Lettice, consisting of a heavy canopy profusely decorated and borne by Corinthian pillars; beneath which, enclosed by iron rails, are the recumbent figures of the earl and his wife. The earl is clad in armor, over which is a mantle bearing the badge of the Order of the Garter. The countess is dressed in the robes of a peeress, with a band of jewels around her head, and a ruffle of Queen Elizabeth's time. We found by reading the inscription on the monument, that he occupied the following positions of honor during his lifetime, and thought so many titles was enough to kill any man: Earl of Leicester, Baron of Denbigh, Knight both of the Order of the Garter and St. Michael, master of the horse to Queen Elizabeth, steward of the Queen's household, privy counsellor, justice in eyre of the forests, parks, chases, etc., lieutenant and captain general of the English army, sent by Queen Elizabeth to the Netherlands, governor general and commander of the provinces united in that place, and was lieutenant governor of England against Philip II. of Spain, in 1588, when he died.

At the church door we with our friends took a cab and were driven to Kenilworth, a distance of five miles. The scenery was charming all the way, and our driver anxious to give us all the information possible called our attention to everything of historic interest. We stopped opposite Guy's Cliff, a most romantic spot, to admire the elegant mansion visible through the long avenue of overhanging trees. We drove on a little distance and then alighted from our carriage; and passing by an old ruined mill we reached a rustic bridge across a pebbly stream, shaded with leafy trees, from which we had another fine view of Guy's Cliff. We drove on and our attention was soon directed to a monument on Blacklow Hill, erected on the spot where Piers Gaveston, Earl of Cornwall, was beheaded. We passed many beautiful residences, wreathed with ivy, adorned with flowers and foliage, so characterestic of English homes.

We soon reached Kenilworth and entered the castle walls. What a contrast between the splendid magnificence of Warwick and the deserted ruins of Kenilworth, with nothing but the walls remaining, yet the thrifty, large-leafed ivy clings to it fondly as if seeking to hide its decrepitude and cover its unsightliness with her mantle of green in kindly remembrance of her former greatness. And yet these gray old towers, made illustrious by Scott's Kenilworth, attract more visitors annually than many of her more favored sisters. No sooner does the visitor catch sight of these venerable walls than the celebrated visit of Queen Elizabeth in 1575, the sorrowful tale of Amy Robsart's wrongs, Robert Dudley's unfaithfulness, and Varney's villainy, crowd upon the mind in quick succession. Let me quote from Walter Scott, where Queen Elizabeth approached the castle in all her pomp and glory, attended by her grand retinue: "The splendid procession advanced along the avenue that led to the Gallery Tower, lined on either hand by the retainers of the Earl of Leicester. Onward came the cavalcade, illuminated by two hundred thick waxen torches, in the hands of as many horsemen, which cast a light like that of broad day all around the procession, but especially upon the principal group, of which the Queen herself, arrayed in the most splendid manner, and blazing with jewels, formed the central figure. She was mounted on a milk-white horse, which she reined with peculiar grace and dignity, and in the whole of her stately and noble carriage you saw the daughter of a hundred kings. The ladies of the court, who rode beside Her Majesty, had so arrayed themselves that no inferior luminary might appear to approach the orbit of royalty. Her favorite, Leicester, who glittered like a golden image with jewels and cloth of gold, rode on her right on a black charger."

Enough of Cæsar's tower is still standing to tell of its former immensity and strength; and a portion of Mervyn's tower remains. The latter is the one in which Amy Robsart was concealed during the visit of the Queen. We climbed the stone staircase to its summit, and there, seated on a remnant of the wall, looked about over these ruins. Adjoining Mervyn's tower was the great banqueting hall; the windows of lofty height are filled with tracery and transomed. The space of wall between them is paneled, and the fire-places on each side still bear traces of exquisite ornamentation.

After spying out each nook and corner, we bade our friend good-bye and took train for Manchester. We passed through the large manufacturing city of Birmingham, and reached Manchester late in the evening. It is a large manufacturing city also, full of smoke, people, and cart-loads of cotton cloth. Mr. Culler spent the next morning in hunting up and calling upon an uncle and aunt of one of our Newton bankers, to whom he carried messages from their kin across the sea, and found them hospitable, pleasant and courteous. I wisely occupied the time in resting, and at three in the afternoon we pursued our journey as far as Hassop station.

The next day we, with several others, went in a large excursion wagon a distance of about three miles to the Chatsworth estate, owned by the Duke of Devonshire. This is the largest and finest estate in England, being eleven miles in circumference. In the lovely park were hundreds of sleek cattle and tame deer beneath the broad low branches of the beech trees, and lazy sheep

> "Nipping grass and daisies white
> From the morning till the night."

As we approached the Chatsworth house, we passed a small stone structure in which Mary Queen of Scots was imprisoned at intervals for twelve years. There used to be an underground passage connecting this prison with the old ancestral mansion of the Cavendishes. The entrance to this princely mansion, built of cream-colored sandstone, beautifully veined, is by the Porter's Lodge, a structure forming three archways, ornamented with carved roses and having large iron gates. The length of the palace is five hundred and fifty-seven feet, and its architecture is of the Ionic style. We entered the Sub-hall, the ceiling of which is embellished with a copy of Guido's Aurora, the general conception of which is in the highest degree poetical. The figure of Apollo, seated in his chariot drawn by fiery steeds, unites grace with dignity. He is attended by figures representing the Hours, whose actions are playful and simple, and the expression of their faces sweet and lovely. The figure of Aurora flying before and strewing flowers in his pathway seems buoyant as the morning breeze itself. The Great Hall is a spacious apartment, with a mosaic floor of white and black marble, and its wall and ceiling paintings represent the history of Julius Cæsar. In the centre of the room is a very handsome fossil marble table, and on the floor is a long ornamental canoe, presented to the late Duke of Devonshire by the Sultan of Turkey. A corridor, beautified with statuary, paintings, antique and historical objects, leads to the chapel, which is exceedingly handsome, having a marble floor, walls of cedar wood bordered with garlands of roses delicately carved from wood, and further ornamented with paintings illustrating scenes in the life of Christ, and the pure altar of white Derbyshire spars and marble is accompanied with graceful figures of Faith and Hope. One room contains more than one thousand original drawings and sketches by the most distinguished masters of the Flemish, Venetian, Spanish, French and Italian schools. The old State bedroom contains the bed in which George II. died, and the chairs and footstools used at the coronation of George III. and Queen Charlotte. The State Music Room contains a splendid cabinet of minerals, fossils, fluor and calcareous spars, etc., and an emerald said to be " the finest specimen of its kind for purity of form and uniform depth of color." It was purchased by the sixth Duke of Devonshire from Dom Pedro, Emperor of Brazil. This room is elaborately ornamented with paintings, portraits, miniatures in porcelain, handsome mosaic tables, and rare china of various and striking designs. The State Drawing Room is also fitted up beautifully, the decorations and appointments including many costly works of art. One table of mosaic work composed of different colored precious stones is indescribably beautiful. Here is also a most excellent full-length portrait of Mary Queen of Scots. The Library rooms are wonderful! In elegant book-cases are the rarest literary treasures, handsomely bound, consisting of twenty-five thousand volumes, and many valuable illuminated manuscripts. The Dining Room is ornamented in the most gorgeous manner, and in the centre is a table which will seat fifty persons. We next passed into the Sculpture Gallery, which is one hundred and three feet long, and is beautifully lighted by skylights. It contains forty fine pieces of sculpture, placed upon costly pedestals and pillars. Adjoining it is the orangery, where we saw trees laden with the golden fruit.

We then took a walk through the immense gardens, which take sixty men to attend to them. We were very fortunate in being there that day, as the Earl of Rutland with a small party were guests at the mansion, and all the fountains were playing for their special benefit. The French garden is gay with brilliant flower-beds, lovely walks, creeping vines, statuary and superb vases. We came in sight of an artificial cascade, which is situated on a sloping hillside. On the top of the hill is a stone temple adorned with sea-lions and dolphins, and when the water is turned on at this point, it flows over a long series of broad stone steps reaching from the top to the bottom of the hill, thus producing a picturesque cascade; its flood of water being conveyed under the garden to the Derwent river. Its beauty is enhanced by a line of stately trees on either side. We walked on until we reached what appeared to be a romantic valley in a natural forest, surrounded with high cliffs and rocks and secluded retreats. But what was our surprise when told that all this is artificial! That high towering cliff is made of stone laid together with mortar, and creeping vines ingeniously planted in the crevices, to cover the deception. The immense boulders which lie scattered around promiscuously, have all been placed here by the hand of man. We entered a grotto, formed of huge rocks, and when about to retrace our steps, the attendant placed his hand on a large boulder which blocks up the end of the grotto, and turned it around on a pivot, thus allowing the party to pass through. We soon came to a weeping willow which the attendant declared was always moist. We were looking at it intently, not noticing that our guide had slipped from us, when suddenly from every sprig and leaf came a shower of water. We found upon close inspection that the tree is made of copper; but so skillfully done as to resemble a natural tree. Passing through an archway of rocks we found ourselves in an open garden, in the centre of which is a grand conservatory. This large glass-house covers nearly an acre of ground. It is filled with the rarest and choicest plants, flowers and trees, from Europe, Asia, Africa and America. Here we saw the citron tree filled with its delicious fruit; banana, orange and palm trees growing as luxuriantly as if in a tropical clime. There are thirty green-houses in all. The grandest of the fountains is called the Emperor. It sends up the water with great force to a height of two hundred and sixty feet, forming a grand spectacle. Further on we came to an oak tree planted by Queen Victoria in 1832, a sycamore tree planted by the Prince Consort in 1843, and a Spanish chestnut tree planted by the Emperor Alexandria of Russia in 1816. We strolled through the Italian garden, adorned with choice cedars and artistic parterres of flowers, arranged after the fashion of sunny Italy, and finally reached the archway through which we had first entered, scarcely able to believe that all this wealth belonged to one man. Whereupon we were told that he owned two other estates besides, and only spends a few months of the year here.

In the churchyard of the little village of Edensor, not far distant, we found the grave of Lord Frederick Cavendish, the second son of the present Duke of Devonshire, interred here May 11, 1882. He was appointed Chief Secretary for Ireland on May 4, and was cruelly assassinated two days later in Phœnix Park, Dublin. We again entered our carriage and were off for Haddon Hall, the property of the Duke of Rutland. Its exterior presents a most imposing and picturesque appearance, with its massive walls, embattled parapets and towers wreathed with ivy, rising majestically above the surrounding hills, studded with trees. But the interior has been shorn of its glory for nearly a hundred years; for at the beginning of the last century this old mansion ceased to be the family residence, and was abandoned for the more magnificent castle of Belvoir. There are still a few traces of its former grandeur in the faded, decaying tapestry in some of the rooms, and in the wood carvings and armorial bearings in its bay windows. It serves as a memorial of the olden time, and is said to be "one of the most perfect examples in England of an old baronial mansion of the feudal ages." We climbed to the top of its highest tower, from which we had another of those pretty landscape views for which England is so celebrated.

At Hassop we took the train for York, reaching there late in the evening. We passed through the town of Sheffield, noted for its steel and cutlery works. Next morning we went to see the grand cathedral of York, whose foundation was laid in 1291. Its west front has two uniform towers one hundred and ninety-six feet high, surmounted by eight pinnacles. The Lantern tower is situated near the middle of the building, and is square, plain and massive. The length of this superb edifice is five hundred and twenty-four feet. It is composed of five different styles of Gothic architecture. The interior consists of a nave and aisles, transepts, choir and side aisles, the Lady Chapel and Chapter House. It was a grand sight as we stood near the central entrance of the nave and looked up the long vista of pillars, seven on either side, forming eight pointed Gothic arches, the eye taking in a portion of the central tower, the organ screen, surmounted by the organ, and above it rising the great east window. The screen separates the choir from the nave, and is of stone, ornamented with statues of the kings of England, from William the Conqueror to Henry VI., in royal costumes, each bearing the name and time of reign. The vaulting is of wood, the ribs or groins of which form a delicate tracery, and are adorned with carved knots. The pillars are quite plain, but the capitals are highly ornamented. The cathedral is remarkable for its rich stained-glass windows. In the south transept the windows are in three tiers, and the large circular one at the top, called the marigold window, twenty-seven feet in diameter, is particularly beautiful. At the end of the north transept is also a handsome window divided into five lights, called the five sisters, because it was given to the church by five sisters, who themselves made the pattern for it in embroidery. The colors are very subdued, the general effect being that of olive green, although there are many colors intermingled, and a rich velvety tinge pervades the whole. The choir is unusually large and much more ornamented than the rest of the building, the wood carving of the stalls being very elaborate. The side aisles of the choir and Lady's Chapel are filled with monuments. The noble east window back of the choir is considered the finest in the entire edifice. It is seventy-five feet high and thirty-two broad, and consists of about two hundred divisions with delineations of the leading events of sacred history. The figures are a little more than two feet high, and are beautifully executed. The upper part of the window is divided from the lower by a stone gallery. It is so high up and the window is so large that to a person standing on the floor it looks like the centre piece of a common window-sash, but we were informed by the verger that fifty people could stand in it. In the crypt we were shown the remains of Norman and Saxon churches, over which the present structure had been built, such as pillars, beautiful mouldings and groined vaultings. The Chapter House is octagonal, having seven of its sides occupied with splendid stained-glass windows. The ceiling is exceedingly handsome, but it would take an architect to describe it, the workmanship is so very elaborate, and is supported without pillars. Forty-four stalls of the finest marble are arranged around it, with canopies supported by slender columns, having elegantly carved capitals, in some of which are representations of leaves, animals and men in antic postures, some crying, others laughing. On one capital is an old friar kissing a young nun; and on the capitals near by are several figures of nuns, laughing at the loving couple. Tradition informs us that over the doors to this Chapter House stood thirteen figures of solid silver, about a foot in height, representing the twelve apostles and the virgin Mary, the latter being two feet high; and Oliver Cromwell ordered them to be taken down and melted into money, so that it might go about doing good. Of course Mr. Culler ascended the Lantern tower, and of course I didn't.

At three o'clock in the the afternoon we started for Edinburgh and arrived there between eight and nine in the evening. We took the East Coast railway line, and the greater part of the way could look across the water of the North Sea, dotted with vessels and boats. As night drew near, the sun modestly sought to hide himself behind the distant hills on our left, while his beams tinged the great pile of fleecy clouds with gold and purple, as they appeared to rest on the bosom of the water.

CHAPTER IX.

Our first day in Edinburgh was the Sabbath. We attended the College Street United Presbyterian church in the morning. In the afternoon my husband went to St. George's Free church, and in the evening to the Dublin Street Baptist church. This city is remarkable for its church-going people. Everybody goes to church, rain or shine. They are not so afraid of being drowned or melted, or even sprinkled with rain, as people in America. They always expect rain, and go prepared for it, even if the sun does shine. The church pews have an umbrella-holder attached; and rain would be the last thing that would keep them from church. I think the spark of divine grace must be very feeble in a person when a few drops of rain will put it out. Omnibuses and street cars in Europe have seats on top where ladies as well as gentlemen ride, when they wish to obtain a good view. One day we rode in this manner about the city, and were much pleased with Edinburgh. It has many magnificent buildings, fine private residences, imposing churches, delightful gardens and parks, and almost every foot of it is historical. Here is where John Knox, the reformer, lived and labored; where Walter Scott's Heart of Midlothian was located; and where Mary Queen of Scots held her brief, but stormy reign. As early as 854 Edinburgh was quite a village. It now has a population of more than two hundred thousand. A sort of ravine separates the old town from the new, which is traversed by railroad tracks. The Mound, a large embankment, connects the two parts of the city, its descending slopes transformed into flower gardens. Upon this mound is the Gallery of Fine Arts, and the Royal Institution. The old town is the most picturesque and historical. Its principal street stretching from Holyrood Palace up to the castle is a mile in length, its various portions called the Lawnmarket, the High Street and Canongate. This street has as many as one hundred closes, miniature streets, some of them not more than four or five feet wide, running at right angles to the main street. They were built as defences against the invasions of the Highlanders, and could formerly be closed by means of portcullises. The old town has also the picturesque old Castle, lofty Arthur's Seat, Salisbury Crags, Holyrood Palace, and the Queen's drive around the base of the hills. The new town slopes to the sea, and its finest street is Princes street, ornamented with Walter Scott's magnificent monument.

Taken as a whole, Edinburgh is a most beautiful city, with its handsome buildings, of gray sandstone; its wide, clean, well paved streets; its handsome squares; elegant monuments, ten in number; its terraces; the Castle perched upon its rocky eminence; hills, crags, and blue stretch of water. It is noted for its seminaries of learning, possessing stimulants for the intellect, and many advantages for studying the fine arts. We ascended Calton Hill, a high rocky eminence, rising abruptly from the heart of the city, where we could look all over Edinburgh and far out on the water. Here is Nelson's monument, a lofty, massive, circular tower used as a time signal, which looks more like a light house than a monument. On the flag staff, a large ball is rigged, which, moved by machinery adjusted to the observatory, drops every day at one o'clock, Greenwich time. Just opposite is a square Grecian monument in remembrance of Prof. Playfair, a noted philosopher; also a monument to Dugald Stewart; and an unfinished national monument, intended to be a copy of the Panthenon at Athens, and a memorial to the Scots who fell in the Napoleonic wars. Twelve pillars stand on a foundation; this is all and nothing more. It was never completed.

Further down the hill is a monument to Robert Burns, a sort of Grecian temple, surrounded by twelve polished marble pillars. Within is an interesting collection of relics: letters written by the poet, some of his poems, a marble apple, perfect and true to nature in form and coloring, presented to his brother's wife at her wedding, two paintings representing the story of Tam O' Shanter and the Witches, and many other things.

At the foot of Calton Hill is the old Calton burying-ground. Here we saw the Martyrs' Monument, an obelisk erected in 1845 to the memory of several persons who were banished for advocating Parliamentary Reform; and also a round tower in which is the grave of David Hume, the historian. Although he was an infidel, over his tomb are these words:

"Behold, I come quickly. Thanks be to God, which giveth us the victory through our Lord Jesus Christ."

Early one morning, after a substantial breakfast, feeling vigorous in body and fresh in mind, we climbed up to the top of Arthur's Seat, so called because from this eminence King Arthur looked down upon the scene of his victory over the Saxons. In making the ascent, we passed the ruins of St. Anthony's Chapel, and also a well by the same name, a little below the chapel, where we took a good, cool draught from the spring whose overflow helps to supply the artificial St. Margaret's Loch. When perched on an irregular mass of rocks, which caps the climax, eight hundred and twenty-two feet above the sea level, we had a magnificent panoramic view of Edinburgh, which repaid all our toil of climbing; and here, away up here, were two table-cloths, spread on the ground, covered with cakes, buns, lemonade, ginger-ade, etc. And two women presided over these funny little refreshment stalls. From this point of view a small low cottage was pointed out to us as the one in which Jeanie Deans (Helen Walker) used to live; and over there, the Salisbury Crags form a beautiful picture with their sharp peaks distinctly outlined against the sky. We bought some excellent ginger-snaps, which gave us sufficient snap to descend this gigantic hill in a lively manner, and were soon at Holyrood Palace, which is situated near the foot.

It is a grand quadrangular structure, with a double battlemented tower on each end of the front. In the centre is the grand entrance, ornamented with four Doric columns on each side, and above are carved the royal arms of Scotland. It was founded by James IV. in 1501. A portion of it is fitted up sumptuously as the royal apartments, as Queen Victoria and the royal family make it their stopping-place on the way to the Queen's castle, at Balmoral, in the north of Scotland. We immediately ascended to the picture gallery, a large room filled with fictitious pictures of both fabulous and reputed kings of Scotland, painted in 1684. Lord Darnley's rooms contain several portraits, one of himself when a child, and the walls are hung with tapestry covered with trees, leaves, Cupids and landscapes. Another flight of stairs brought us to Mary Queen of Scots' apartments. The first is called the audience chamber, the ceiling of which is ornamented with armorial bearings, and the walls are hung with very old tapestry, dropping to pieces with age. Here is an ancient bed, with old gold silk drapery, said to have been occupied by Charles I. while stopping at the palace; and some handsome embroidered chairs. This is the room where John Knox had many warm discussions with this most beautiful Queen, each contending for their faith. The adjoining apartment is Queen Mary's bed-room, twenty-two by eighteen feet. Her bed is just as it was three hundred years ago, excepting that old Father Time has stolen the richness of color from the crimson damask hangings and beautifully wrought silk counterpane. They are slowly mouldering away, and look so light and porous that a breath of air might blow them to pieces. A small bit of moth-eaten blanket lies on the pillow. Here are her old-fashioned, high, straight-backed chairs, and the baby-linen basket sent her by Queen Elizabeth. Portraits of Henry VIII., Queen Elizabeth, and Mary herself, adorn the walls. At the southwest corner of this room is a door leading into her dressing-room, which is only about ten feet square, and hung with faded tapestry. On the north side of the bed-room are two doors close together; one opens on a private staircase, and the other leads into a very small room twelve feet square, in which Queen Mary used to take her tea, called a supper-room. In this room is a block of marble, brought hither from the chapel, on which Mary and Lord Darnley knelt when they were married. In a glass case are pieces of the old decayed tapestry which formerly covered the walls. History tells us that on the night of March 9, 1566, the murderers of David Rizzio (the Queen's foreign secretary) ascended to the royal apartments by this private staircase, entered the supper-room, dragged the ill-fated Rizzio from behind the Queen, to whose skirts he clung for protection, through the bed-room and audience chamber, during which he received more than fifty wounds, and was at last killed at the head of the stairs by the daggers of the Earl of Morton, Lord Ruthven, Lord Lindsay, and several others. There he lay weltering in his blood for some time; and large dark spots, whether occasioned by his blood or not, were pointed out to us, which stain that part of the floor. Scarcely anything but the walls and a few pillars remain of the chapel in which Charles I. was crowned, James I., II., III., and Queen Mary and Darnley were married; and where James II. and V. and Lord Darnley are buried.

Leaving Holyrood, we walked up High Street, so full of historical interest, formerly the residence of the nobility, but now occupied by the lowest classes. The houses preserve their antique appearance, with peaks and gables and outside stairs. Passing many closes now filled with squalor and filth and vile perfumes, we came to Canongate Church. Dr. Hugh Blair, whose rhetoric is used in many of our colleges, used to preach here. In the churchyard we found the tombstones of Dr. Adam Ferguson, historian of the Roman Republic, Adam Smith, the author of "The Wealth of Nations," and Dugald Stewart, Professor of Moral Philosophy.

A little further up the street we reached Canongate Tolbooth, which used to be the court-house and jail of the burgh, and was built in the time of James VI. It has a tower and spire, flanked by two turrets in front, and between these turrets a large clock projects over the street, bearing this motto, " Sic itur ad astra" (this is the way to the stars). This is *not* the Tolbooth referred to in Scott's novel.

We next saw Moray's house, with its old balcony, made historical by the following occurrence:

"On the thirteenth of May, 1650, the marriage of the Earl

of Moray's eldest daughter took place, and during this merry festival the great Marquis of Montrose was dragged a prisoner up the Canongate street; and it is said that the wedding party so far forgot their dignity as to step out on this old stone balcony that overhangs the street, to gaze on the degradation of their fallen enemy, who was hanged two days after."

Passing on, we came to the house of John Knox, the reformer, one of the oldest houses in Edinburgh. He lived here thirteen years, and died here in 1572, at the age of sixty-seven. On the front of the house, in large letters, is the following inscription:

"Lufe God abufe al and yi nychtbour as yi self."

The first floor is occupied by shops, the case with all the houses on this street. We ascended to the second floor by a flight of stairs on the outside of the street, and entered a large room with a window facing the street, from which John Knox often addressed an audience in the street below; also the room was filled with people during the preaching, and is, therefore, called his audience-room. On the third floor is his bed-room, sitting-room, and little study, the latter in the corner of the building, with a window on each side. It is about four by eight feet in size, with a small cupboard for books. The panes of glass in the windows are the smallest I ever saw. In this study is a funny little old chair, which is the only thing in the house that belonged to John Knox. But in the sitting-room and bedroom are several pictures of him and a bust, also several old and interesting books. In this quaint and old-fashioned house John Knox wrote his History of the Reformation.

Still walking on, we came to St. Giles Cathedral, a massive Gothic structure in the form of a cross. We entered and found that the whole interior was being restored. It was built about 1214, but at the time of the Reformation it was divided into four separate places of worship. They are now tearing down all the partitions, scraping off the plaster from the stone vaulting, and revealing the handsome original stone-work. It is henceforth to be used by one congregation—the Established Church of Scotland. In the crypt we were shown the tombs of Regent

Moray and the Marquis of Montrose. John Knox used to preach in this church, and we were shown the place where his pulpit stood; and this is the church where Jenny Geddes hurled her stool at the head of the Dean of Edinburgh, in 1637, upon his attempt to introduce the Liturgical Service. At the northwest corner of St. Giles Cathedral, on the stone sidewalk, is the figure of a heart made with stones shaped like bricks, which marks the site of the old Tolbooth, the "Heart of Midlothian," as it was called, and which has been immortalized in Walter Scott's novel of the same name.

Just back of St. Giles, in the open square between that building and the Parliament House, is a small surface-bronzed stone in the ground with the initials J. K., indicating the spot where on November 26, 1572, John Knox was buried; and over his grave the Regent Morton pronounced this eulogy: " Here lies he who never feared the face of man."

The last Parliament held in Edinburgh was in 1707, when the treaty of union between England and Scotland was ratified. The great hall in which the Parliament met, now used for the sitting of the courts, is one hundred and twenty-two feet long, and forty feet wide. It has a pendant oak roof springing from a series of exquisitely sculptured corbels of different designs. The windows are of stained glass; the walls covered with fine paintings of distinguished statesmen and lawyers who have been connected with the Scottish bar, and a row of marble statues and busts of distinguished personages also ornament the room. Adjoining are two fine libraries, one containing two hundred thousand printed volumes, and the other sixty thousand.

From here we walked to the castle. On the esplanade in front of the castle, more than three hundred feet square, the soldiers were drilling before a military inspector. We watched them for some time and admired their uniformity of movement, and the dexterity with which they handled their weapons. Their uniform of red jackets, white belts, dark plaid pants, and small caps, is very pretty, but must make conspicuous targets for their enemies. The castle, situated on the summit of a stupendous rock, more than four hundred feet above the level of the sea, is the most prominent object in all views of the city. It is a massive structure, very plain in architecture, but a strong fortress. Its only approach is through this open square, which I have mentioned. Passing the outer barrier we entered the fortress itself by a drawbridge which spans a deep moat. Beyond this is the guardhouse, and still higher up is the portcullis gate. Finally we reached the citadel or highest platform of the castle, and were shown the apartments which visitors are allowed to enter. The Crown-room contains the ancient regalia of Scotland. It consists of a crown set with diamonds and precious stones, sceptre and sword of state, also the royal jewels studded with diamonds. The last monarch crowned with this diadem was Charles II. In this room is a large, oaken, iron-bound chest, in which these treasures were locked up and forgotten for more than one hundred years. We next entered the room in which Queen Mary gave birth to James I. of England, June 19, 1566. The room is very small and irregular, it being only eight feet long. On the wall is the following inscription, in old fashioned letters and spelling:

> "Lord Jesus Christ, that crownit was with Thornse
> Preserve the Birth, quhais Badgie heir in borne
> And send Hir Sonne successione, to Reigne still
> Long in this Realme, if that it be thy will,
> Als grant, O Lord, qubat eber of Hir proceed.
> Be to thy Honer, and Praise Sobied.
>
> 19th IVNII, 1566."

From the window of this room the baby king was let down to the street, in a basket attached to a rope, and secretly taken to Stirling Castle to be baptized in the Roman Catholic faith. In the room through which you pass to the above-described room, is a very handsome painting of Queen Mary, when she was only eighteen years old, and also a good one when older. The queer little Norman chapel is the oldest part of the castle, having stood for eight hundred years. Opposite, on the King's Bastion, is a large cannon, called Mons Meg, used by James IV. in the siege of Dumbarton in 1489. The view from the bastion is very pretty on a clear day. Just below, is the beautiful park with its shaven lawn and lovely flower beds; the rich monuments in which Edinburgh abounds, elegant buildings, church spires, and beyond, the Frith of Forth, with its surface enlivened with boats and vessels. Below the castle, to the left as you approach it, is a spacious street, called Grass Market, which for centuries was the place of public execution; but a weekly market has been held here since 1477. Cowgate street used to be a fashionable and romantic garden suburb, on the slopes of which stood the mansions of the noble and wealthy; now it is filled with the lowest classes, and is anything but an agreeable place.

The Royal Institution, a building of Grecian architecture has a small Antiquarian Museum on the first floor containing a few relics from every country in the world; many of them curious and interesting. John Knox's pulpit which he used in St. Giles church is here, and also Jenny Geddes' stool which she hurled at the head of the Dean of St. Giles. The upper floor is occupied by a Sculpture Gallery, in which are casts of the celebrated statues of antiquity. Just at the rear of this building is the National Picture Gallery, consisting of two ranges of galleries, lighted from the roof only. In one, the Royal Scottish Academy has its annual exhibition of works by living artists, the other range contains the permanent collection. Here are specimens of the Flemish, Dutch, and French Schools of the sixteenth and seventeenth centuries; the Italian, Venetian, Genoese, Florentine and Scottish Schools. A copy of the Crucifixion, by Rubens, is here, also a copy of Raphael's Transfiguration; several pretty Scottish landscapes with ruined castles and mountain heights; and many other pleasing pictures.

The National Museum is the largest public building in Scotland, being four hundred feet long and two hundred feet wide. It consists of a series of courts opening into a great hall. It has a circular glass roof and two rows of galleries. The Great Hall contains models and specimens of architecture, civil and military engineering, and collateral arts; the first gallery above, glass, pottery, porcelain, ornamental metal work, wood-carving, etc.; and the upper gallery, specimens of food, raw products, etc. The Natural History Hall has on the ground floor a general collection of mammalia; the first gallery, birds, shells, etc.; upper gallery, reptiles and fishes, where we saw the skeleton of a whale seventy-nine feet long. The ground floor of the South Hall contains models illustrating metallurgy, various manufactures from metals, pottery and glass; the first gallery contains specimens and models illustrating the material and processes of manufacturing hemp, linen, cotton, wool, silk; also manufactures from ivory, bone, shells, hair, feathers, and almost everything else; upper gallery illustrates Chemistry and Philosophy; and another called the North East Room, contains an ethnological collection.

Walter Scott's Monument on Princes Street is an elegantly carved stone structure, two hundred feet high. It is in the form of an open Gothic spire, supported by four early English arches, forming a canopy, beneath which is a statue of Sir Walter Scott, in a sitting posture, with his favorite dog Maida at his feet. It was erected in 1840, and cost about seventy-five thousand dollars. In the niches above the arches are figures representing the principal characters in his novels and poems, such as the Lady of the Lake, Rob Roy, the Last Minstrel, Prince Charles, etc. A staircase in one of the columns leads to a series of galleries, which we had sense enough not to ascend. Early one morning we went by train to Melrose, a short distance, to see the Abbey. It is a grand old ruin, a thing of the past, the roof overgrown with grass and weeds; and yet enough remains from which to trace its former splendor. The present Abbey was built by Robert I., and from then down to Cromwell's time it was besieged, battered and burned, until reduced to its present ruinous condition. The front part of the Abbey is totally destroyed, not a vestige of it to be seen except the side chapels, which formed the outer portion of the side aisles. The first three have been roofless for ages, but the others are still good. The organ screen crosses the nave on a line with the division of the fifth and sixth chapels, and from there to the transepts, the entire Abbey is well roofed. The aisles have the original groined roof; but the nave has a roof of common masonry; that part having been fitted up for a Presbyterian place of worship in 1618. Here and there throughout this old ruin remain portions of beautiful carving. The capitals of some of the pillars are exquisite! One especially fine is carved to represent the curly greens or kale, and is so delicately chiseled as to resemble a beautiful pattern of lace. The transepts are open to the blue sky. The ornamentation around the door and window of the south transept are in complete preservation. Above this window rises the small bell tower, containing an old bell, which we heard strike the hour of one. It seemed like a voice from the tomb to hear this bell dolefully break the silence in this old mouldering ruin, surrounded by marble slabs which mark the resting place of many dead. Near the bell is a quaint rickety wooden clock-dial. In the north transept is a round window wrought so as to represent the crown of thorns; and here are statues of St. Peter and St. Paul, high up on the wall; and a delicately carved hand, lightly grasping a bunch of flowers forms the bracket for supporting the groins of the roof. In a corner of the Abbey near the chancel is the grave of the famous wizard Michael Scott, according to the Lay of the Last Minstrel. Somebody is evidently buried there. But the most interesting part of this structure is the chancel; for here a small stone marks the spot where the heart of Robert Bruce is said to be buried. The roof of the chancel is handsomely carved, and its "East Window" with its delicate tracery is the one immortalized by Walter Scott in these lines:

> "The moon on the east oriel shone
> Through slender shafts of shapely stone,
> By foliaged tracery combined;
> Thou wouldst have thought some fairy's hand,
> 'Twixt poplars straight, the osier wand
> In many a freakish knot had twined;
> Then framed a spell, when the work was done,
> And changed the willow wreaths to stone."

Through a door in the north aisle we entered the space formerly occupied by the cloisters; now nothing exists but the walls, the seats and false Gothic arches which covered them. The roof is a minus quantity. The stone carving around the walls in the form of roses, lilies, thistles, oak and fern leaves, is admirable! On the corner of one of the walls is the figure of an angel supposed to be flying away with a message from the church, and a few feet from it is the head of a negro grinning from ear to ear. Whether one has any connection with the history of the other, I am unable to state. We engaged a carriage and were driven to Abbotsford, the home of Walter Scott, a distance of about three miles. Scott's great-granddaughter now occupies this elegant mansion, "a romance of stone and lime," with castellated turrets and lovely surroundings. We were first shown into the study, where we saw Scott's writing desk, and the very large, comfortable chair, covered with leather, in which he used to sit. In a niche is a bronze cast of Sir Walter, taken after death. He must have been exceedingly long-headed in every sense of the word. The library, an adjoining apartment, fifty by sixty feet, has a richly-carved ceiling in oak. The books arranged around the room in glass cases, reaching from the floor to the ceiling, are twenty thousand in number. And here is a fine marble bust of Scott, executed by Chantery, considered the best of all his likenesses: two handsomely carved elbow chairs, the gift of the Pope; and a writing desk, the gift of George III. In the Drawing Room, the woodwork is of cedar, and the walls are adorned with fine portrait paintings of Cardinal Wolsey, Dryden, and Walter Scott, and Mary Queen of Scots' head on a charger, painted an hour after her execution. I recognized it immediately, notwithstanding the face is deadly pale and very much swollen, though not distorted. In a glass case is a very handsome display of presents made to Scott, among which is a gold snuff-box, a silver one, and another of ebony set with diamonds; all indicating that that worthy gentleman must have been very fond of snuff. And here is the knife and fork he used when a small boy. We next passed into the Armory which contained a large collection of weapons of war, suits of tilting armor, Lochaber axes, battle axes, the gun of Rob Roy, the pistol of Claverhouse, pistols taken from Napoleon's carriage after the battle of Waterloo; and in a glass case, the last suit of clothes ever worn by Sir Walter Scott, even his shoes, light plush hat, and walking stick.

An hour's ride brought us back to Edinburgh, and next morning we took another short train ride to Hawthornden.

The Lodge or Mansion, the home of the poet, Drummond, called the "classic Hawthornden," is built on a solid rock or cliff overhanging the Esk River ("where ford there was none"), which winds through a rocky channel thickly shaded with overhanging trees. The oldest portion of the house is six hundred years old. One side of it is completely covered with ivy. Visitors (tourists) are not admitted to the house, which is owned by the Drummond family, but they are allowed to walk through the grounds. A tree called the three sisters is quite a curiosity. Three trees spring out of the ground from one place. They are five hundred years old. Ben Johnson walked all the way from London here to sit in "Drummond's classic shade." Chiseled out of the solid rock, upon which the house is built, are several low rooms not high enough for a tall person to stand upright in, where Robert Bruce, king of Scotland, is said to have hid for safety; and also the redoubted Sir Alexander Ramsay and his followers, at another time. We passed through a long passage at the end of which is a very deep well. Through a small doorway we stepped into another room, which is called Robert Bruce's library. There are small square places cut in the walls for each book. It has a very small window, concealed from the outside by ivy, but the inside commands a view of the entire glen, through this net-work of leaves. Opposite this room is Robert Bruce's bed-room, without a ray of light excepting what steals in from the low doorway. I shuddered to think of spending a night in such a den.

From here we walked about a mile and a half to Rosslyn Chapel, through a shady, romantic pathway along the bank of the winding Esk River, "one of the most beautiful and sequestered spots in Scotland."

At the western extremity of Hawthornden, we reached Rosslyn Castle, situated on a bold, craggy peninsula, beneath which flows the Esk. It was built in the eleventh century, and all that now remains is a pile of mouldering ruins and three tiers of vaults or dungeons—in one of which Mary Queen of Scots hid for three weeks.

We climbed up a long, tiresome hill, and reached the famous Rosslyn Chapel, but had to wait some little time before entering, as a marriage in high life was taking place within. It was a pretty sight, looking for all the world as if it had just stepped out of a picture book, to see the bridal party walk from the chapel to the carriage, while a winsome child lavishly strewed beautiful flowers in their pathway; and truly the lovely bride in her fleecy robe, decked with orange blossoms, seemed fit to tread on roses.

The chapel was founded in 1446, by William St. Clair, and was to be the chancel of a very large edifice, but for some reason the other part was never erected. It is quite small, only sixty-nine feet long, thirty-five feet broad and forty feet high. It is divided into centre and side aisles by two rows of elaborately sculptured pillars, supporting beautifully decorated Gothic arches. There are thirteen different kinds of arches in the chapel, and each arch, pillar and window presents a different ornamentation of the most exquisite workmanship. Even on friezes in bass-relief, are representations of the Apostles feeding the hungry, clothing the naked and visiting the sick. The finest part of the building, however, is the Lady's Chapel. The groined roof is one mass of the most elaborate stone carving. One peculiarly beautiful pillar, ornamented with spiral festoons of delicately-carved leaves, giving it the appearance of a twisted column, is called the Apprentices' Pillar, on account of the story that the master builder thought it necessary to go to Rome to see the original of which this was to be a copy. During his absence his apprentice executed the work so creditably that when the master returned he, in a fit of jealousy, struck the apprentice on the head with a mallet and killed him. The windows are of stained glass. A new organ has lately been placed over the entrance door. It is said of this chapel that "nowhere in the world will such wealth of architectural beauty and detail be found within so small a space."

The next day we left Edinburgh about one o'clock, reaching Stirling in about an hour, and proceeded immediately to the Castle, passing through Greyfriars Churchyard, where among the monuments, we noticed an urn with a sun-dial on it, upon which is engraved:

> "I am a shadow, so art thou,
> I mark time: dost thou?

The Castle is situated on a precipitous rock, and commands one of the finest stretches of landscape. Our attendant took us to the best place of observation and pointed out many historical and interesting spots. The atmosphere was clear and bright (a rare thing for Scotland) and we could distinctly see Ben Lomond, Ben Venue, Ben A'an, Ben Ledi, Ben Voirlich, Uam-Var, the Ochil Hills and the winding Forth River, the Campasie Hills, a ruined Abbey, the Wallace Monument, Abbey Craig, the Bridge of Allan and the old "Field of Bannockburn," where Bruce gained the victory which liberated Scotland.

This castle was the birth-place of James II., and also of James V. The latter was crowned here, and James IV. resided here. In a small room which we entered, James II. assassinated William, Earl of Douglas, and then hurled his lifeless body through the window into the garden below. The window is now filled with stained-glass, representing in the centre, a bleeding heart with a crown above it, donated by Queen Victoria. Mary Queen of Scots was imprisoned here a short time. This unfortunate yet beautiful queen was imprisoned in many castles, and when not caged up was driven about like a hunted deer, seeking shelter in dungeons, anywhere, that she might escape her persecutors; and at last her beautiful head was severed from her body by the cruel axe of the executioner. The next day we attended services in the old Greyfriars Church. Here James VI. was crowned and John Knox preached the coronation sermon, and Queen Mary was also crowned here. We listened to a doctrinal sermon from a clergyman of the Established Church of Scotland.

Early Monday morning we were off by train to Callander. There we found three or four coaches each seating twenty persons, waiting for tourists who were taking the trip through the Trossachs. We went by coach ten miles and had a most delightful time, passing through the country where were located the scenes of Scott's Lady of the Lake, and Doune Lodge, the seat of the Earl of Moray; rode along the banks of Lake Vennachar its entire length; had a good view of Ben Voirlich, passsed close to the base of the lofty Ben Ledi ("the Hill of God") two thousand, nine hundred feet high, and Ben A'an. The latter appeared most beautiful, rising up so distinct in form, seemingly independent of all the others. And here we first saw the pretty pink heather which gayly clothes the mountains of Scotland.

The road took us along the banks of Loch Achray its entire length, and suddenly we entered the Trossachs. This romantic part of the route is about a mile in length and received its name from its perpendicular sides, which "bristle" with a great variety of trees. Emerging from the Trossachs we reached Loch Katrine, where we took the steamer and rode from one end of it to the other. We soon passed a lovely little island, covered with trees, called "Ellen's Isle." On either side rise the lofty mountains, Ben Venue and Ben A'an. The lake is eight miles long and three-quarters of a mile wide, and has many bays and promontories. It began to mist, then rain gently, and by the time we had reached the termination of the lake, it poured in torrents, and continued to do so the remainder of the day. We again mounted to the top of a four-horse coach and rode to Inversnaid on Loch Lomond. Just picture to yourself twenty persons on top of a coach, with the two centre seats back to back, and the rain pouring intensely. Of course there was not sufficient space for all to put up their umbrellas, so many of the passengers were compelled to transform themselves into eaves troughs and carry off the water from the roofs of the umbrellas. One poor man did not recognize his usefulness in this particular until he felt the dampness on his shoulder, and discovered that his heavy overcoat was completely saturated with the drippings of the umbrella behind him. A rib of one parasol conducted the inky fluid directly into the ear of a lady. I felt for the first time in my life that I could not sing from my heart,

"Let some droppings fall on me."

Aside from this little unpleasantness the drive between these two lakes, skirting the edge of a deep ravine, wild and romantic, was delightful, for everybody kept in a good humor and chatted cheerfully. We drove up to Inversnaid hotel, and all marched in like drowned rats. We obtained some fresh sandwiches and hot coffee, while the English and Scotch passengers indulged in something stronger. Our garments were restored to their original appearance when it was announced that our boat was ready, and we launched forth once more on the lake steamer.

Loch Lomond is called the "Queen of Scottish Lakes." It is thirty miles long, and seven broad, and with its wooded isles, shadowy recesses, irregular peninsulas, and old Ben Lomond rising from its eastern shore to a height of three thousand feet, it is certainly most picturesque. We could not think of going down in the cabin, even if it did rain as if the clouds were emptying all their contents just in that particular spot; and so with our gossamers and umbrellas, never before so valuable and much appreciated, we stood on deck and admired all the grandeur visible, and filled in with imagination what the sun's absence had withdrawn from the picture, and contentedly let it rain. The thirty miles were at last ended and we bade farewell to Loch Lomond, to take a dry seat in a railway car for Glasgow.

On the way we passed Dumbarton Castle, perched on the two lofty peaks of a rock, more than five hundred feet high, and celebrated as the place where William Wallace was imprisoned. Arriving at Glasgow late in the afternoon, we were fully prepared, for the good, smoking, hot dinner which we received at the hotel.

Glasgow is the third city in Great Britain in wealth and population, being the industrial and commercial metropolis of Scotland, and numbering more than half a million inhabitants. It is the seat of extensive manufactures, among which is the building of iron ocean and river steamers. It is connected with the ocean by the river Clyde, and is an important sea-port city. The Clyde is navigable by vessels of two thousand tons burden, thus affording facilities for the cultivation of a world-wide commerce. Glasgow has many handsome, lofty buildings of modern date, but owing to the number of cotton factories, chemical works, foundries, and work-shops of all kinds, it is black and smoky, and has little to detain the tourist; so about noon the next day we renewed our journey, passing through Paisley, noted for its manufacture of beautiful shawls, a fact with which the ladies are all acquainted.

About one in the afternoon, we reached Ayr, a pretty seacoast town situated at the mouth of the river Ayr, across which stream are the "Twa Brigs." The "Auld Brig" was built in the reign of Alexander III, and the new one in 1788. From the station we took a charming walk of two miles to the birthplace of the poet, Robert Burns, in the country. It is a low humble cottage with a thatched roof, and had formerly but two rooms; but additions have been made at both ends, making a long low building. These two rooms, however, are kept sacred and are not used by the people who occupy the house. The kitchen was the room honored by the birth of the great poet in 1759, and in a small recess is a bed dating back to that time; and I suppose it will continue to be shown to vistors until it becomes as old and shadowy as that of Mary, Queen of Scots. In this room are two tables, some chairs, and the old-fashioned clock which belonged to his childhood home. The sitting-room is now filled with ornaments, carved out of wood from the trees of the old place, with pictures on them of the cottage, Alloways Kirk and the bridge, which are for sale. We walked on a little distance and came to the Kirk, with nothing left but the side walls and gable ends, a very wee little church, with the inside walls overgrown with ivy, and there is the window through which Tam O'Shanter looked and saw the witches dance. In the churchyard lie Burns' father and mother. On the opposite side of the road, a little farther on, is the new church of Alloway, and near it is a fine monument to Burns, very much the same style as the one at Edinburgh, only higher and more beautiful. Its base is triangular in shape, and the architecture Grecian.

In one part of the pretty garden which surrounds the monument is a small building containing two pieces of statuary carved from stone, representing Tam O'Shanter and Sooter Johnny. The latter with his shoemaker's apron and his toes turned in, tells one plainly what his trade was. These statues have been to America, as well as all over Europe. We walked over the "Auld Brig of Alloway" which crosses the Doon river, where Tam O'Shanter was pursued by the witches, and where the grey mare's tail was pulled off. It is an old arched stone bridge, the top having the same curve as the arch. We slowly walked back to the station and took the train for Carlisle, England; passing through Dumfries where Robert Burns died at the age of thirty-seven years, after a residence of five years, and was buried in St. Michael's church-yard. Here is where he wrote "Tam O'Shanter" and "To Mary in Heaven."

We reached Carlisle in the evening and spent the next forenoon in looking about this old city, which was formerly a Roman station and the seat of the ancient kings of Cumbria. About 900 it was destroyed by the Danes, and for two centuries remained in ruins. It was often involved in the border wars between England and Scotland. We went to the Cathedral and attended the special service of prayer for the recovery of the archbishop of Canterbury. A part of the old wall of the eleventh century has been built into the new wall of the church. The arches are very crooked, the base of the columns on one side having sunk so as to throw the arch all out of shape. The high altar is just new, ornamented with different colored marbles;

the large stained-glass window behind it is very handsome, and the stone pulpit of delicate carving is quite an ornament.

We then took a walk around the Castle, which is a very plain looking structure. It is now used for barracks and military stores. Visitors are not allowed to enter as they are so afraid of dynamite or something of that nature being brought in, since the trouble with Ireland. Mary, Queen of Scots was here imprisoned after the battle of Langside.

We went by train to Keswick, quite a fashionable resort, being the best centre from which to visit most of the wildest scenery in the English Lake District. It contains less than three thousand inhabitants, yet it has multitudes of visitors during the season, and many excellent hotels. It is surrounded by grand old mountains and rests at the foot of Skiddaw Mountain, three thousand and fifty-eight feet high. It is only a quarter of a mile from Derwentwater, one of the most charming lakes. Immediately after selecting our hotel we started out for a walk to the "Falls of Lodore," a distance of two and a half miles. We walked along the shore of the lovely Derwentwater, dotted with row boats. It is three miles long and one and a half broad, and has seven or eight pretty islands. One is called the floating island, because at irregular intervals of a few years, it rises to the surface of the water. It is seven years since it made its last appearance. "It is a mass of earthy matter six feet thick and varying in size in different years, from an acre to a few perches, covered with vegetation and full of air-bubbles which buoy it on the surface of the water." This remarkable phenomenon is supposed to be caused by gas escaping from decayed vegetable matter. A beautiful range of mountains stretches along the shore of this lake with many, many peaks, of various shapes and heights, covered with the lovely pink heather; and August is just the month to see it in all its glory. It is so thick that it gives the whole mountain a pinkish tinge. Trout, salmon, eels, perch and pike, are found in this lake. Our road lay through the valley with the lofty Wallow Crag and Falcon Crag at our left, and on our right the lake with another lofty range of mountains for a background; the different peaks named Cat Bells, Cansey Pike, Grisedale Pike and Barrow. We so much enjoyed this quiet, shady path with a low stone wall on either side, overgrown with pretty moss and in many places adorned with a rich growth of ivy. It seemed as if we were in fairy land, every spot was so replete with nature's beauty. We rested occasionally on rocks by the wayside and at last reached the Falls of Lodore. Here between two immense perpendicular cliffs, Shepherd's Crag on the right and Gowder Crag on the left, are scores of huge boulders interspersed with smaller ones, thrown together in the wildest confusion, and over these, the water forming an innumerable number of small cascades comes tumbling down a distance of one hundred and twenty-four feet, with a tremendous roar, "dizzying and deafening the ear with its sounds." But I will not attempt to explain how the water comes down at Lodore, since Southey has done it so well in his musical poem ending thus :

> "Retreating and beating and meeting and sheeting,
> Delaying and straying and playing and spraying,
> Advancing and prancing and glancing and dancing,
> Recoiling, turmoiling and toiling and boiling,
> And gleaming and streaming and steaming and beaming,
> And rushing and flushing and brushing and gushing,
> And flapping and rapping and clapping and slapping,
> And curling and whirling and purling and twirling,
> And thumping and plumping and bumping and jumping,
> And dashing and flashing and splashing and clashing,
> And so never ending but always descending,
> Sounds and motions forever and ever are blending,
> All at once and all o'er, with a mighty uproar,
> And this way the water comes down at Lodore."

Mr. Culler gathered some heather here, which we brought home to America. We walked leisurely back to our hotel and felt somewhat weary after our five miles stroll. The next morning, very early, we started by coach, or wagonette, as it is called there, on the Buttermere excursion. We went over the same road that we did the previous day as far as the Falls of

Lodore. From that point of the twenty-three miles' drive the scenery was new to us. We soon had a grand view of the Borrowdale Mountains in front of us, with Great End and Scawfell Pike. The latter is the highest mountain in England, being three thousand two hundred and ten feet. At the entrance to the Borrowdale Valley, rocks are thrown together promiscuously, scarcely leaving room for the road along the river's edge.

We soon came to the famous Bowder Stone, an immense boulder which has fallen from the adjacent crags. It is thirty-six feet high and eighty-nine feet in circumference; and rests on so small a base, that persons on its opposite sides may shake hands, through a hole under it. Pieces of carpet are placed on the ground, so that people may perform this ceremony without soiling their garments. Ascending it by a wooden stair-case we took a survey of the surrounding country. Once more seated in the wagonette with our hands full of pretty heather we rode through the most charming scenery. I had no idea there was anything like it in England. Tourists who go through the English Lake Region, and do not take this lovely ride to Buttermere, miss the grandest scenery in the whole district. Long ranges of mountains, one peak rising above another, covered with beautiful heather, form a magnificent panorama!

At Seatoller we all had to alight from the coaches and walk to the top of Honister Pass, as it was all the horses could do to draw the empty coaches. It is the worst carriage road in the Lake District, being steep, rough and stony. We walked for a distance of about three miles, steadily climbing up at a slow pace; admiring the bold mountain scenery as we went; and gathering flowers of different varieties, some meekly lifting their heads in a secluded spot, half hidden by the scattered stones, "born to blush unseen, and waste their fragrance on the mountain air." Close to the road on our left, all the way, ran a pretty mountain stream, with now and then a miniature cascade lightening our toilsome journey with its laughing waters.

During the ascent Mount Helvellyn comes in view, and on reaching the summit, Honister Crag, the grandest in the district, among the trees, formerly the residence of Mrs. Hemans, the poetess. Our attention was attracted to a white marble cross rising above the waters of the lake, and were told that it was placed there as a memorial to three young men who at that spot found a watery grave. We had the company of a very pleasant English lady and gentleman, by the name of Fleming. We landed at Bowness, and rode a mile and a half to Windermere. The towns of Keswick, Ambleside, Bowness, and Windermere are fashionable places for summer resort in the English Lake region, and are very pretty, quaint looking little villages, built mostly of rough slate stone of all sizes, apparently laid up without mortar, presenting a rustic appearance, nicely suited to the picturesque mountain scenery around them. We were delighted with this part of England, the home of the poets, and really its Switzerland.

At Windermere we took train for Liverpool, and in passing through the town of Kendal saw the Castle, or rather its ruins, where Catherine Parr, last wife of Henry VIII. lived. Upon reaching Liverpool, we went to the North Western Hotel, one of the grandest in Europe, with its highly-polished granite pillars, handsome parlors, elegant private rooms, etc. The next morning we ran down to Chester, a distance of sixteen miles, and alighted from the train in the longest depot in England, being one thousand and fifty feet in length, and having an iron roof. It rained fearfully, but we sallied forth, and walked to the old part of the city, where we ascended the ancient city wall, which was first erected A. D. 61, afterwards rebuilt in 907. It is built entirely around the old part of the city, and is seven feet thick, and nearly two miles in circumference, having four gates. On the inside is a nice stone pavement, where two people may walk abreast, higher than the tops of the houses, where we had a delightful (?) walk through a drenching rain half-way around the city, taking in the old Cathedral and the Tower, from which King Charles I. saw his army defeated on Rowton Moor, four miles away, in 1645. We also walked through some of the old arcades, or rows, as they are called. The houses in these streets are arranged thus: The front part of the second stories, as far as sixteen feet back, form a continuous paved walk or covered gallery, open in front, and is reached by steps from the street below. The better class of shops are in these rows, and there are dwelling rooms above, and inferior shops below them. These "rows" and the "old wall" are things peculiar to Chester, and we were glad that we had seen them, although not under the most favorable circumstances.

We returned to Liverpool, and in a short time a tap came at our door, and there stood Mrs. Marsh, a lady with whom we had spent the day at Chatsworth Estate, who came to take us to her home in the city, where we spent the time pleasantly for a day or two, until our departure for America.

On the 6th of September, at 2 o'clock in the afternoon, we took the tender on the river Mersey, which conveyed us to the steamship Egypt, where we bade a final farewell to the Marshes, and once more greeted Miss Camp and Mrs. Pritchard, who took passage on the same steamer. The day was bright and beautiful, so we had a delightful send-off. My cousin, James Holder, a florist, had deposited with the steamship company a basket of choice plants from my native place (which I am happy to state to my readers are at the present blooming gayly), and his sister Mary, with her deft fingers, had beautifully embroidered a present for each of us.

We landed in New York City on Sabbath, September 17, 1882. How grateful and refreshing was the sight of Staten and Coney Islands, clothed with verdure, as we approached our own glorious country! And no less pleasing were three happy faces on the pier, belonging to a bride and groom and their brother, members of our own flock at Newton, Iowa, who had come to welcome us home from across the seas.

If any of my readers wonder why I have said so little concerning the agriculture, manufactures, commerce, customs and habits of the people, and political affairs of the countries which we visited, please remember that this is EUROPE THROUGH A WOMAN'S EYE.

www.ingramcontent.com/pod-product-compliance
Lightning Source LLC
Chambersburg PA
CBHW021812230426
43669CB00008B/720